# Turning the Pages

## Books by Peter Schwed

*Turning the Pages: An Insider's Story of Simon & Schuster 1924–1984*
*Hanging in There!: How to Resist Retirement from Life and Avoid Being Put Out to Pasture*
*Test Your Tennis I.Q.*
*God Bless Pawnbrokers*
*The Serve and the Overhead Smash*
*Sinister Tennis: How to Play Against and With Left-Handers*

As Collaborator

*The Education of a Woman Golfer* (with Nancy Lopez)

As Coeditor

*The Fireside Book of Tennis* (with Allison Danzig)
*Great Stories from the World of Sport* (with Herbert Warren Wind)

# Turning

An Insider's Story of

## PETER SCHWED

# the Pages

SIMON & SCHUSTER 1924–1984

Macmillan Publishing Company · New York

Macmillan Publishing Company
866 Third Avenue, New York, N.Y. 10022
Collier Macmillan Canada, Inc.

Library of Congress Cataloging in Publication Data

Schwed, Peter.
Turning the pages.

Includes index.
1. Simon and Schuster, Inc.—History.   2. Publishers
and publishing—New York (N.Y.)—History.   I. Title.
Z473.S577S38   1984      070.5′09747′1      84-7947

ISBN 0-02-607790-6

Macmillan books are available at special discounts
for bulk purchases for sales promotions, premiums,
fund-raising, or educational use. Special editions or
book excerpts can also be created to specification.
For details, contact:

Special Sales Director
Macmillan Publishing Company
866 Third Avenue
New York, New York 10022

10  9  8  7  6  5  4  3  2  1

Designed by Jack Meserole

Printed in the United States of America

Again and Always for Antonia

# Contents

WITH A PARTIAL CAST OF CHARACTERS, TITLES, AND EVENTS

Author's Note, xv

Preface, xvii

I   Publishers—of What? 1

*That First Miracle Year on a Shoestring*

Crossword Puzzles, J. Haldeman Julius and Will Durant, and What Next?

2   Give the Reader a Break! 17

*Mostly about Richard Leo Simon*

George Gershwin, Ludwig van Beethoven, and Rodgers and Hart, Contract Bridge and Its Consummate Rascal, Photography, Golf and Alex Morrison, Fitness and Artie McGovern, Artur Schnabel, Margaret Halsey and "With Malice Toward Some," Peter Arno, Hendrik Willem Van Loon.

3   PAAIMA and "Dinkelspiel," 45

*Mostly about Max Lincoln Schuster*

"The Story of Philosophy," Max Eastman, Clifton Fadiman, Robert Ripley and "Believe It or Not," Thomas Craven, John Cowper Powys, Leo Tolstoy, Justin Kaplan, Jerome Weidman, and the Pink, Blue, and Green Slips of Paper.


4   How to Win a Publishing House and Influence Profits, 66

*Mostly about Leon Shimkin*

"Our Little Golden Nugget," the Celebrated Ping-Pong Table, Dale Carnegie and "How to Win Friends and Influence People," J. K. Lasser and "Your Income Tax," Clarence Lovejoy, Joshua Loth Liebman and "Peace of Mind," the Peoples Book Club, Pocket Books, Fathers and Sons, Frustrated Financial Flirtations.


5   From "The Inner Sanctum" to Outer Space in Advertising, 87

*Stories of Fair and Foul Weather*

"The Inner Sanctum," Schuster's "Windswept" Ads, the Jack Goodman–Nina Bourne Touch, Strome Lamon, the Founding Father of Book Publicity—Alexander King, Promotion à la Jacqueline Susann and Jane Fonda, Richard Snyder and Dan Green, a Modern Dreyfus Case.

6  Fun and Games in the Classless Society, 117

*The Closest Thing to the Garden of Eden*

Office Shenanigans, the Jones Beach Parties, the Barney
Greengrass Spoof, Walt Kelly and "Pogo," Kay Thompson and
"Eloise," Reprise on Alexander King, and Some Occasionally
Serious Notes.


7  On Shaky Ground, 134

*Yes—In God We Trust, but Not Always in Authors or Fate*

"Trader Horn," Joan Lowell and "The Cradle of the Deep,"
"Casanova's Homecoming," Eric Hodgins and "Mr. Blandings
Builds His Dream House," "The Passion Flower Hotel Affair,"
Dr. Herman Taller and "Calories Don't Count," "Quotations
from Chairman LBJ," General George C. Marshall,
"Catch-22," Henry Morton Robinson and "The Cardinal,"
"The Secret Diary of Harold L. Ickes," "Pat the Bunny," and
the Headaches of Helen Barrow.


8  The Tails That Wagged the Dog, 162

*Pocket Books, Little Golden Books and Records*

Robert de Graff, Dr. Benjamin Spock, Georges du Plaix,
Western Printing and Lithographing Nuptials, Albert Le-
venthal, Robert Bernstein, Bing Crosby, "Dr. Dan the Bandage
Man."

**9** Gulliver Captured by the Lilliputians, 173

*The Taking Over by—or Possibly of—Marshall Field*

A House Divided: "Would You Sell Joanna?", the First
Absentee Ownership but Business as Usual, Joseph Barnes,
Wendell L. Willkie, Seymour Turk, Quincy Howe, Wallace
Brockway, James R. Newman and "The World of Mathemat-
ics," P. G. Wodehouse, Evan Hunter, Chas Addams, Bertrand
Russell, J. Robert Oppenheimer, S. J. Perelman, Cornelius
Ryan, Irving Wallace, Meyer Levin, James Thurber, and the
Female Hands That Rocked the Cradle.

**10** A Last Brave Fling, 190

*The New Ventures Project of Richard Simon*

Richard Grossman, Postcards and Photography, William Holly
Whyte and "The Organization Man," Sloan Wilson and "The
Man in the Gray Flannel Suit," Philippe Halsman and Fer-
nandel and "The Jump Book."

**11** Damon and Pythias, 201

*An Extraordinary Relationship*

Jack Goodman and Albert Leventhal, the Goodman-Leventhal
Corporation, Tom Bevans, Norman Corwin, the End of an
Era, and "Dirge Without Music."

**12** Across the Far Atlantic, 216

*Mostly but Not Exclusively about Our British Cousins*

The Early Years from John Cowper Powys and Bertrand
Russell to Bernard Berenson and Nikos Kazantzakis, Felix
Salten's "Bambi," Charlie Chaplin, "The Way Things Work,"
Punch Magazine and Malcolm Muggeridge, William L. Shirer,
Hugh Johnson, John Hedgecoe, "The Joy of Sex," Graham
Greene, Changing Times and Attitudes.

**13** The Phoenixes That Rose from the Ashes, 234

*You Lose Some and You Win Some*

Robert Gottlieb, Anthony M. Schulte, Nina Bourne, Robert
Bernstein and Bennett Cerf, Michael Korda, Harold Robbins,
Richard E. Snyder, Catastrophes in Couples but the Opera Isn't
Over Until the Fat Lady Sings.

**14** Big Fish That Got Away—and Some Faithful
Galley Slaves, 254

*A Rueful Retrospective and an Appreciative Present*

Rachel Carson, Mary McCarthy, Herman Wouk, Shel Silverstein, Christina Stead, "Lolita," plus the Other Side of the Coin:
A Loyal Band.

**15** Render unto Caesar the Things That Are Caesar's, 270

*Mostly about Richard E. Snyder*

Growth and the Philosophy of Never Leaving Well Enough Alone, Eugene McCarthy, Gulf & Western and the Conglomerate Effect, New Imprints, David Obst and "All the President's Men" plus the other Watergate books, the State of the Unions, the Korda Connection.


l'Envoi, 289

*"To an Unknown Mortal of 2936 A.D."*

Notes to Be Left in a Cornerstone.


Photograph Acknowledgments, 293


Index, 295

# Author's Note

The reader may be perplexed by the fact that there seems to be a lamentable lack of consistency in these pages about what the name of the book-publishing firm seems to be. Originally the founders, Dick Simon and Max Schuster, named it "Simon and Schuster" and strenuously resisted any shorthand attempts by anyone to make it "Simon & Schuster"; their efforts have been rewarded even to this day by the fact that the firm's imprint on the spine and title page of every hardback book continues to be written with the "and" rather than the offensive ampersand. Also the cable address, almost immediately adopted as the signature on the old famous Inner Sanctum advertising columns, was "Essandess"—not "S & S." It wasn't until years later, when publishing divisions were merged and corporate thinking mushroomed, that the ampersand really took over (except for those spines and title pages), so that today "Simon & Schuster" is the official name on the letterhead and everything else, from catalogues to the name of the building on the Avenue of the Americas where the executive offices are housed.

As a result, in writing this book the author has purposely thrown consistency to the winds and uses one or the other of the names as it seems suited either to the chronology of the story or to his whim. Not that it matters very much: it's always the same company, and, in *Romeo and Juliet*, no less an authority than Shakespeare proclaimed that a rose by any other name would smell as sweet. Or was that in *Romeo & Juliet*?

# Preface

January 2, 1984, was Simon & Schuster's sixtieth birthday, and I have known its owners, executives, editors, staff, and authors intimately for fifty-two of those sixty years. Only two other people— Leon Shimkin, who owned the firm before selling it to Gulf & Western, and Sam Meyerson, the mail-order director—have longer ties to the company, and neither of them is a professional writer or has any inclination to be one. That leaves me as the one person uniquely qualified to write this book, and what a joy every aspect of it has been. Research often involves little more than drudgery, but in this case I've had the opportunity to visit with old friends and associates, some of whom I hadn't seen in decades, to reminisce, and to unearth both dramatic and delightful material about which I'm certain no one presently at Simon & Schuster or I myself had been aware. From its very beginning right up through the years until now, this has constantly been an unusually lively publishing house, and the story of its incredible growth, highlighted by a multitude of personal anecdotes, reflects that. Nor did the fact that I did not know the firm during those first eight years of its existence, when I was in school and at college, turn out to be any handicap, for that period is documented far better and more extensively than any other.

Therefore, in extending my appreciation and acknowledgments, I do so first to Kenneth Lohf, chief of the rare books and manuscripts section of Butler Library at Columbia University, and his staff. Both Dick Simon and Max Schuster were Columbia graduates; their publishing records and memorabilia, left to the university, were a veritable gold mine to me of both information and illustrative material. Max Schuster had the acquisitive instincts of a squirrel and saved and filed virtually everything he or anyone else ever wrote about the company or himself, from extensive correspondence with authors like Bertrand Russell and Bernard Berenson almost to his laundry lists. So the collection of Schusteriana is truly formidable. Dick Simon's bounty isn't too far behind, even though he, having none of the squirrel's characteristics, simply tossed his records into large boxes and left Mr. Lohf and his people to put them in order and catalogue them. Dick, a most enthusiastic and talented photographer himself, left some enchanting pictures of the people who populated the early years. Some of the photographs repose at Columbia, but several that you will see in this volume were graciously supplied by his widow, Andrea, from albums and wall hangings in their home in Riverdale. Where new photographs had to be taken of the latter, it was done by Andrea and Dick's professional-photographer son, Peter.

I should explain why I, who worked at Simon & Schuster for only [*sic!*] thirty-seven years, claim to have known everyone intimately for fifty-two years. It was because by happenstance Jack Goodman and Albert Leventhal had become my closest friends in the early 1930s in New York, where I, fresh out of college, was working for the Provident Loan Society in my first job. Although Jack and Albert were both still very young men, they had already established themselves as major figures at Essandess, and the Provident Loan, located in the Twenties on what was then called Fourth Avenue— even now it's hard for me to think of it as Park Avenue South—was all of two blocks away from their office. So I would join Albert and Jack, and other Simon and Schuster people like Tom Bevans and Clifton Fadiman and Jerome Weidman and Nina Bourne, for luncheon at least a couple of times a week. We all were such good friends that I spent a majority of evenings with Jack or Albert or both and our respective women friends and, as an outsider who had no personal stake in office gossip, I think I was privy to as much inside and intimate information then as I've ever picked up in the years when I actually worked at Simon and Schuster. In those later thirty-seven years, however, I had everything from peripheral to close contact with a host of publishing people and authors. I've interviewed all those who are still alive, and I could reach, and whom I thought likely to be able to contribute. They all did to a greater or lesser extent, but to try to list them here would be repetitive, because if you look at the index to this book you can properly assume that every living person in it talked to me generously and freely, and I am immensely grateful to them all. I should also tip my cap to the *New Yorker*, which graciously let me review Geoffrey Hellman's splendid 1939 three-part Profile of Simon and Schuster, giving me background information I would have had great difficulty matching elsewhere; to Tony Schwartz, who consented to my using a certain few direct quotes he obtained in interviews with Dick Snyder and Michael Korda that appeared in his stories about them in the *New York Times*; and to unidentified writers for *Publishers Weekly* who conducted in-depth question-and-answer sessions with Mr. Snyder.

It would be remiss of me not to point out that for a comparatively short period of time, Simon & Schuster had a president other than the four S's who are the chief protagonists in this book: Richard Leo Simon, Max Lincoln Schuster, Leon Shimkin, and Richard E. Snyder. He was Seymour Turk, who in January 1973, when Leon Shimkin made himself chairman of the board and chief executive officer, moved up from his prior role as executive vice-president and acted as president during the couple of years before the firm was taken into the Gulf & Western conglomerate and Snyder was named president. Seymour was a talented, loyal caretaker for Leon and he earned widespread respect for his performance, but his term was short and his work almost exclusively in the business area of publishing. I have been assured by Sy that he takes no offense in not being grouped among the four S's as a dominating figure of the course of Simon & Schuster's history. Like so many other S & S alumni and alumnae, he moved on to bigger and better things after resigning in 1975. After filling major posts first with the Viking Press and then with Harry N. Abrams, Inc., he is today the general manager and senior vice-president of the Book-of-the-Month Club.

P.S.

# Publishers—of What?

I

THE DAY was January 2, 1924, when twenty-five-year-old Richard L. Simon and twenty-seven-year-old M. Lincoln Schuster opened the door of their first office, a small three-room affair at 37 West Fifty-seventh Street in New York. They didn't have much to do that first morning except to admire the fresh paint on the door that read "Simon and Schuster, Publishers." Having no one to go to lunch with except each other, they did. When they returned, someone had inscribed a dash and two words under the proud name: "—of what?"

It was a good question. Although in the decade that followed World War I a book-publishing company could be launched for next to nothing, unless it came up fairly quickly with something successful, it wouldn't be around long. Dick and Max had funds that seemed ample enough at the time to pay the rent and the telephone bill, and to dole out salaries of $20 a week to each other—they had each saved up $3,000 to pour into the enterprise, and at 1924 rates, that should carry them a reasonable period of time. Their families had also promised that they'd chip in if more money was needed, but everyone fervently hoped that wouldn't occur.

It was Richard Simon's aunt who came up with a practical if dubious suggestion about what the new firm might publish first. She had developed an enthusiasm for crossword puzzles, which up to then had been a modest feature in the morning *World*, and she thought a book of them would appeal to people like herself. Dick had his reservations but, for lack of anything else on the horizon, approached the newspaper's three crossword editors, F. Gregory Hartswick, Prosper Buranelli, and Margaret Petherbridge, and arranged to pay them $25 each to collaborate and produce such a book. (You can appreciate how the boys were forced from the outset to spend their money like water.)

The result was that *The Crossword Puzzle Book* was published on April 10, three months after the company had set up shop, with what must have seemed a justifiably conservative first printing of 3,600 copies. The name of Simon and Schuster didn't even appear in this initial printing—a prominent bookdealer had warned the fledgling publishers that putting out a game book as their first venture might work against their being considered serious publishers, so they used "Plaza Publishing Company," a modest name inspired by their office telephone exchange. Dick Simon was less modest about thinking of ideas to put the book across. In the first of the inspired promotional tie-ins that later became a hallmark of the firm, he talked the Venus pencil company into giving him 3,600 rubber-eraser-topped pencils, one to be attached to each copy of the first printing. He also shot the works by having a one-inch advertisement inserted on the puzzle page of the *World* reading: "Out today! The first Crossword Puzzle Book!" Over the next few days, all hell broke loose.

The orders poured in at an unbelievable pace. Five more cautious printings of about 5,000 copies each were rushed through the presses and disappeared from the bookstore shelves like snowflakes on a hot stove before Dick and Max decided to start ordering 25,000 copies at a time. Over 100,000 copies were sold in the first wild rush, and an equal pace was achieved by a second collection put together hastily as *Crossword Book No. 2*, now proudly bearing the imprint of Simon and Schuster—as did all printings of the first book after the initial one. Bookstores were not going to be contemptuous of any firm that had produced such whopping bestsellers, and the Plaza Publishing Company was buried permanently. Before Simon and Schuster was a year old it had put out four crossword puzzle books; all four reached the top position on the nonfiction bestseller list. By the end of that first full year more than a million books had been sold and the profits were dizzying. Dick and Max never had to turn to their relatives for more financing.

Max Schuster and Dick Simon with the first copy of their first book

Almost immediately more than twenty clerks were hired to handle the orders; by the second year, the staff had grown to fifty and the office space had been expanded to a second floor. Although the crossword puzzle books continued to sell well and have done so ever since (Simon & Schuster has published more than two hundred of them to date), the skyrocketing craze was over. The fifty clerical employees had to be let go and the Essandess payroll was cut back to essentially three people, Dick and Max and a seventeen-year-old boy prodigy named Leon Shimkin, who had appeared on their doorstep in the middle of the frenzy in August 1924 with such convincing credentials that he was hired at $25 a week, the same salary Dick and Max were now paying themselves.

Through 1925 the crossword boom continued, and no one needed to worry too much about the future. Dozens of fascinating stories surfaced through these first two years about crossword puzzle books.

Here are a few that were reported in the *New York Times*.

• A New Yorker named Welz Nathan spent more than three hours at a table in an Upper West Side restaurant trying to solve a puzzle. Asked to leave, he refused to do so, was arrested, and was given his choice of paying a $5 fine or spending one day in jail. He chose the latter, saying it would give him undisturbed time in which to finish the puzzle.

• The Los Angeles Public Library put a time limit of five minutes on the use of a dictionary by any person at any time, since the puzzle craze had precipitated long waiting lines throughout the day. A sign posted above the dictionary section requested patrons to "Please settle difficulties at the librarian's desk."

• All crossword puzzles appearing in Hungarian newspapers had to be submitted to the censor, together with the solutions, prior to publication. This measure, taken to insure the stability of the Horthy government, was promulgated because a Royal Legitimist newspaper had published a puzzle in which the solution of the three horizontal words along the top line read "Long Live Otto."

• In England, London Zoo officials sent out a letter saying that the zoo would hereafter refuse to assist crossword puzzle addicts by giving scientific names of animals. (Queen Mary and several other members of the royal household were among those who confessed they were addicted.)

• Warner Fite, Professor of Logic, and Robert K. Root, Professor of English, both at Princeton University, formulated plans to use crossword puzzles in their respective courses, feeling that it could make the perpetually bored student find interest in his work.

• In Cleveland, a legal-aid organization received an average of ten letters a day, all very much the same. A typical one read: "We were happy until recently. Then my husband became absorbed in crossword puzzles. Since then he has no time to even look at me or the children. He no more gets his hat off than it is crossword puzzles. If I talk to him he gets angry. If we do go out for the evening he takes a crossword puzzle along with him. Morning, noon, and night—it's breaking up our home. He will either have to give them up or I will obtain a divorce."

• The first Intercollegiate Crossword Puzzle Tournament was held before several thousand spectators in the ballroom of the Roosevelt Hotel, the finalists performing on giant blackboards, screened from each other, trying to work the deciding puzzle while the audience, supplied with the definitions, suppressed the desire to shout an answer. Yale alumnus Stephen Vincent Benét, Pulitzer Prize poet, led the Elis to a narrow victory over Wellesley, while Harvard, represented by columnist Heywood Broun and Pulitzer Prize playwright Robert Sherwood, came in third. Princeton, Vassar, Smith, City College, and Bryn Mawr, represented by comparable intellectual notables, were also-rans.

Apart from the newsworthy incidents cited above, some charming, more personal anecdotes were recounted in the halls of Simon and Schuster by the delightful woman who was then, and still is more than half a century later, the guiding genius of the crossword puzzle books. That is Margaret Petherbridge, who married John Farrar, the eminent book publisher. When Margaret was asked if crosswords ever contained mistakes she replied that the rare ones were almost invariably merely typographical errors. But she had to confess to one unusual case: the nine-letter answer was "wooden leg," but since a recent puzzle had used Long John Silver in a definition, Margaret changed the name in the new puzzle's definition and made it "Captain Ahab's distinguishing characteristic." A letter was received from an eight-year-old boy complaining that while he had

Prosper Buranelli, Margaret Petherbridge, and F. Gregory Hartswick

worked out the puzzle and found the answer to be "wooden leg," didn't the creator of the puzzle know that Captain Ahab had an *ivory* leg? Margaret had to concede, but wondered rather testily what an eight-year-old was doing reading *Moby Dick*!

On another occasion a woman telephoned Margaret to say that she had solved a puzzle some time before that contained a word meaning "housewife" but she couldn't remember the word and now needed it desperately to use for a special important purpose. Told that the world was "oikologist" and, out of curiosity, asked what that very special purpose might be, she replied: "To use on my passport."

The profits that rolled up as a result of the fantastic success of the crossword puzzle books were more than enough to give the owners some security in the future of their new firm. It is intriguing in today's inflated economy to look back and see the size of the financial obligations that the watchdog, Leon Shimkin, was controlling for the non-fiscally-minded bosses. Remember that 1925 was not a year in the Great Depression but rather belonged to an era of a constantly climbing stock market and general prosperity.

The bill for the luncheon at which Dick Simon entertained his first authors, the three creators of crosswords, came to a staggering $5.85. His four-day selling trip to Washington, Philadelphia, and Atlantic City ran up an expense account of $27.30. Shimkin, as will be noted, had to be paid the same $25-a-week salary that Dick and Max themselves were now drawing, and the secretary they shared actually got $1 more. Essandess had already built up a reputation among book publishers for spending money like drunken sailors on advertising; that impression seemed well justified—the books reveal that $736.70 had been splurged in that fashion. The annual rent for greatly enlarged quarters had really soared and was now up to $3,000 a year. Despite all this the profit before taxes wasn't too bad—about 24 percent of sales. But the cruelly high federal taxes of 13.5 percent plus the state bite of still another 4.5 percent were enough to make businessmen like Simon and Schuster wonder if it all was worthwhile.

Simon was pretty unhappy as well about a policy he had instituted himself, the practice of allowing bookstores to return unsold copies for credit. The return policy was so successful in encouraging bookstores to order and display S and S books that the entire industry had to follow suit, but it's a policy whose results in later years has aroused many regrets as the percentage of returns has kept mounting. These days a hardcover publishing house that can keep returns down to 20 percent is doing about as well as can be expected, while mass-market paperback publishers suffer returns like 40 or 50 percent. But two years after S & S started its business, Simon scribbled a bold *"Bookstore returns too high!"* on the margin of that year's financial statement, and what he was referring to was a 3 percent return. He wasn't quite as miserable about the slightly less than $11,000 the firm had paid out to thirty authors as advances on thirty unpublished books that had been contracted for, even though $11,000 was a somewhat uncomfortable risk. (Today such a sum might be the advance paid for a single book with quite modest commercial potential; really hot properties now command advances that each run into the hundreds of thousands of dollars and, on occasion, even into the millions.)

Still, despite such burdens, life could be pretty good back then when the best theater ticket cost two dollars, a double-feature movie a quarter or not much more, a small candy bar a nickel and a huge one a dime, the morning newspaper two cents, and the subway fare a nickel.

The horizon was rosy, even though, apart from the puzzle books, the company's first real list had not produced too much. It consisted of one novel, *Harvey Landrum* by Ridley Wills, about which the most impressive thing to be said was that it was the only work of fiction accepted out of 241 novels submitted, but it sold less than 500 copies. A biography of Joseph Pulitzer, a collection of poems by Irwin Edman, and a children's illustrated game book didn't fare much better. The two books that sold moderately well were both "Common Sense" titles, one on the common sense of investing by Merryle Stanley Rukeyser, and the other on the common sense of tennis by the world's champion player of the day, Bill Tilden. With the crossword puzzle bonanza declining fast, despite money in the bank, Simon and Schuster had to come up with something else good—and quickly. Max Schuster did.

He had read a series on philosophy, tiny paperback five-cent Little Blue Books, published by E. Haldeman-Julius in Kansas, and written by a young instructor at Columbia University named Will Durant. Schuster bought the copyright to the series from Haldeman-Julius and then had Durant turn them into one big book, which he titled *The Story of Philosophy*. He then backed up its publication with the first of the overpowering "windswept" Max Schuster copy that became a hallmark of the firm's advertising for its more important books. The ads were almost invariably a full page in size, which was almost unheard of before that time, and always had an unusually arresting scream headline running across the top: one for *The Story of Philosophy* read *"Give me not millions,"* cried Mitya, *"but the answers to my questions!"* Even if the reader of the advertisement didn't know that Mitya was a character out of Dostoevsky, that headline grabbed his attention. *The Story of Philosophy* hit the bestseller list almost immediately after its publication in 1926, kept selling more copies each week as favorable word-of-mouth got around, and achieved the Number One spot on the bestseller list the following year. It established S and S as a firm capable of taking on and making a success of a distinguished book, and not merely a couple of lucky entrepreneurs who had stumbled onto a freak gold mine with crossword puzzle books. Simon and Schuster never looked back from that time forth, nor did Durant, whose earnings from that first book were enough to launch him on the gigantic project that would occupy him and his wife, Ariel, for the next half-century and would bring them and S & S both prestige and wealth—the massive *Story of Civilization* series.

As the 1920s drew to a close, it was clear that Simon and Schuster had arrived to stay, but admiration and even envy of the firm's obvious flair didn't completely erase some traditional old-time publishers' reservations about those young upstarts. Added to a continuing supercilious feeling about crossword puzzle books having been their origin, the house had published two extremely successful nonfiction books of adventure, *Trader Horn* and *Cradle of the Deep*, and in both cases the authors had been accused of being fakes. Those stories belong a little later in this book, so for the moment it is enough to mention them and that they engendered scandals. However, in 1934,

John Cowper Powys and Will Durant

ten years after the birth of the house and during the depths of the
Great Depression, *Fortune* magazine ran an admiring lead article
about S and S, about how in a decade they had turned $6,000 into
$800,000. Admittedly, *Fortune* is interested in financial rather than
artistic success, but the author tipped his hat constantly to the character the firm had established in so short a time, and he attributed the
partners' success to certain hard facts.

"They knew something the larger houses didn't know, or
couldn't live up to: never, never expand the business beyond the
capacity of the partners to care for it personally. There is little to
Simon and Schuster except Simon and Schuster. They have, it is true,
a genius in Leon Shimkin, their business manager, and another in
their editor-in-chief, Clifton Fadiman. But in the last analysis it is
Richard Simon and Max Schuster, following their hunches with or
without theorizing about them, who turn every trick. . . . They have
brought a healthy atmosphere of business to a profession overly
sentimental about itself. Without them the book trade might be in a
worse state than it is today—though God knows it's bad enough. The
publishers carry the booksellers, the banks carry the publishers, the
RFC carries the banks, and Mr. Roosevelt carries the RFC. But Simon and Schuster carry few, are carried by nobody. That's something."

Then five years later, in 1939, the *New Yorker* magazine, whose
editorial god has never been Mammon, ran a long three-part Profile
of the firm, written by that very elegant author, Geoffrey T. Hellman, which, while poking gentle fun at some of the characteristics of
the principals and not slighting the two embarrassing fiascoes of the
early years, *Trader Horn* and *Cradle of the Deep*, was equally unstinting
in its overall praise of the firm and its effect upon the book industry,
its creativity, and the individuals who made it tick. First impressions
die hard, however, and as late as 1944 there were some who were still
haughty about Essandess even though, by that time, it was universally accepted as a true prodigy of twentieth-century book publishers, one which in twenty years had taken a deserved place among
the leaders in the industry. Alfred Harcourt, expressing a possibly
typical feeling among the more conservative publishers, wrote to
Ben Huebsch, a fellow publisher: "It's the books and not the schemes
that give a list distinction and a real publisher his satisfactions—that

makes the business fun. You have always, I think, exhibited that fundamental characteristic of a real publisher. What really distinguished books have S & S published?"

With all deference to Alfred Harcourt, who was unquestionably a distinguished publisher, the implication was unfair then and even less fair today. Admittedly the house has had from its very beginnings a dichotomous approach to book publishing, and the catholicity of its lists, past and present, reflects that attitude. Always aware that publishing and selling books is their way of making a living, they do seek out and exploit the commercial book, and always have. But literary quality meant the world to Max Schuster and almost as much to Dick Simon, and even back in 1944 an effective rejoinder could have been given to Harcourt if his query had been public. In addition to *The Story of Philosophy*, by 1944 Will Durant had also turned out the first three volumes of *The Story of Civilization* series—*Our Oriental Heritage, The Life of Greece,* and *Caesar and Christ.* Ernest Dimnet's *Art of Thinking* was a notable book. So were, to name just a few more, John Cowper Powys's *Wolf Solent,* Leon Trotsky's three-volume *History of the Russian Revolution,* Leonard Ehrlich's *God's Angry Men,* Felix Salten's classic *Bambi,* the Viennese novelettes of Arthur Schnitzler, Hans Fallada's *Little Man, What Now?,* Artur Schnabel's *Beethoven's 32 Sonatas for the Pianoforte,* Albert Einstein and Leopold Infeld's *Evolution of Physics,* Rachel Carson's *Under the Sea Wind,* Millen Brand's *Outward Room,* and Wendell Willkie's *One World.* Although some of these were substantial bestsellers, it would be difficult to maintain that they were not all distinguished books. Simon and Schuster had even had one Pulitzer Prize winner in 1935—*Now in November,* by Josephine Johnson.

Today, with sixty years of publishing behind the firm and forty years after Harcourt's question, Richard Snyder could reply to a modern skeptic equally convincingly. Simon & Schuster continues to publish the exploitable, nonliterary work of what are essentially nonauthors, such as national celebrities, but while its backlist does not match that of the outstanding literary houses such as Knopf and Farrar, Straus, and Giroux, few publishers' backlists do. Simon and Schuster's record of distinguished books can compare with most others without apology, and it is a very definite and important part of Richard Synder's approach to see to it that quality books are never

Josephine Johnson

lost in the admittedly unabashed scramble for bestsellers. The house has had two more of its publications honored in the winning of the most prestigious book awards of the nation in the years since *Now in November* carried off the Pulitzer fiction laurels. Justin Kaplan, a former editor at S & S, swept the boards in 1966 with his magnificent *Mr. Clemens and Mark Twain*, which won both the Pulitzer Prize and the National Book Award. A little over a decade later, in 1977, David McCullough's monumental depiction of the creation of the Panama Canal, *The Path Between the Seas*, also won the National

Book Award as well as the two most prestigious of scholarly-history honors, the Francis Parkman Prize and the Samuel Eliot Morison Award.

Furthermore, two factors often work against an eminently deserving book winning these prizes. The first is that each award has its own set of rules about books that can even be nominated, such as nationality of author, subject matter, and type of production. Sec-

Justin Kaplan

David McCullough

ond, it's a matter of common knowledge that the choices made over the years by the committees of the Pulitzer Prize and National Book Award (now replaced by the American Book Award) have just as often been criticized as they've been applauded. Let us look at some Simon and Schuster titles that could have been notable candidates or winners if merit had been the sole consideration.

We might begin with William Shirer's *Rise and Fall of the Third Reich*, the uncontested classic history of Nazi Germany, which at least did win the distinguished Carey Thomas Award. What about

Bertrand Russell's *History of Western Philosophy*, as well as other of his thought-provoking books? Will and Ariel Durant's eleven volumes of *The Story of Civilization* are recognized as monuments of scholarly history, any one of which might have won one of the major prizes; but none did, perhaps because they are so readable. Then there is Harold Schonberg's *Great Conductors* and *Great Pianists*. James R. Newman's four-volume *World of Mathematics* may not have been a suitable entry both because it dealt with too special a topic and because it was, for the most part, an anthology, but what publisher would not have considered it a shining ornament on his literary list? The same could be said of the wonderful series of books prepared by the editors of *Scientific American*, which ranged over subject matter so erudite as to be incomprehensible to the general reader (including this one), but regarded as classics by the scientifically knowledgeable. Truly distinguished fiction has never been S & S's strongest point, but for more than a decade the house has been the proud publisher of that master novelist, Graham Greene. John Cowper Powys was Max Schuster's idol and Schuster published all his books, including the previously mentioned *Wolf Solent*, often classed as a landmark of English fiction. Vilhelm Moberg is probably the most outstanding novelist ever to come out of Sweden and his *Emigrants* is a book that could hardly have been overlooked by American prize-bestowing committees if it had been eligible, and the same is true of Nikos Kazantzakis's *Zorba the Greek* and *The Odyssey: A Modern Sequel*. Joseph Heller's *Catch-22* had a remarkable effect upon readers, lasting well past the acclaim it won when published, and is regarded as a modern classic. If I also tossed in P. G. Wodehouse and his work, Alfred Harcourt would probably have been as irritated as Hugh Walpole is reported to have been when Hilaire Belloc stated that Wodehouse was "the best prose writer of the age" when Oxford University bestowed an LLD on Wodehouse for distinguished writing, but what author has brought more joy to readers in this century? Wodehouse, unlike most authors, has been proven to be truly inimitable, and while we're at it, and for much the same reasons, let's nominate the work of another classic S & S author, S. J. Perelman. Coming up to more recent times, the house now boasts the fiction of Joan Didion, Margaret Atwood, John Gregory Dunne, Francine du Plessix Gray, Larry McMurtry, and Anthony Burgess, and I've left out a few less recognizable names whose work I personally consider superior to some of those. Still, it's not an unimpressive list for a house that is much better known for nonfiction than for fiction.

Finally there is a category of books that deserve being termed "distinguished," but not because they are essentially literary. They are important books that had considerable effect upon readers and even upon the nation—books like Wendell Willkie's *One World*, John Henry Faulk's *Fear on Trial*, the Boston Women's Health Book Collective's *Our Bodies, Ourselves*, Bob Woodward and Carl Bernstein's *All the President's Men*, Woodward and Scott Armstrong's *Brethren*, Seymour M. Hersh's *Price of Power* (published by S & S's sister company, Summit Books). Distinguished, by Alfred Harcourt's standards? I think so, because while popularity and big sales don't make books distinguished, they should not disqualify them either.

# Give the Reader a Break!

# 2

D ICK SIMON was just as keen about books as his more scholarly and even pedantic partner, Max Schuster, but his was the passion of a born salesman whose products happened to be ones that stimulated and interested him—books. An extrovert with a winning way of turning on the charm and attracting people when he was so minded, he had an equally effective way of snubbing others, which his admirers ascribed to excessive shyness. Most of the people that Simon and Schuster hired over the first quarter of a century were Dick Simon's protégés. The result was that the office was top-heavy with talented extroverts, with everybody constantly engaged in everyone else's business—and this closely knit body found such an atmosphere stimulating and rewarding. Dick had four guiding principles in hiring people, the first of which was the least important and the least admirable. With few exceptions his inclination was to staff the secretarial ranks with single, beautiful girls. His other three tenets were to take on compatible and talented people regardless of what their experience had been in the past, to let them grow into book publishing, and finally to be sure that they were able to write anything from jacket blurbs through advertising copy to sales letters to the trade.

Dick brought in a great many good and profitable books to the firm, but being a most personable man without Max's academic leanings, he acquired his books largely through sound instincts and personal contacts. A *Fortune* article of the time said that all publishers hated all booksellers and that all booksellers hated all publishers—but it certainly couldn't have been said of Dick Simon and his relationship to the trade. Booksellers were his best friends and he theirs. He visited bookstores constantly, giving advice and seeking it, asking opinions from owners and clerks about forthcoming Essandess titles, their jackets, the approach that advertising and promotion should take. In 1980, a score of years after Simon's death, Carl A. Kroch, the president of Kroch & Brentano's and very possibly the dean of American booksellers in this century, paid high tribute to Dick in addressing a conference at the Library of Congress. After saying that booksellers and publishers need not be natural enemies, he said:

"The publisher who I feel had the greatest impact on my business career was Richard L. Simon, co-founder of Simon and Schuster. Dick was the most innovative publisher I have ever known. He had a tremendous influence on the entire industry. It was he who experimented, so successfully, with the odd price for books. He reasoned that when you went into a drugstore and bought a tube of toothpaste for 79¢ you felt that it was marked down from a dollar and that you were getting a bargain. Why not do the same thing with books? So he priced his books at $4.95, $7.95, and $14.95. I don't have to tell you that ever since it has been a standard practice in the industry.

"Simon and Schuster was just about the first publisher to use coupon advertising with the orders directed to them and not to dealers. Booksellers were incensed: Essandess was stealing sales from them and they wouldn't sell their books, but that wasn't Dick's idea. He was merely creating a bigger demand, which meant more sales for booksellers. And that theory has been proven true.

"Dick made two suggestions to me that I believe have been most useful. He said that the public generally is afraid to go into bookstores. They fear that some salesperson will correct their pronunciation of an author's name or that they, the customers, will show some degree of ignorance and embarrass themselves. Dick said, 'Make people want to come into your store, make them feel at ease and welcome.' I have stressed that point to our sales staff continuously. Dick also urged that we advertise consistently. Not every ad will pay out but the cumulative result will be a recognition of your store as the place to buy books."

Dick Simon always had his customers, be they booksellers or the general public that bought books, foremost in his mind. He had brass paperweights made for all editors; they were seven inches long and two inches high and heavy enough to hold down a loose manuscript in a strong wind. Beautifully and boldly embossed on their face was Richard Simon's creed for editors: "Give the Reader a Break." He meant to see to it that the printer used a typeface and spacing that were easy to read, and was particularly generous in those respects when the book's audience was likely to be older people with fading vision. He meant that cookbooks should be bound in material that could be wiped clean with a damp kitchen cloth. He meant that books containing musical scores should be bound so they would lie flat on a music stand, that books needing illustrations or an index or glossary or notes got them, and so on down the line. I still have my paperweight and I'd hate to lose it: it's ornamental, functional, and a constant reminder of what should be a very important awareness on the part of any book publisher.

In bringing authors and books to the house, Dick Simon catered to his personal enthusiasms and talents. He was a superb musicologist and so expert a pianist that he might well have become a concert performer; one of his early Simon and Schuster book successes was his persuading an old Columbia University friend, George Gershwin, to allow a book to be made of his musical works. This was the first time such a project had been conceived: music publishers sold sheet music in stores like Schirmer's and felt that such a book would be competition, cutting into sheet-music sales. Dick finally persuaded them that the proceeds from a book's publication, which would be shared between the composer and the music publisher, would simply be found money, since the overlap between music-store customers and bookstore patrons couldn't be too significant. What is more, new exposure to a different audience would build interest in the purchase of other sheet music that wasn't available in a book. His argument was that the potential for expanded sales grows with each new exposure, even if, at first blush, it appears competitive. The truth of his contention has been borne out since in many areas of publishing, such as in the running of coupon advertisements and in the leasing of book-club rights, both of which were regarded initially with enormous suspicion by retail booksellers. In the case of *The George Gershwin Song Book*, Dick had to enlist Gershwin's help to persuade the music publishers; in the end, no one lived to regret such eventual cooperation. The book was a very considerable success and Gershwin's sheet-music sales continued to prosper.

That experience was the catalyst for another fruitful idea. Dick was devoted to classical music as well as popular, so he next turned to his friend, the great pianist Artur Schnabel, and had him edit a two-volume paperbound edition of Beethoven's *32 Sonatas for the Pianoforte*. It was because of Simon's devotion to music that he took on this obviously noncommercial project. When the first printings were exhausted some years after and the cost of running off more copies of one of the volumes would have made the retail price prohibitive, the work went out of print. Ever since, copies have commanded huge prices in the rare-book market. A gratifying concluding note to the affair is that today Belwin-Mills, the music publishers, have decided to print the work themselves, since the demand continues strong in their retail music stores, but they have granted bookstore distribution rights to S & S.*

Simon realized that real book successes were more likely to be found in collections of songs by the top hit-show composers, and once again he had to turn no further than to friends in the Columbia Alumni Association, Richard Rodgers and Lorenz Hart. The publication of *The Rodgers and Hart Song Book*, a much more sumptuous volume than the Gershwin book and embellished with delightful four-color illustrations, turned out to be a smashing success, and paved the way to an entire series of such books, all very successful. Simon and Schuster had proved that they could put across this sort of book and as a result obtained absolute domination in the field. The Rodgers and Hart volume was followed by *The Noël Coward Song Book*, *The Cole Porter Song Book*, the *Rodgers and Hammerstein Song Book*, *The Jerome Kern Song Book*, *The Frank Loesser Song Book*, *The Bacharach and David Song Book*, and *The Gilbert and Sullivan Song Book*. Each of these enchanting books contained the music, specially arranged for the piano, the lyrics, and sprightly illustrations; all over America virtually every home that boasted a piano owned one or more of these volumes. The big music companies that owned the copyrights often put up a struggle, but Dick was persuasive. He was aided considerably by a member of the S and S staff, Norman

*The Belwin-Mills edition changes the title to *Beethoven Complete Piano Sonatas*, and prints the text in five languages.

Monath, who was also a devoted musicologist, a composer himself, and a man who had connections in the music industry. So Simon and Schuster latched onto virtually every popular musical-show song-writer of note—since, as each new one saw what lovely books Essandess produced to immortalize the works of other composers, he saw to it that his music company yielded and allowed a song book too. The one lamentable and obvious gap in the long line was the failure to persuade Irving Berlin, who was his own music company as well as composer and lyricist of his songs, to go along. Berlin always listened to Essandess's blandishments courteously, and several times a marriage seemed simply to be waiting for the organ music to start, but in the end Berlin always pulled the plug. So the greatest of all such books, *The Irving Berlin Song Book*, still remains to be done. Nor did Simon and Schuster ever try for what might have been an obvious next-in-line in the series, a Simon and Garfunkel book; by the time that team had become so popular, Dick Simon was dead, and the taste and enthusiasm that ran so strong among the earlier owner and staff had run its course.

Individual books that achieve super sales successes are exciting and great, and a new publishing house needs its share of them to produce sufficient cash flow to keep going for a while. But a firm cannot survive if it depends too solidly upon another bestseller popping up with regularity. No matter how brilliant and imaginative and attractive its principals may be, a new publishing house has no backlist, and backlist sales, which require little or no continuing advertising and promotion, not only constitute a very big portion of a healthy publisher's business, but sustain it when inevitable fallow periods come along. Few American publishers in this century enjoyed a more brilliant beginning than did William J. Sloane Associates just after World War II, but, despite the fact that Bill Sloane had a real flair for publishing and proved it for a while with the authors he attracted, the sales his books made, and the unusually high number of major book-club adoptions those books gained, Sloane failed and was merged into the solid house of William Morrow and Company. Sloane's firm did not have enough backlist to support it when the dawn faded and bad weather arose, and there are many similar cases.

No one at Essandess appreciated this potential danger more than Richard Simon; seeing what could be achieved in one of his areas of passionate interest, music, he decided to try his hand with others. He had three other hobbies that were close to obsessions: photography, contract bridge, and sports. His plan was to seduce a big-name author to write a book on each of his specialties and, if any or all of those books turned out to be successes, to follow up with other books by other big names on the same topics. That way, through the ensuing years, the spine of a solid backlist could be established.

Simon had laid the groundwork for his plan very early in the firm's history, as far as contract bridge was concerned. From 1926 through 1931, years that led into a decade when it seemed every household in America played bridge most evenings of the week, Essandess published a new instructional book almost every year by the then Number One bridge player in the country, Sidney S. Lenz; they were all very successful. By the early 1930s, not only was Lenz quite old, but he'd run out of things to say. A new king of contract bridge had been crowned, Ely Culbertson. Dick made a stab at trying to get Culbertson to write for him, but Culbertson, who fancied himself as being as canny a businessman as bridge player, had signed up with a very small publisher who, in order to get the great man on its list, offered him such excessively high royalty rates that Dick wouldn't have thought of matching them. Since there was no pretender to Culbertson's throne on the horizon, there was nothing for S and S to do but bide its time.

Then a picaresque, Gargantuan figure named P. Hal Sims emerged, formed a team he named the Four Aces, and in tournament after tournament proceeded to destroy all opposition, including Culbertson's. And the lovely thing was that Sims wasn't using the Culbertson system of bidding, which had become the one all bridge players at that time employed. Sims had devised his own new and completely different system and was proving it was better. Not only was Simon convinced of that but so were the three employees he had hired (according to many) primarily because they were top-grade bridge players, Albert Leventhal, Jack Goodman, and Lee Wright. They all ganged up on Sims one day after a tournament and told him he simply had to write a book for Simon and Schuster. They had even dreamed up a title for it, *Money Contract*, but Sims said he had no intention of writing a book. It was too much work for the amount of money that might come out of it; he'd rather win bigger

The frightening countenance of P. Hal Sims in action

money playing bridge. But the Essandess contingent persisted, finally pleading that at least he should have a contract with them so that, if he ever changed his mind, he wouldn't do a book for anyone else. Hal seemed to feel that the whole thing was academic but he agreed that if he ever were to write a book, his pals were entitled to publish it.

When the contract was put down in front of Sims, he immediately flipped to the final page and started to sign his name. "Hey, wait a minute, Hal!" cried Albert Leventhal. "Aren't you going to read it?" Sims gave Albert a sly smile.

"This is your turf, boys," he said, "and I'm playing your game. If you decide to do right by me, well and good. If you decide to take me to the cleaners I'll be taken, and there won't be anything I can do about it. If we were dickering for partners or bets or anything else in my territory, like contract bridge or a golf match, I'd play it a lot cozier, but not here and not on this." He then did proceed to sign the contract without even glancing at the terms. He did write *Money Contract*, it was an enormous success, and since the terms of the contract were standard ones, he made a great deal of money.

Flamboyant rogues have always held a special appeal for people who are inclined to find an imaginative scamp more interesting than a stodgy hero. The Simon and Schuster crowd would have been bored to death by the tight-lipped, precise Ely Culbertson had he turned out to be their contract bridge bestselling author, but they were enchanted by Hal Sims even when they were his victims and even when his tactics approached the villainous. Being the best bridge player in the world was less important to him than winning money at anything, and although he was a gifted performer at everything he undertook, he derived particular pleasure if his streak of larceny had been a factor in setting up his "pigeon." An unregenerate gambler who played cards for very high stakes, he saw nothing wrong in sneaking a peek into an opponent's hand if he had the chance, and he freely admitted it. He held his cards close enough to his chest, never spreading them and often not even sorting them, so that no one had a chance to do that to him—but his philosophy was, let his opponents try if they could. Once when Lee Wright and her partner were about to engage in an important tournament game against Culbertson and his wife, Sims gave Lee a piece of Simsian strategy. "Smoke cigarettes constantly, Lee, and blow the smoke at Josephine. She's allergic to it."

Sims was so gifted at so many things that a normal person might wonder why he needed to stoop to chicanery, but Hal wasn't normal. He wanted to bet on anything and everything—but even more important, he wanted to be as sure of winning as he could. So although he was truly accomplished at golf, tennis, billiards, shooting, gin rummy, and heaven knows what else, he was never satisfied with what his natural endowments might bring him but manipulated all sorts of ploys to give himself anything from an edge to a sure thing. Once, playing in a golf foursome composed of Dick Simon, Albert Leventhal, Jack Goodman, and himself, on the first tee he proposed a substantial bet on each hole but agreed, since he was so excellent a golfer and they were all comparative duffers, that no pairing of two against two would be fair. (Some years later Jack developed into a very respectable golfer, but at that time he was as bad as Dick and Albert, which was quite bad.) So with a bland display of justice that would have done credit to Solomon, Sims proposed the following:

"Let's make it an even thing for all three of you. I will be the partner of each of you in turn for six holes out of the eighteen." Leon Shimkin might have had the sort of mind that would spot the flaw in the proposal immediately, but the ingenuous trio thought that sounded just fine. It wasn't until it was too late that the realization came to them that an excellent golfer paired with a duffer against two other duffers was going to win every hole, while each of them would lose twelve holes while winning only six.

Carrying through the principle that lightning, far from never striking the same spot twice, was quite likely to do so, after the Lenz and Sims successes Dick Simon went after every big contract-bridge name he could entice onto his list. There were Richard Frey and Albert Morehead, and finally the most dazzling of all contract bridge bestsellers written by Charles Goren. Goren had become the new world champion of the game and his success was attributable to a completely new and better system for bidding that he had devised, the Point Count system. So when S and S published Goren's *Point Count Bidding in Contract Bridge* in 1949, its sales topped a million copies in a few years. That book and a subsequent Goren book entitled *Contract Bridge for Beginners* are still extremely strong sellers

Charles Goren

on the backlist and seem destined to continue to be so, for the Point Count system remains the one used by the overwhelming majority of bridge players. In later years, after Richard Simon's death, despite some falling-off of the game's popularity from its peak in the second quarter of the century, S and S continued to look for and publish the best of contract-bridge authors: Terence Reese, Jeremy Flint, Ernest Rovere, Alfred Sheinwold, Howard Schenken, to name a few. But the real bloom was off the rose after the days of Sidney Lenz, P. Hal Sims, and Charles Goren.

In the meantime, what about Simon's other two enthusiasms, photography and sports? In the 1930s, high-speed photography with miniature cameras like the Leica was a new thing and most amateurs were a little afraid of its expense and complications, but Dick Simon was fascinated by it. He soon became a real expert, with a knowledge about the art that transcended that of many professional photographers, so he decided to write a basic beginner's book about it. Published in 1939 with the title *Miniature Photography*, it immediately established itself as the book on the subject, and it sold well in both bookstores and camera stores. At the height of its reputation and success, however, Dick had Simon and Schuster withdraw the book and destroy existing copies and the plates; today you will not even find the title in the general catalogue listing all the titles ever published by the firm.

Why? The year the book was published, 1939, was also the year World War II broke out. Germany blitzkrieged Western Europe and even threatened to invade England across the Channel. Dick knew that practically every fine miniature camera at that time, and all the accompanying paraphernalia, was made in Germany, and he was damned if he as an individual, or his firm as the book's publisher, was going to do anything to promote German goods. So he killed *Miniature Photography* forever. Two years later, after Pearl Harbor and America's entrance into the war, Simon ordained another change in S and S's business that sprang from the same sort of motive. The firm's colophon of the Sower had evolved a number of slightly different forms over the years, but a basic one displayed a background of the sun's rays behind the Sower. To Dick it looked much too much like the Rising Sun on the Japanese flag, so that particular logo was discontinued immediately and has never been resurrected since.

Despite his abortion of his own book, its reception and success had enforced Dick's instinct that a good thing deserves being repeated, so over the next two decades he actively pursued the best and most distinguished photographers and he came up with a flock of photographic books, some stunning and some intriguing. Dick was a fanatic about having such books reproduced by the finest printing processes existing, and although as a rule he endeavored to keep the price of a book as low as possible, on such books he spared no expense. He insisted upon maintaining those standards all through

The original 1924
Sower

The "Inner Sanctum"
column logo

The modern Sower

Parody for
Charles Addams book

Parody for
*The French Cat*

Parody for
*A Treasury of Hymns*

Parody for
George Price book

Parody for
*Treasury of Gilbert
and Sullivan (Mikado)*

The 1941 Sower,
dispatched after
Pearl Harbor

Parody for
*Pogo*

The S & S colophon of "The Sower" has gone through many mutations over
the years including occasional parodies of it used on special books. A few
examples are shown on this page.

the years including his final ones, when he had lost his health and his power in the firm. It was then that he published his finest books of photography, as you will learn later.

Simon's first venture into sports books had been William T. Tilden's *Common Sense of Tennis*, a title that appeared on Essandess's very first list back in 1924 and which, although no one was paying much attention to anything but crossword puzzles, sold better than anything else on the list. Although Dick's game was tennis, he knew that the real fanaticism for sports instruction was in golf. Every country club employed a golf professional who made a good living giving lessons, while professional tennis instruction was almost non-existent. There had never been a really successful golf-instruction book, but Dick was acquainted with Alex J. Morrison, a very well-known teaching professional who had developed a radical theory of how to play the game well. His pupils, both other professionals and amateurs, swore by him. Morrison was persuaded to put his golf lessons down on paper and, in 1932, Simon and Schuster published his *New Way to Better Golf,* and the first golf bestseller was on its way. It went into more than two dozen printings and sold ten to twenty times as many copies as any previous golf-instruction book.

Simon made up his mind that he was onto a good thing. If it worked so well once with golf, it could work again, and if golf worked, so could other excellent sports books. What needed to be done was to secure star sports performers as authors even if they couldn't write—you could always get a decent writer to listen to them and run off a manuscript on the typewriter, and then advertise and promote the book the way Essandess had the Morrison. This decision that a sports line well done could be a strong feature on a publisher's list turned out to be a good thing for Dick and the early S and S—and later for me. One of the presumed attractions that inclined the firm to hire me originally was my reputation as a sports authority, particularly in those sports which seemed to have the greatest appeal to book buyers: golf, tennis, baseball, and football. Consequently for some three decades an important and enjoyable aspect of my job was to bring into the house and edit virtually every such book the firm published. The perquisites that frequently were offered me by authors with whom I worked rank high among my most enjoyable experiences in publishing. I've played on the same tennis court with Big Bill Tilden, Bobby Riggs, Rod Laver, and perhaps surprisingly, Jack Nicklaus. (Jack loves to play tennis and is a good player. I'm good enough not to be embarrassed, as I clearly would be on a golf course.) But I have played golf with Tommy Armour, who tolerated my game because we were such good friends, and watched many a major tournament with that most knowledgable and companionable dean of golf writers, Herbert Warren Wind. Johnny Unitas and George Allen have invited me to sit in the press box with them at football games, Leo Durocher and Branch Rickey at baseball games. Sometimes I felt I should be paying Simon and Schuster for the pleasures my job afforded me, but I manfully resisted the impulse.

Dick Simon's inspiration was the spark that ignited S and S's pursuit of so many major sports authors, and in publishing Morrison's *New Way to Better Golf*, he proved for the first time that an instructional sports book could be a national and international bestseller. In some respects the book was almost a course in elementary physics, what with lots of information about the arc of the swing and centrifugal force, and Dick brought all of his inspired advertising flair into extolling its unique features. I cannot vouch for what Morrison's book actually accomplished in lowering scores for the world's golfers, but it certainly salvaged S and S's fiscal year of 1932, a year that old-timers will ruefully recall as the very bottom of the Depression. It was an equally big hit in England, where Charles Evans, chairman of the London publishing house of William Heinemann, had purchased British Empire rights from Simon. On both sides of the Atlantic, Alex J. Morrison was revered among golfers as a prophet and deliverer from evil, rather as Allah was in the world of Islam.

Charlie Evans was the most fanatical worshipper of all, being a really good amateur golfer who, as the result of studying Morrison's theories, had been able to cut a half a dozen strokes off his already good scores, but he had never met Morrison or even exchanged letters with him. All the material needed to publish the book successfully in England—the manuscript, illustrations, and advertisements—had been furnished by Essandess, and Simon knew that Evans was wistful about never having had anything to do personally with the Great Man. When Dick learned that Evans was coming to the United States on one of his regular book-scouting trips, he thought it would be a nice idea if he arranged for the two of them to play a round of golf with Morrison, and casually suggested it in a letter to London. Instantly cables flew westward over the ocean in great profusion as Evans went about changing a number of publishing appointments so that he could take advantage of this magnificent opportunity. Simon was going to meet his ship at the dock in New York with a car and whisk him off to the Holy Land where the ceremonies would take place, the Winged Foot Golf Club in Mamaroneck, N.Y.

The appointed day arrived and the only slight hitch was some difficulty encountered in fitting Evans's huge golf bag, jammed with so many new Alex Morrison clubs, into Dick's small car—these were the days before the fourteen-club limit. It was accomplished, however. About an hour later the scene moved to the first tee at Winged Foot where Morrison, the host, politely said to midair between the two publishers, "Your honor, gentlemen."

Dick Simon looked inquiringly at Charlie Evans, who motioned to him to proceed. So Dick teed up his ball and, knowing quite well that if he squared off facing the fairway his inevitable slice would carry the ball further toward the ninth fairway than toward the first green, sensibly faced Long Island Sound and swung. His slice was enough to make the ball trickle into the rough on the right, but at least it was some 170 yards out. Satisfied, Dick stepped back and ceded the tee to Evans.

Evans teed up his ball. Evans took his stance. The day was seasonably cool but the perspiration that had broken out all over his brow was clearly visible. Evans stood there. He had literally frozen at the thought of flubbing his first shot completely before Morrison's all-knowing eyes.

A full minute passed and Morrison said: "All right, Mr. Evans. Step away and start all over again. This is just a casual round with good friends—no one cares how any of us play or what we score. We're here for fun."

Evans looked at him gratefully but he didn't stop sweating. He did step back, breathed deeply, and resumed his stance. The same thing happened again. He simply could not bring himself to take a swing. At the end of another minute he straightened up and apologized. He explained that the whole thing had meant too much to him

Charley.

The Right Comets, Dec.
Swiss Schris to Vienna
So Rio
May 28 19

for too long a time and that now he just couldn't face it. He was sure that he would perform ignominiously all the way around and he didn't want to expose his companions to that. So would they please excuse him because he wanted to go back to New York right now. No, thanks awfully, he wasn't going to change his mind. No, he didn't want them to give up their round. No, he didn't want to walk around with them and have lunch in the clubhouse afterward. He wanted to get off the golf course and out of sight. Thank you so much, Dick, Alex, and so dreadfully sorry things turned out this way.

Deaf to all attempts at persuasion, Charlie Evans did indeed take off and, believe it or not, actually canceled his American business trip and instead caught the first ship home to England.

Successful books that fit into a category pave the way for a publisher to continue with others of the same nature, and sports books constitute merely one example. Cookbooks and diet books that work are inevitably followed by other cookbooks and diet books, authoritative medical books for laymen about one topic are followed by others on different medical topics. In recent years perhaps the outstanding example may have been the plethora of books about fitness published in what would have seemed to be overabundance by just about every firm in the business, but the results have clearly contradicted that first assumption. The United States has become so fitness-conscious that every new, or authoritative, or unusual, or celebrity-sponsored book of any merit more than justifies its publication. Simon and Schuster is by no means the only house to recognize this and benefit by it, but it's one of the outstanding ones. George Butler and Charles Gaines's *Pumping Iron*, featuring strongman Arnold Schwarzenegger, was a huge bestseller, and so was Dr. George Sheehan's *Running and Being*. *Total Fitness in 30 Minutes a Week* by Dr. Laurence E. Morehouse and Leonard Gross actually topped the nonfiction bestseller lists in 1975, and the most notable case has been the

Charlie Evans and Dick Simon

To Leon Shimkin
my friendly antagonist
Artie M. Govern
June 6, 1936

Leon Shimkin sparring with Artie McGovern

recent Number One status of Jane Fonda's programs for fitness, starting with her incredibly successful *Jane Fonda's Workout Book* and followed by a similar work for pregnant women and spinoffs taking the form of calendars and desk diaries. The national mania for buying books about attaining physical fitness may appear to have been born at the outset of the last quarter of this century, but *plus ça change, plus c'est la même chose.* Back in 1925 the eighteen-year-old Leon Shimkin attended a gymnasium run by a boxing trainer, Artie McGovern, and out of that peripheral contact encouraged Dick Simon to get McGovern to write a book, *The Secret of Keeping Fit.* There was no such craze about attaining the body beautiful then, but McGovern's book could barely be kept in stock throughout the year, so great was the demand. It's a little puzzling why Essandess and other publishers didn't leap onto the bandwagon more ardently in the years that followed and waited to do so until half a century later. Perhaps it was felt that McGovern had said the last word on the subject, but how wrong that feeling has turned out to be!

Even a good experience with a title, or a word or portion of a title, can give rise to further inspirations. The first use of the word "Fireside" was when Jack Goodman put together a lovely anthology in the early 1930s entitled *The Fireside Book of Dog Stories.* It sold extremely well and was a Book-of-the-Month Club choice; from then on the word "Fireside" was used almost indiscriminately for an amazing number of variegated gift books. There were Fireside books of love songs and of American songs, a *Fireside Cook Book,* a *Fireside Chess Book,* a *Fireside Treasury of Modern Humor.* A series of Fireside sports books appeared over the years: *Fireside Baseball* (so successful that it was followed by a second and third volume), and Fireside books on boxing, golf, tennis, horse racing, football, fishing—even cards and guns. As a result the name "Fireside" became so identified with S & S publishing that about fifteen years ago, when the firm was eager to create substantial lines in the burgeoning quality-paperback market and was looking for names to give identity to the separate divisions, "Fireside" was the choice for one. The name for the other quality paperback list, "Touchstone," was dreamed up afresh.

There are many other examples of this sort of treading in the footsteps of previously proven title successes, such as *A Treasury of _____, Invitation to _____, The Best of_____,* and *The Education of a*

_____. The grandaddy of them all, which Dick Simon surely didn't invent but saw that his firm utilized often and profitably, was *How to* _____. In the early years of this century there was a well-known bookman's gag based upon the notion that the ideal book title would combine topics known to be bestselling ones and, at that time, the proposal was for *Lincoln's Doctor's Dog*. Much later Albert Leventhal came up with one that better suited the smash hits of his day, even though it didn't include *How to*, namely, *A Treasury of Filthy Religious Art Masterpieces*. But even if Albert had not been jesting and even if the idea had viability, Dick Simon, really quite a puritanical publisher, would never have gone for it. He was a very solid family man.

Dick had three brothers and one sister, and although all five children were musicologists, forging so solid a clan as to be close to airtight, Papa Simon's pets were clearly Dick, the firstborn, and Elizabeth, the only girl. He often ignored and even worked a degree of humiliation on the other boys, Henry, Alfred, and George, but later all of them surmounted any early traumas and each became notable in the world of music. The one who became involved with Simon and Schuster, and so with this narrative, was Henry.

Henry was a very different type of man than Dick, an introvert rather than an extrovert, a scholarly academic. Versed in the classics and one of the country's outstanding experts on both the opera and Shakespeare, he had enjoyed a very brilliant career as a teacher, greatly admired by the institutions at which he taught and almost adored by his students. But brother Dick's publishing enterprise was flourishing and it looked more exciting to Henry, so he left the groves of academe and became an editor. Almost certainly it was a mistake—not that Henry wasn't a fine editor, but his interests and his style never fitted too comfortably into the S and S pattern. He actually was most respected and used by Max Schuster because, although Dick Simon loved his brother, he wasn't Dick's idea of an editor. Dick's idea more closely resembled a jumping bean.

Yet peripherally Henry was involved in one of Dick's most rewarding book successes. Henry married a secretary in the office, Margaret Halsey, and they went off together to live for a year in a small town in Devon, England, where Henry had been offered an exchange professorial scholarship. Peg Halsey wrote back extremely funny, acid letters about her disenchantment with the English and

Henry W. Simon

Margaret ("Peg") Halsey (*Copyright by Philippe Halsman*)

country living in England. She wrote, for example, that British ladies' shoes seemed to have been made by someone who had read what a pair of shoes were but had never seen any. Dick received letters and so did Peg's other friends at S and S, and each one that came in made that office day a merry one, being passed back and forth. Finally Dick collected them all and wrote Peg to keep them coming, because at the end of the year he felt an extremely good book could be fashioned out of them. Peg did, and Lee Wright, who had been Dick's secretary but was beginning to blossom as an editor, helped Peg and Dick turn the letters into a coherent, felicitous manuscript. Dick came up with a wonderful title, *With Malice Toward Some*, and it was launched toward bestsellerdom.

The fact is that although everyone in the firm chuckled over Peg's wicked humor in the letters, it was Dick and Dick alone who had unbounded confidence in the book. When galleys were sent to the Book-of-the-Month Club for consideration, a routine procedure, it was made a "C" book, which meant that one judge would be asked to take a look at it but that its chances were very slim. Yet Dick was not one to accept defeat easily on a project dear to his heart. He collared Harry Scherman, the president of the BOMC, and Dorothy Canfield Fisher, one of the judges, and read sections of Peg's manuscript aloud to them, then argued that in simple justice, so absorbing and unique a book simply had to be upgraded by the club. Make it an "A" book, which would mean that all the judges would be reading it. Dorothy Canfield Fisher took the bait, read the entire book, and was convinced that Dick was right. The rest is history: *With Malice Toward Some* was taken by the club as a main selection and, largely attributable to that prestigious acceptance, became one of the bestselling books of the period.

After that Dick Simon, whose enthusiasms were likely to exhibit the characteristics of a Yo-Yo, lost interest in Peg Halsey. She sensed it and would have taken her next work elsewhere, but Albert Leventhal, a devoted fan, persuaded Peg to stay with the firm and come under the wing of Lee Wright. Lee was always the most constructive and supportive of editors, and Peg is unstinting in her praise of how Lee worked with her on the five other books she then wrote under the S and S imprint. All were solidly successful, although not in the same commercial class as *With Malice*—primarily because of the seriousness of their topics. Although Margaret Halsey invariably wrote with a light touch, her later books all reflected her deep concern about civil rights, reform, and other matters of national importance, and they won more recognition from serious reviewers than from the compilers of bestseller lists.

When Lee Wright was promoted to senior editor and given her own sizable office, there was an aspect that might well have puzzled an outsider who had occasion to visit S & S frequently, such as an author who was working with another editor. Passing Lee's office, day after day, he or she would see two men at a table in the corner, crouched in chairs and pondering over a chessboard. Lee's husband, Jack Bassett, had serious health problems and it wasn't advisable for

Lee Wright

him to be alone at home when Lee went off to work. So a spot was created for him in that corner, initially to allow Lee to keep an eye on him. Jack was passionately devoted to the game of chess and he knew he was in a climate sympathetic to lovers of games. S and S had already seen to it that the firm had an outstanding line of contract bridge books but, after all, chess was the game of games, and Bassett was close to the Master classification. So was another Essandess staff member, Norman Monath, a particular favorite of Simon's because they shared two intense side interests, games and music. Norman, an accomplished pianist and composer, had been invaluable to Dick, with his contacts among musicians and his skill in securing book rights from music publishers, and if Norman wanted to spend hours with Bassett working out chess problems and helping build a chess line for the house, it was all right with Simon. So the two of them did and between them produced a series of instructional chess books that for years dominated the category in American book publishing, with authors that ranged from Capablanca through Irving Chernev and Fred Reinfeld to Bobby Fisher. If an efficiency expert had ever happened to spot Jack and Norman apparently goldbricking at a chessboard over hours of office time, he would have learned that there was more there than met the eye.

Henry Simon was not the first member of the family to marry an S & S employee—Dick was. A few years after the firm was founded, Leon Shimkin, who acted then as office manager as well as business manager and had charge of personnel, hired a new switchboard operator named Andrea Heineman. She was a lovely young woman but she didn't have the vaguest idea of how to run a switchboard. It didn't take very long for everybody, and in particular Richard Simon, to discover that fact. He called Leon on the carpet and issued an order to fire that impossible girl, but Leon defended her, saying she was indeed completely inexperienced but that she was very bright and would catch onto the switchboard in no time. Dick, only half-convinced, relented sufficiently to agree to give her a short trial. It turned out to be a lucky decision. In 1934 Richard Simon married Andrea Heineman, and soon they had four children. The best-known one is Carly Simon, the popular rock singer, but the two other daughters, Joanna and Lucy, have also each made notable musical reputations, Joanna in opera and Lucy in folk singing, while the one son, Peter, is a professional photographer.

One of Andrea's treasured memories in connection with the birth of her children concerned an Essandess author who became so close to the Simon family at home, and to the Simon and Schuster family in the office, that he was practically a member himself. That was the massive, gregarious, warm-hearted Dutchman, Hendrik Willem Van Loon.

Van Loon not only wrote several exceptionally attractive and successful books for the company, including *Van Loon's Geography*, and his *Ships, Arts,* and *Lives,* but he illustrated each copiously with his delightful watercolors. A man who much preferred writing letters to using the telephone, and one who never wearied of drawing, he would invariably dash off at least a little sketch or even something considerably more ambitious on the front of the envelopes containing his letters, next to the address or framing it artistically. On each of the four occasions when Andrea went off to a hospital to have a baby, Van Loon wrote her a letter every day; thus Andrea became the owner of about two dozen Van Loon originals, which she has lovingly preserved to this day. They were all rendered in various shades and colors, of course, and are much more striking than the sampling in the black-and-white illustration here—which I selected and Peter Simon photographed as a montage—but the illustration does at least convey an idea of the talented Van Loon's very special maternity offerings over the years to Andrea Simon. The office staff loved Van Loon as well, for if it was known he was coming in—which he did frequently—no one had to eat breakfast. Heedless of his own forty-four-inch waistline, Van Loon would invariably appear loaded down with a huge bag of hot-cross buns rushed over from his pet bake-shop.

Although from the very beginning Max Schuster was the member of the team more likely to be attracted to serious or literary works the firm could publish, Dick Simon contributed some entries as well. He was particularly effective on scouting trips he made to Germany and Austria, and one particular gem was Felix Salten's classic story of a deer, *Bambi,* which was a huge seller in that original form long before Walt Disney bought motion-picture rights. Disney cutie-pied it up and made it so very much his own that it takes a historian to remember Salten at all. (The translator S & S used is still well remembered, though, but for a different reason. He was Whittaker Chambers, the informant whose testimony destroyed Alger Hiss's career.)

Simon loved people and things that made him laugh, and I don't believe he ever hired anyone lacking a sense of humor. Simon and

A sampling of the many Hendrik Willem Van Loon envelopes

Schuster's reputation as the outstanding publisher of funny books didn't reach full flower until the forties, but it was Dick who started it all. He had Peter Arno, first and perhaps greatest of all *New Yorker* cartoonists, collect his early work for a book. *Whoops, Dearie* was published with such success in 1927 that for the next forty years, whenever Arno had amassed enough cartoons, another tremendously popular book was issued; there were six more, the most fondly remembered of which is probably *The Man in the Shower*. Simon and Schuster's triumphs with Arno inclined both the house and the *New Yorker* to proceed in later years with book collections of virtually every one of the magazine's cartoon artists, and that publication so dominated the field that there virtually was no competition. Simon and Schuster usually had the best sort of Christmas book, what with its many volumes of Charles Addams, Whitney Darrow, Jr., George Price, Alan Dunn, Otto Soglow, Carl Rose, and William Steig, to which could be added Thomas Craven's standout anthology, *Cartoon Cavalcade*, and the work of a few non–*New Yorker* geniuses of comparable stature such as Walt Kelly, H. T. Webster, and the best of the *Punch* group. Jack Goodman, Albert Leventhal, Nina Bourne, Bob Gottlieb, and others carried on the tradition of publishing humor when their turns came, but it was Dick Simon who lit the torch.

# PAAIMA and "Dinkelspiel"

# 3

ANYONE starting to write about Max Schuster is almost certain to be seduced into dwelling upon his personal methods of operation and foibles, to the disadvantage of extending proper credit to him as the devoted and even inspired bookman he was. One had to be around Max for quite a period of time before being able to appreciate his love affair with books and his resolution to be the best publisher possible. On short or less intimate acquaintance, Max seemed such a figure of affectionate ridicule that the temptation to begin characterizing him in that light is almost irresistible.

Let's start with his name, which his parents bestowed upon him—Max. In high school Schuster became such an admirer of Abraham Lincoln that he adopted Lincoln as his middle name and even dropped his first name on his signature, so that forever after it read "M. Lincoln Schuster." This, of course, never stopped anyone from calling him "Max" except for people who hardly knew him.

Then, when he was sixteen years old and gained entrance to the Columbia School of Journalism, it turned out that he was not only the youngest member of the class but the only one wearing short pants. He was not quite five feet tall and did not weigh ninety pounds; one classmate, who had been looking forward to college as a mature experience, was utterly disgusted at the sight of Max, and even considered leaving. Two or three years later, Schuster suddenly gained some seventy pounds and grew almost another foot, feats which he attributed to sheer willpower.

Thomas Edison liked to say that genius was one percent inspiration and ninety-nine percent perspiration. In Max's case the figures may be topheavy but surely it was dogged work that enabled him to accomplish what he did. Each evening he read every newspaper and magazine thoroughly, marking with a heavy blue grease pencil any item that seemed even remotely interesting as the basis for some unforeseen book. The next day he would bring in his briefcase bulging with these publications, and three secretaries would spend the day clipping the items, sorting them, and then mounting them in separate albums according to the subject matter, with cross references and duplicates when they overlapped. It was this tactic of Max's that inspired one of the better jests in an office parody about a mythical book's progress—the epic story of Barney Greengrass, the Sturgeon King, which will be described in a later chapter. Max's supposed contribution recounted in this elaborate fictional prank was a three-inch-thick folder of clippings simply labeled "Fish."

Max might well have had such a folder, for the topics he had those poor secretaries clipping and building up in albums were encyclopedic. He further extended and complicated his gigantic files by seeing to it that his bundles of colored three-by-five pieces of paper, which he accumulated in his pockets throughout the day, were classified and stored in similar fashion. Whenever he saw or heard anything that he thought might conceivably be of interest some day, he jotted a note to himself on either a pink, blue, or green slip, having filled his left-hand coat pocket with a batch of such slips each morning. The pink slips were used when he thought he had an idea for a projected book, the green ones were reminders of people to see and things to do, the blue ones for what he termed "MQ's,'" or maxim quotations. Those were short statements or ideas that he found sufficiently arresting to think they might serve him in the huge treasury of wisdom that he intended to put together when he had the time. Once he had written on a pink, green, or blue slip, he transferred it to his right-hand coat pocket so that, at the end of the day, he could pull out the day's batch and hand it over to one of the harassed secretaries to type up and fit into the next morning's regimentation of stored background information. Max Eastman, a great friend of the firm and a man whose sense of humor was evident in the writing of his popular book, *Enjoyment of Laughter*, once got hold of one of Max's

Max Eastman

pink slips, scrawled "Dinkelspiel" on it in a fair imitation of Schuster's handwriting, and managed to plant it in Max's right-hand pocket. It baffled Schuster for some time and he couldn't recall what had inspired him to write "Dinkelspiel." Finally, even if considerably troubled by it, he gave up.

Schuster loved to use abbreviations for office routine work and, after exposure to them for a while, the staff started to use them too. An editorial memorandum was labeled "EM," and while most were likely to fit on a typed page, one of Schuster's once ran to 192 pages in outlining a fifty-year plan and schedule for S & S's publishing.

Instructions to write somebody a polite answer bore "PA" across the top of an incoming letter, but if the response was to be a brief rejection the label was "BR." For a time no one could figure out why Max's "LL" seemed to mean that the person should be sent a form rejection but it eventually became clear: the form rejection used the excuse that the submitted manuscript was too special for Essandess's limited list. "FU" did not mean what you think, but rather instructed the recipient to follow up. The most elaborate of Max's code initials was "PAAIMA," which utterly baffled the first people to see it but which Maria Leiper, a young woman schooled in the exquisite etiquette practiced at Vassar, finally managed to decode. It meant "polite answer as in my absence."

In the beginning, both because it fitted their natural energies and inclinations and because Simon and Schuster had not yet achieved the sort of literary reputation that inclined too many agents to send the house their best manuscripts, both Max and Dick were likely to think of ideas for books and then assign them to authors they felt could do the best job. Max's sometimes ludicrous tactics may have wasted energy and driven his secretaries and his editors crazy, but they often bore fruit. First of all they gave rise to the concept and creation of Essandess's first great success with a book of distinction, Will Durant's *Story of Philosophy*. Then, Max spotted another that turned out to be a Golconda.

Clifton Fadiman has over the years become one of the giant names in books, but back in the late 1920s he was simply a Columbia graduate who had been hired by Henry Simon, then a teacher at the Ethical Culture Schools in New York, to be an instructor. That was fine for a first job, but Fadiman, who to the best of my knowledge has never been called anything but "Kip" by those who know him, had always had his eye upon book publishing, and there he was, an associate of the brother of one of the partners of that young, jazzy firm called Simon and Schuster. Couldn't Henry effect an introduction to Dick?

Henry could and did, but Dick, who had good instincts but laid no claim to being literary, realized that this young man was much more cut to Schuster's pattern, and suggested that Max interview him. An appointment was arranged. Max's first question was to ask Kip what he thought he could contribute to the expanding company,

Leon Shimkin, Max Schuster, Dick Simon, and Clifton ("Kip") Fadiman

probably expecting the usual reply that applicants for editorial jobs invariably give—their love of reading and confidence in their taste and judgment. Instead Kip pulled out a brown folder, extracted a sheaf of papers, and said: "I have typed out one hundred ideas that I think might make books."

No answer could have appealed more to Max Schuster, and the magic number of 100 must have been the clincher—ever so much more appealing than prosaic numbers like 83 or 109. Kip was hired before the day was out, though he now admits he wasn't at all sure that very many of his ideas were any good at all, or for that matter ever came into being. He did know that Max Schuster spotted one in particular that turned out to be a fantastic winner with Simon and Schuster in hardback, and with Pocket Books in paperback. Kip's idea, like his others, had been expressed in a single sentence: "I believe that an intriguing and successful book could be compiled out

Robert "Believe It or Not" Ripley

of a selection of the Robert Ripley cartoon features for the Hearst papers, *Believe It or Not.*" That one inspired idea of Kip's, singled out by Max Schuster as the gem of Fadiman's 100 proposals, certainly more than justified the something less than $20 a week Kip was first paid. The first Ripley *Believe It or Not* sold close to 200,000 copies, a huge hardback sale in those days—or even, for that matter, today— and in subsequent reprints, further compilations of the feature published by Pocket Books, and worldwide editions, the Ripley books have a total sales record bordering on 30 million copies. Max Schuster, who always liked to feel that anything he did had cultural overtones, is quoted as having said: "We projected Ripley not only as a cartoonist but as a figure comparable to Marco Polo." That statement had something of its highflown tone diminished when a man named Norman Pearlroth died a year or so ago at the age of eighty-nine, and rated an extensive obituary in the *New York Times.* Then the world learned that Pearlroth had spent virtually seven days every week in the New York Public Library on Fifth Avenue working up research for Ripley's feature. Indeed Ripley did travel to almost two hundred countries to scout truths stranger than fiction, but his travels were invariably based upon Pearlroth's research. A marvelous cartoonist with a smashing idea, but hardly Marco Polo.

Pearlroth had been working in a bank in 1923 when he was twenty-nine years old. He met Ripley by chance and learned that he was looking for someone who could read foreign publications. Pearlroth, who grew up in Poland, was fluent in fourteen languages, was an avid reader of foreign journals, and had an unusual memory for miscellany. He got the job and stayed with Ripley, handing in his research every Friday. With Ripley's death in 1947, the feature was purchased by King Features Syndicate, but Pearlroth kept working for Ripley's replacement until he retired in 1955.

Max Schuster's next coup was to assign Thomas Craven the task of writing about the lives and works of great painters, not only resulting in the book *Men of Art*, which sold over 75,000 copies, but attaching Craven, an exceptional man, to the house. He later wrote another equally successful art book, *Modern Art*, edited a delightful compilation of humor, *Cartoon Cavalcade*, and achieved his greatest fame as the editor who supervised and wrote the text for a true landmark in Simon and Schuster's history of publishing, the superb

Max Schuster, Thomas Craven, and Dick Simon

first collection of the greatest paintings the world knew, *A Treasury of Art Masterpieces*. That book, originally published in 1939 with a $10 list price (a comparable book done today would surely be priced at $50 or more), was perhaps the most spectacular example in the firm's history of brilliant sales performance, involving huge expenditures on full-color brochures and intensive advertising and collateral publicity. Albert Leventhal is credited with being the brains and spirit of the operation, and from the sales angle he was, but he had something to work with—Schuster's dream and Craven's execution.

Schuster had filed away an old EM for over a decade before he one day decided to breathe life into it. He knew that the Bible was by far the world's bestselling book, but he thought it could be improved by judicious editing. A professor at the University of Oregon, Ernest Sutherland Bates, agreed; if the King James Version were rearranged by time and subject matter, with redundancies eliminated, with prose printed as prose and verse as verse, drama as drama, letters as letters, and with spelling and punctuation modernized, "the noblest monument of English literature" could be fully appreciated and clearly understood by readers of all faiths. Bates went to work, and in 1936 *The Bible Designed to Be Read as Living Literature* was published. It was an instantaneous hit, was adopted by the Book-of-the-Month Club, and sold close to a quarter of a million copies in the hardcover trade edition in this country alone. And that, as masters-of-ceremonies are fond of saying, reminds me of a story, even if it falls out of place chronologically.

Some twenty-five years later when I was publisher of Simon and Schuster and the brilliant young Robert Gottlieb was editor-in-chief, an Israeli gentleman with a letter of introduction to me presented himself at our offices. He was carrying two huge, obviously very heavy suitcases, one in each hand, and as he staggered down the hall he might well have been cast as a dispirited Willy Loman in *Death of a Salesman*. When he finally managed to reach my office and tottered in, Gottlieb was there talking to me and stayed on to see what was in those massive bags.

They turned out to be huge photographs of the Holy Land, and the idea was to publish them in a luxurious, oversize volume. We decided such a book was not practical and then helped the gentleman repack his gear and showed him out to the elevators. After he was gone Bob turned to me and said: "Too bad—I had a great idea for a title for his book. *The Bible Designed to Be Read as Living Luggage!*"

Apart from his persistent prodding of other people whom he considered potential authors to write books for which his own voluminous files could supply background material, Max counted that day lost whose low descending sun viewed from his hands no worthy action done. No doubt a lot of his editorial energies were wasted motion, but he truly was the busy bee who strove to improve each shining hour. So on two occasions, instead of stimulating others to use the incredible files he amassed so compulsively, he turned out books himself. The first was a photographic history of 1934, *Eyes on the World*, which S & S published the following year. Others might have been daunted by the work Schuster and his assistants put into this project. Over 30,000 clippings were scissored from newspapers and magazines and 20,000 photographs unearthed, out of which 4,000 were considered strong enough to have reproducible copies made and filed. Max then personally winnowed those down to about 700 and dummied up his book. *Eyes on the World* was not much of a commercial success but the project had two good results. Schuster had a ball, and Henry Luce has been quoted as saying that *Eyes on the World* was his inspiration for founding *Life* magazine in 1936.

A few years later Schuster closeted himself again for many months to prepare another book. He had been collecting material for it for well over a decade, and this time he turned out a work that was not only prestigious but also commercial, *A Treasury of the World's Great Letters*. Mixing impeccable taste with an advertising man's instinct for what would capture a browser's interest, Schuster included in the table of contents a provocative fragment of each letter listed. Perhaps someone had done this before Max, but if so, nobody seems to be aware of it. In any case, his choices of fragments were inspired. For example, the Contents entry for Lord Chesterfield's letter to his illegitimate son is followed by, ". . . even polished brass will pass upon more people than rough gold"; and the quotation from Michelangelo's negotiating terms with His Holiness the Pope for the art he proposed for the Sistine Chapel, reads; ". . . it will be a work without equal in all the world. . . ." The technique was so clearly effective in the pages of the book when copies were available that it was used virtually intact as the basis for all the advertisements that ran after publication.

Simon and Schuster's personnel policy back in the early years was a remarkably free-wheeling affair. Apart from the solid business types whom Shimkin would occasionally take on because he investigated their credentials, gave them tests, and found them good, the bulk of the staff was built up by other methods. People were rarely brought in for so dull a reason as to fill a specific job. Dick Simon, around whom most of the action swirled, hired people he found imaginative, or funny, or excellent contract-bridge players—which, to him, was the mark of a good mind that could be turned to good effect towards publishing matters. Dick's philosophy was to engage personable, lively people without book-publishing experience and toss them into the middle of the office ocean, being sure that the really good ones would come to the surface and swim confidently to whatever he or she could do most effectively. On the whole that's the way he built up the group that eventually took over most of the day-to-day publishing functions from himself and Max, people like Albert Leventhal, Jack Goodman, Tom Bevans, Nina Bourne, Lee Wright, Joseph Barnes. They in turn took on the group who became the overlapping-to-next generation, and among many others that included me, Helen Barrow, Bob Gottlieb, Tony Schulte, Milly Marmur, Richard Kluger, Michael Korda, Strome Lamon, Dan Green.

Once Dick Simon had established his particular coterie of associates, Max Schuster became to some extent a loner. He had little interest in the high jinks that enlivened daily operations at the office, and even less in the occupations of Dick and his crowd after hours. Max wanted to work on books, usually serious books, with help from serious assistants, so that is what he looked for on the fairly few occasions when he hired someone specifically for that role. The first of them, as has been noted, was Clifton Fadiman, who turned out to be a winner. Even in his apprenticeship it was immediately apparent that Kip had rare sensitivity and taste and, in working for Max on his books, was obviously a standout among editors. One of his first jobs was to do the huge cutting job on John Cowper Powys's enormous manuscript that would enable that book to be published at a reasonable list price; he did this so successfully that the book, *Wolf Solent*, stands alone in S & S's first decade as the work of fiction of which the house could be completely justified in being proud. Assigned to being the working editor for Essandess's pet author of the time, Hendrik Willem Van Loon, Fadiman did yeoman's work in steering that learned historian's manuscripts into channels more palatable for the general reader. Van Loon, a true Renaissance man, often wrote in such an ebullient style as to need toning down. On the other hand, Kip is quick to admit that the cheerful Dutchman once taught him a great lesson about editing. In reading the manuscript for *Van Loon's Geography*, Kip ringed about a hundred words with red ink. He felt they were difficult words for the young adult audience at which Van

Loon's deceptively simple style was aimed. Why use "supercilious" when "proud" would serve equally well and some readers would not know the meaning of the longer word? Why "ambiguous" when "doubtful" would do?

Van Loon looked at Fadiman and smiled gently. "How will young people ever learn the language and expand their vocabularies unless you give them intriguing words to look up? I use such words on purpose." Kip was immediately convinced; the words stayed in as written.

A gathering at Ripley's publication day party. *From left to right:* George Gershwin, Count Felix Von Luckner, Gene Tunney, Max Schuster, Robert Ripley, Dick Simon (pathetically trying to conceal his height!), Sidney Lenz, Hendrik Willem Van Loon, and Sir Hubert Wilkins.

Fadiman's reputation as a perceptive, incisive book critic grew steadily during his years at S & S and, in 1933, the *New Yorker* asked him if he'd be interested in becoming its book editor, which meant he would be writing most of the major reviews in that weekly and most prestigious publication. It was understood that this would not be a full-time occupation and that Kip would continue in his role at Essandess but, appealing as the offer was, both he and the *New Yorker* were troubled by the obvious conflict of interest that would arise whenever a Simon and Schuster book seemed a good candidate for a major review. The matter was discussed with the S and S bosses and they quite generously if somewhat ruefully agreed that Fadiman could take on the *New Yorker* job and that he would not review any of the firm's books. It was a proper decision, even though it would be hard on a few of the house's best authors not to have a chance for a major review in the magazine. From the firm's standpoint it meant that their young editor would be expanding his reputation and might well attract top-level authors to the house as a result.

All this worked out well enough for a while, but some time later Fadiman opened his pay envelope and found in it a sum considerably smaller than the usual one. He went to the financial boss, Leon Shimkin, to say that there had been some mistake, but Leon replied that there had not. He had been thinking over the fact that, in order to perform his other function, Kip had been taking off the equivalent of one working day a week, so Leon had deducted that proportion of Fadiman's weekly salary from the paycheck to compensate. At the time Kip was so outraged by this action that it was a major factor in his resigning a short while later. Today, half a century later, he confesses that he thinks Shimkin was justified by business standards even if the pay cut wasn't a wonderful example of extending tender loving care to a valuable employee.

Regardless of how irritating the docking of salary may have been, Fadiman was due to leave Simon and Schuster around then in any event. He had branched out and was fast becoming a national figure. The *New Yorker* loved his work and showed it in generous paychecks over the decade Kip wrote reviews. But even more important from the standpoint of fame, Fadiman became the master-of-ceremonies of one of the most successful of all radio programs, *Information Please*, and continued with style and flair from 1938 to 1948. In the middle of that stint, in 1944, he was also appointed to the position he still holds, a judge of the Book-of-the-Month Club. Just before the BOMC connection became fact, Simon and Schuster asked him if instead he'd consider returning to the firm as editor-in-chief, but that onetime dream no longer paid enough to compete with his other pursuits. In that connection, Kip maintained that working in book publishing without being an owner was the world's most luxurious way of starving to death. He meant that the perquisites were splendid—luncheons in the best restaurants, attending conferences at lush resorts, and so forth—but the salary check wasn't likely to be up to paying the rent, eating other meals, raising a family, or doing much else. That certainly was true then even if it is less true now, but it is still undeniable that people blessed with the sort of intelligence, talent, and energy that distinguishes good book editors could make more money in another business.

Nonetheless, Fadiman remembers his tenure at Simon and Schuster and his confrères there contain more admiration and affection than many of the old-timers I interviewed. Kip is often an outspoken man about matters that don't please him, but in this case his words were nothing but upbeat.

"Max and Dick were mercurial geniuses who dreamed up ideas for book publishing that may seem conventional now but which were completely fresh and novel then. They sensed the emergence of a new audience composed of people who hadn't bought books in the past. They kept abreast of the news of the day and tied in book ideas that related, finding celebrities, often from show business, to be the authors. Eddie Cantor's *Caught Short* about the 1929 Wall Street Crash was an example. Cantor wasn't enthusiastic about taking time out to do such a book, but Schuster got it out of him by sending a high-pressure stenographer around every night to the New Amsterdam Theatre, where Cantor was starring in *Whoopee*, and armed with Max's copious notes and suggestions, she got him to dictate during intermissions. *Caught Short* sold 70,000 copies within its first two weeks of publication.

"Max had a fantastic feel for advertising and the Inner Sanctum columns, which he originally wrote and which were later carried on in the same great style by Jack Goodman and Nina Bourne, were enjoyed as avidly by newspaper readers as if they were columns by such favorites of the period as Heywood Broun and Franklin P. Adams (FPA). Dick wrote wonderful Inner Sanctum columns too, but his were chiefly for *Publishers Weekly* and were directed to the book trade rather than to the general reader. They were the first to splurge with full two-page-spread advertisements in the *New York Times Book Review*, and the first to conceive of a handsome checkerboard type of advertisement of that size that presented their leading gift books for Christmas—a technique that most publishers eventually copied and still use today. The unusually arresting headlines in bold type that were a feature of their full-page advertisements created a sensation in what had been a much more sedate approach to book publishing. Max was particularly adept in the lead-offs he gave his 'windswept' ads but Dick was no slouch either. Here are examples of each, first Schuster's headline and following copy for *The Evolution of Physics* by Albert Einstein and Leopold Infeld:

IF EINSTEIN CALLED AT YOUR HOME TONIGHT
willing to stay and explain to you the
mysteries of the Universe and the
Theory of Relativity,
WOULD YOU LISTEN TO HIM?

"Dick Simon didn't contribute anything to the fantastic bestselling golf book, *How to Play Your Best Golf All the Time*, except for the headline of the first big advertisement, but that's a little like saying that Churchill didn't contribute much to World War II except for speeches. The headline ran:

WHACK THE HELL OUT OF THE BALL
WITH YOUR *RIGHT* HAND!

along with a line drawing of a golfer obviously doing so.*

*Note: for the benefit of nongolfers, until then every golf professional had been preaching that golf was essentially a left-handed game for right-handed golfers. Tommy Armour was the undisputed golf instructor genius of the day, and his pronouncement was reassuring for right-handed golfers, seeming much more natural, but it was blasphemy to the right-handed traditionalists who had always been told that the left hand should control and dominate their swings. In any event, the book sold half a million copies in its first year and is still selling more than thirty years later, and while most of its success is due to its being recognized as a classic in the field, a good part of its initial surge to the top of the bestseller lists was undoubtedly due to that headline, which Norman Monath dug up out of Armour's text along with half a dozen other possibilities, but which Dick Simon recognized as the one that might make the book take off.

"When Max or Dick had a new idea about which they were enthusiastic, they plunged ahead without any quibble. They didn't ask for extended outlines or plans: if they had ever even heard of test-market research they didn't believe in it. They trusted their instincts, they trusted the people who were to carry out their ideas, and backed them to the hilt. That is what made working for Simon and Schuster in those days so exciting. You could take the ball and run with it. Of course now and then for some reason or the other they would veto something you desperately wanted to do. In my case once it was telling me to reject Viña Delmar's *Bad Girl*, which they considered too risqué. Harcourt, Brace took it on afterwards and sold 100,000 copies, to say nothing of what the big results must have been when the mass paperback edition came out. Quite honestly, probably because it came to nothing as far as we were concerned, I don't remember the whole thing that well, but Geoffrey Hellman wrote about it in his *New Yorker* Profile and I'll certainly accept his reporting as accurate. He wrote that the rejection prompted me to pull all the books off my shelves onto the office floor, jump on them, and disappear for three days.

"But it was rare that the boys didn't go along with a really passionate enthusiasm that any highly valued associate came up with. Even Leon Shimkin, the only one of the three partners who tried to keep the boat steady and thought about the future by keeping a tight rein on salaries and expenses, never tried to curb costs on a hot new idea that Max or Dick were eager to try to exploit. A good example was the very expensive four-color Christmas brochure, printed in the hundreds of thousands and furnished free to major book accounts to mail to their customers with their own imprint and address so that orders came back to the stores. This was an immense gamble and there was no real way to measure its effect except for the fact that year after year, while this tactic was used, Simon and Schuster gift books dominated the Christmas season. It would be interesting to know how many people, receiving a handsome mailing piece from, let us say, Brentano's, which didn't say 'Simon and Schuster' anywhere on it, realized that all the books featured in it were indeed S and S publications.

"Then in 1942 Max Schuster came up with another publishing inspiration. The translation of Leo Tolstoy's masterpiece, *War and*

*Peace*, done by Louise and Aylmer Maude, had long been regarded as the best one in the English language and had been published for years by the Oxford University Press. It had sold steadily but quietly for a long time as classics invariably do after their original issue, but 1942 was the year of Hitler's Russian campaign in World War II and it occurred to Max that the analogies between that and Napoleon's Russian campaign as described in *War and Peace* were striking. So Max made an arrangement with Oxford for Simon and Schuster to use the Maude translation in a new edition that would embody a number of intriguing features and to pay a royalty for such permission. Then he turned to me, although I had left the firm some years before, and commissioned me to write a very long Foreword—more than 15,000 words—about the book and the parallels in the campaigns. He had maps prepared that pointed up the similarities and then conceived an idea which exemplified perhaps more than anything else the firm ever did the Dick Simon notion of 'Give the Reader a Break.' A 12-page 'Reader's Guide and Bookmark' was prepared that first presented the principal characters arranged in family groups, followed by the dates of the principal historical events along with the maps, and finally listed the characters in the book again but this time in the order of their appearance. Printed on a page slightly smaller than those in the volume, this 12-page pamphlet was an invaluable help to readers plowing their way through the 1,350 pages that comprised the Inner Sanctum Edition of *War and Peace* and trying to keep the seventy-odd characters straight, particularly with their unfamiliar Russian names. The pamphlet also served as an excellent bookmark, most useful when the reader returned to the book after putting it aside for a while which, I would imagine, was true of almost every reader since *War and Peace* is not likely to be read at one sitting. Then, in case the pamphlet was lost and to preserve the material in permanent form, it was all printed again and bound into the back of the actual book. Beautifully packaged and effectively advertised and promoted with its unique features emphasized, this edition breathed new life in Tolstoy's great work and became a bestseller.

"People are apt to think of great editors as being men whose basic function is to use a blue pencil while making a manuscript better. That is certainly part of the role but creative brainwaves like those

I've recalled are what make great publishers out of great editors."

In Clifton Fadiman, Max Schuster had exactly the sort of scholarly editor with popular instincts who complemented his sort of publishing. Years later he acquired another, Justin Kaplan, who performed comparable yeoman service for Max before he doffed his editor's robes and became a full-time author. This turned out to be a fine decision for Justin to make, both for himself and for Simon and Schuster, who have had the reward of being Kaplan's publishers since his departure, for Justin's very first book, the biography entitled *Mr. Clemens and Mark Twain*, was the outstanding nonfiction work of 1966, capturing both the National Book Award and the Pulitzer Prize. Kaplan followed up his Mark Twain classic with two other extremely distinguished biographies, one of Lincoln Steffens and the other of Walt Whitman. He is currently engaged upon an exciting long-range project that has aroused great interest throughout the publishing world, a biography of Charlie Chaplin for which, for the first time, Chaplin's widow, Oona, and the Chaplin estate are making all the records and correspondence available.

One other top-notch editor was assigned as Max Schuster's assistant—Jerome Weidman, who came after Fadiman and before Kaplan. Jerry was a different breed of fellow than Kip or Justin, and his personality, private enthusiasms, and general aura were much more in keeping with the Dick Simon crowd than they were with the sort of aide that Max Schuster might have selected for himself. But Dick had become a little uncomfortable and even embarrassed by the fact that all the very highly placed people in the firm were either directly or indirectly "his boys." All the action swirled around that group, and since Max was not an office hail-fellow-well-met type, it lost the firm a lot of the unquestionably good imput that Max could have contributed. So Dick Simon engineered a well-meaning plot to give Max what he needed.

Jerry happened to be out of the country at the time, the result of an earlier Simon brainstorm. Simon, bemused by Weidman's talents and personal flair, had been an important catalyst in Jerry's becoming a succesful novelist, but Dick felt that his potential could more fully develop if Jerry experienced something more of the world than his previous background of the Bronx and the New York garment district had afforded him. So Dick suggested that Jerry go on an around-the-world-trip and keep his eyes open; to make it possible, he gave him a contract for the travel book that would emerge. Eventually *Letter of Credit* was written and published and even came close to earning back the advance Dick had given, but that is incidental.

Jerry was in Singapore when Max, who had taken the bait gently dropped by Simon, sent him a three-page cablegram. In Max's grandiloquent style and signed "M. Lincoln Schuster," it offered Weidman the honored position of becoming MLS's "ambassador without portfolio" and "representative plenipotentiary." In other

Jerome Weidman

words Jerry was to get a steady, considerably higher-paying job, and it wasn't to interfere with his writing career. Jerry, being human and flattered, had his turn at taking the bait and, under Max, at least to a reasonable extent thrived. True, when he returned he once again became an intimate in the Simon and Company circle and spent most of his free time with them rather than with Max, but he, as always loyal to Max, respected his integrity about books and publishing, and did his level best for him. That has been true of other fine editors who were more Simon's personal friends but did most of their work for Schuster. Although most were conscious of Max's eccentricities, they found them more amusing than irritating, and no one could fail to appreciate that Schuster was the one who really cared about literature. Apart from Fadiman and Kaplan and Weidman, who were officially linked to Schuster, splendid editors like Quincy Howe and Maria Leiper and Henry Simon and Wallace Brockway were more oriented to Max's type of books and worked effectively with him. It is interesting to note that almost every person who either got enticed into taking what most of the freewheeling staff felt was a sucker's job—being Schuster's assistant—or even worked with him closely on certain projects was an editor of real academic and literary quality. Jerry Weidman had quality too, but of a somewhat different nature.

Although Jerry's primary interest clearly was in being an author, writing a book every year while he was with the firm and very nearly keeping up that pace ever since, in the office he acted as a sparkplug. Among his chores for Schuster was the regular hand-holding of Essandess's continuing pride and joy, Will Durant, who was just embarking upon his monumental *Story of Civilization* series. Now Max and his wife, Ray, were generous and lavish hosts upon many occasions, with sumptuous parties festooned with dignitaries and celebrities—either at their summer estate on the North Shore of Long Island or, more frequently, in their winter residence in the old Pulitzer mansion on Manhattan's East Seventy-third Street. The latter was an imposing edifice, with the highest of ceilings and crystal chandeliers, and although the Schusters occupied only a substantial part of it, they had all the advantages that Joseph Pulitzer had put into the building at the turn of the century. So painfully sensitive to sound that the pouring of water into a glass produced a spasm of suffering, Pulitzer dictated that the mansion be made as soundproof as possible.

It was built of limestone and granite with floors laid on ball bearings, walls packed with mineral wool, and some windows insulated with three sheets of heavy plate glass; there was never any chance of the conversation at one of Max and Ray's soirées being disturbed by traffic noises. The Schusters enjoyed entertaining immensely, the Durants were invariably favorite guests, and they always saw to it that a gossip columnist or two was invited to chronicle the event and report on the guests, but Max had little taste for daily chitchat in the office with authors, no matter how distinguished or successful they were. As a result, one day when Will Durant made an unscheduled appearance, Weidman took over from Schuster the host's duties. Knowing that Durant's daughter was soon to be married, Jerry asked what she might like to receive as a present from S and S. Durant replied, "What she'd really like would be a Steinway grand piano."

I could get no confirmation of the story from Leon Shimkin, who, had the piano ever been purchased, would have been the person to write the check, so I assume that no one had the nerve to suggest that amount of author-pampering to Leon—not even Max Schuster.

# How to Win a Publishing House

# and Influence Profits 4

L EON SHIMKIN'S business career might have come
straight out of the pages of one of Horatio Alger Jr.'s rags-to-
riches novels. "Rags" is not the exact term for his boyhood
background, but it was certainly no more than a modest
middle-class one in the Rockaways, where the young Leon's after-
school and summer jobs were a definite factor in family living.
"Riches" is completely appropriate.

In 1923, when Richard Simon and Max Schuster were formulat-
ing their plans to start a publishing house, Shimkin, then sixteen
years old, was picking up summer money by door-to-door selling of
subscriptions to *Cosmopolitan* and other Hearst magazines. Looking
for a career in business, he started attending New York University
School of Commerce. At the end of his first year, once again looking
for a summer job, he applied to Arthur Pell, business manager of the
then prominent publishing firm of Boni and Liveright; he secured the
job convincing Pell that he could perform any number of services in
substituting temporarily for members of the staff who were on vacation. He could too. He was adept at bookkeeping, credit and collections, and stenography, and was a positive wizard at handling the
telephone switchboard. Pell was impressed, and as the summer came
to an end he told Shimkin about the new firm on West Fifty-seventh
Street, which as the result of some fluke success with crossword
puzzle books had expanded and needed an office manager. Leon
hustled over to the fledgling publishers, who offered a salary of $20
per week; but he held out for the $25 that Boni and Liveright had

been paying him, and succeeded in pulling off his first publishing business negotiation. Elated by the wide vistas he saw opening before him, he decided to drop conventional schooling and go to work full time. Nevertheless, after each long day at Simon and Schuster, he attended NYU night courses. When he finished, he tacked on a year of night courses at Brooklyn Law School.

Max Schuster and Dick Simon might very well not have been able to survive those early years so well had not this boy prodigy fallen into their laps, for neither one of them had much in the way of money instincts at the time, nor did they ever develop very sophisticated ones. It is said that in 1944, when Marshall Field bought the firm, Dick Simon didn't immediately invest his personal share—a million dollars—or even put it in a bank to collect interest. Instead, for many months, he simply hung onto Field's check so that he could revel in the sight of it. As for Max Schuster, when he too had become a millionaire, and maintained a luxurious life style both in Manhattan and out on Long Island, he still made it a practice to toss odd pennies from the change he had in his pocket each evening into a bowl, with one bowl kept in each of his two homes. Whenever he left one to go to the other at the beginning or end of summers, despite the fact that each residence was jammed with costly furnishings, he secreted the bowl of pennies that he was leaving behind deep in the corner of a closet under a pile of clothes.

Neither of these stories should be interpreted as showing that Simon was avaricious or Schuster miserly, for those were not their characteristics. They simply were innocents about handling money, and Dick's pride in actually owning a million-dollar check and Max's insatiable instinct for collecting, which in this case took the form of collecting pennies, were merely quirks of generous men.

In any event, back in 1924 neither man was geared for the sort of office-management and business practices that Shimkin did with such competence that Simon dubbed him "Our Little Golden Nugget." Apart from his daily duties he was literally bursting with ideas. He started Essandess in the subsidiary-rights business by selling parts of the crossword puzzle books to newspapers to be run as a daily feature. Anticipating that the house's early success was going to create a sizable tax liability, and resultant cash problems, in the following year, he devised a way of alleviating the burden with the

Internal Revenue Service that became a part of the tax law. It was soon evident that Shimkin was a vital cog whose appointment as secretary-treasurer of the firm was delayed only by the New York State requirement that a person in that position had to be twenty-one years old; but he was financed by the boys and allowed to buy stock in the firm, and it wasn't long before he became an equal partner with the two founders and was known as "the third S." In later years, for a decade after Dick's death and Max's retirement, he was the only one. His eventual sale of the firm to the Gulf & Western conglomerate in 1975 was only one of several financial operations through the years that made him a multimillionaire.

Having survived the first years well enough in the tight quarters on West Fifty-seventh Street, and now having proven themselves enough to feel that it was time to expand, in 1930 Simon and Schuster moved to considerably bigger quarters at 386 Fourth Avenue—later elegantly renamed Park Avenue South, although it still looks its old shabby self. At that time it was where all the action was, and was known as "Publishers' Row." The offices were certainly bigger than before but not much fancier, the heart being a large bare room that contained an open Ping-Pong table.

The Ping-Pong table served many functions throughout the day, but it was most important in the early-morning sessions, where Leon Shimkin was indispensable. The time had passed when the morning mail contained little else but coupons with bills attached ordering crossword puzzle books, but Simon and Schuster sold many books by mail, and scrutinizing the morning mail to see what it had brought was the excitement and delight of everybody in the office. Everyone flocked around the table to open envelopes and sort orders into the separate piles for each book that was currently going to make the reader wiser, or stronger, or improve his bridge game. Dick and Max liked the fervor that swept among all the people clustered around the table—it was a little like that at a gambling casino—but the important man in the room sat off by himself at a table in the corner. That was Leon Shimkin, the only one who could be counted on to compile the tallies correctly and the one who, as the supervisor of the firm's money, was eager to see if enough had come in to make Simon and Schuster's bank balance sufficient to cover the checks he had written or was about to write.

By noon the table had been cleared and the staff Ping-Pong experts had a chance to rip off a few games before lunch. Dick Simon, always a handy performer at any racquet game, was a threat, but the standout star was Jimmy Jacobson, then simply in the business department under Leon but later his partner in Pocket Books. Jimmy was so good that he once won the National Table Tennis title; even Dick had to be given a substantial handicap to make a game close.

Once that was over, the Ping-Pong table became the gathering place for those who chose to eat brown-bag luncheons. Very often, late in the day, it was transformed into a bar for the parties that were thrown on impulse—a book's publication day, a sale to a book club, somebody's birthday or engagement, or simply because people felt like having a party. In an interview many years later Albert Leventhal said: "There was electricity in the air, it was fun to come to work, fun to be in the office, and we hated to leave at the end of the day."

Those musty offices were appealing then to those who had come into book publishing with most of their ideas gleaned from Charles Dickens. Publisher's offices should be cluttered and messy and should be located on Fourth Avenue, not on Fifth or Park. Furnishings and decor that was too fancy not only cost money that might better be spent elsewhere, or pocketed, but also gave authors the wrong idea. And anyway, who needed such stuff? But as the years passed and not only the publishing industry but the commercial world thought it important to upgrade images, even Leon Shimkin was persuaded eventually to spend much more money and to move uptown into the new Rockefeller Center skyscraper complex, into what was then the U.S. Rubber Company building. Strangely enough, after a decade there and then another fifteen years in the International Building (you know, where you get your passport), when Gulf & Western took over the company, Richard Snyder arranged that it be moved back to its first Rockefeller home which, since Essandess was now the major tenant, was renamed the Simon & Schuster building. Let's peek inside and see what the offices look like now.

A prospective author first visiting the present offices, unless quite hardened to the Hollywood or the Jet Set scene, may be overwhelmed and even intimidated. Perhaps the traditions of old Publishers' Row with brown offices and rolltop desks still exist in some places on Fourth Avenue (excuse me, Park Avenue South), but not at 1230 Sixth Avenue (excuse me, Avenue of the Americas, New York, N.Y. 10020). I don't mean to imply that it rivals William Randolph Hearst's San Simeon palace, but the offices are pretty dazzling generally, and the author with prestige enough to be shown into Richard Snyder's private preserve is in for even more of an eyeful than the very considerable one available in simpler visitations to lowlier folk such as the editor-in-chief or the publisher. The offices were designed by James Stewart Polshek, dean of the Columbia School of Architecture, and wherever you wander you are apt to come across a spot of magnificence, such as expensive tapestries and paintings of museum quality. There are floor-to-ceiling mirrors angled at 45 degrees along the halls and equally tall glass walls flanking the doors to offices. During the early days people settling into their new business homes

Felipe *(© 1974 Helene Gaillet)*

kept crashing into them. Subsequently life-saving horizontal bands of gleaming white, or tasteful contrasting deep-toned mirror bands bearing the name of the department that lay behind, have probably forestalled lawsuits.

Let's say you do gain admittance to the Holy of Holies, Snyder's domain. To be brief, after passing the outside door that leads only to his enclave, on the right is a kitchen, a lot smaller than the one at Lutèce but equipped with everything that Felipe, the haute-cuisine chef who oversees it, requires to turn out dishes of Lutèce standards. Felipe is also in a position to cater unusual gourmet provisions, being a consultant to SoHo's famous specialty food shop, Dean & Deluca. One of his regular functions is to prepare the three-course luncheon each Thursday for the weekly deliberations of the editorial board, aided by a modern Jeeves in white jacket who serves, acts as bartender, and pours the vintage wines.

On the left, behind glass walls, is a huge, rather gloomy, but extremely impressive conference room with a long table that can seat twenty comfortably in plush office armchairs and leave room for another fifty or so along the walls. There is projection equipment for movies or slides. Next on the left, before you come to Snyderland itself, is his private bathroom, quite tiny and perhaps not as luxurious as Nero's was, but probably considerably more plush than any you have at home.

Now the enclave fans out in both directions to the sides, where the presidential work is done. On the left two private secretaries guard the outer area of Dick's gorgeous office, with its large, tasteful worktables, couches, armchairs, small decorative tables, and handsome wall hangings. An ordinary desk would be an eyesore in these surroundings, and Dick sits behind a large, highly polished wooden table. Flanking Snyder's office, in the center, is his administrative assistant's office, and past that, on the extreme right, is the large executive dining room to which Felipe's delicacies are brought. This features a handsome nine-foot-diameter circular dining table that comfortably accommodates the four to six people that Dick may be entertaining any day and, somewhat more tightly, the eight or nine members of the editorial board that gather around it for the Thursday business sessions. If the board were ever expanded to ten people, there would be a crisis. The dining table has regular changes of the floral arrangements that are supplied by Rockefeller Center's best, and the linen, china, glass, and silverware are everything that the most persnickety debutante would demand. Grant me poetic license—I am admittedly exaggerating everything to some extent—but I promise you that's the general picture. It is certainly a long long way from the Ping-Pong-table days.

As a matter of fact I have a stunning precedent in embellishing the facts about the marvelous spectacles to be seen in the Simon & Schuster offices, but it has to do with the office of Michael Korda, the editor-in-chief. That is simply one very large room, but in one of his riotously funny *New Yorker* pieces entitled "Under the Shrinking Royalty the Village Smithy Stands," S. J. Perelman wrote about a visit to Michael which was only thinly disguised by calling the protagonist "Mitchell Krakauer" and the firm "Diamond & Oyster." Although in recent times Korda has made his office more conventionally eye-catching but consequently much less horsey, it once was chockful of equestrian paraphernalia and Sid Perelman was inspired to write about as only he could:

"Krakauer's passion for horsemanship was a byword—he was besotted with the sport. His office was filled with stirrups, snaffles, and trophies attesting to his equestrian skill; he wore riding breeches to work, swished a crop against them as he conferred. . . . However, so startling was the transformation I beheld that my mouth fell open. The burled-walnut desk, the luxurious easy chairs and sporting prints, the equestrian memorabilia—all had vanished, and in their place was a scene straight out of Longfellow: a miniature nineteenth-century blacksmith shop. Garbed in a leather apron, Krakauer was bent over an anvil, his hammer busily tapping a horseshoe. Spread all about were the traditional accoutrements of the smith—the forge heaped with glowing coals, the bellows, pincers, a workbench strewn with tools, and bundles of iron bars."

But the modern-day digressions have taken us away from the protagonist of this chapter, Leon Shimkin.

In the past decade since Leon Shimkin gave up control and sold the firm to Gulf & Western, he has been completely out of the Simon & Schuster picture; although he still maintains a modest but pleasant office in the building, he has no involvement with the business. He comes in usually two or three times a week, and devotes his time to personal interests, chief of which for many years has been New York University. Shimkin has affectionate memories of NYU and is so grateful to his alma mater for its part in launching him upon his career that he gave the university $3 million a while back, the result of which is a building on the Washington Square campus named Shimkin Hall, primarily devoted to continuing adult education.

Nor is NYU the only item of nostalgia for Leon. The Simon & Schuster building in which he sits today is on the very site where the Boni & Liveright offices once existed, and that firm has a strong place in S & S's history. The partnership dissolved when the two men who had founded it in 1917 fell out in the early 1920s and agreed that one would have to buy the other out. They could think of no more sophisticated a way to decide the matter than to flip a coin, and Liveright won. Boni retired into subsequent modest publishing, but Horace Liveright carried on, retaining the Boni & Liveright imprint, and built the country's liveliest and one of its most prestigious publishing houses, where Dick Simon, as a salesman, received his baptism into the publishing business. He left to form a partnership with Max Schuster as, almost at the same time, did two other of the firm's salesmen—Bennett Cerf, who with Donald Klopfer founded Random House, and Harold Guinzberg, who with George Oppenheimer founded the Viking Press. Boni & Liveright must have been a fantastic training ground.

Many years later and after Dick Simon died, Max Schuster and Leon Shimkin also came to what both thought should be the parting of the ways. They had come to disagree about too many things, and each man was seriously considering whether he could buy out the other's share. Fortunately each had his own lawyer, both of whom were most unhappy about the prospect of so vital a partnership splitting up—and they came up with an ingenious suggestion.

"If one of you, say Max, decides he wants to buy out the other, he will offer what he thinks the half-share is worth—let's say three million dollars—and then the other man, Leon in this case, will have a very short period of time in which either to accept, and go away, or instead to say 'No thank you, I'll give *you* three million dollars for your half-share,' in which case Max will *have* to accept." Whether or not this ruse was officially adopted is uncertain, but it had the effect intended—to keep Max and Leon together—for it set up a stalemate.

Neither man could ever dare to take the initiative unless he was prepared to pay too much for the half-share. If he offered a fair price, he was more than likely to be matched and lose out. So neither man ever served the ball over the net, so to speak, and Messrs. Schuster and Shimkin remained reasonably amicable partners until many years later, when Leon had the idea that might shorten his wait to take control. That was in 1966, when Max was approaching his seventieth birthday. Leon pointed out that since Max had no children to whom to leave his interest, might it not be sensible to sell out now to Leon and receive enough money in return to live comfortably the rest of his life? Max thought it over for a while, considered the pros and cons with his lawyer, and finally decided to accept Shimkin's offer, which was reported to have been $2 million. Once settled, Max left the S & S scene completely and, though he lived almost another five years, was never seen in the office again. Shimkin, now having acquired the entire stock of the company, almost immediately merged Simon and Schuster with Pocket Books to form a new public-issue company named Simon & Schuster, Inc., with Pocket Books being a division of it. That is the point where the ampersand really took over from "and" between the two names.

Shimkin, even in his retirement today, almost surely gets a nostalgic kick over the fact that last year, with Simon & Schuster bursting at the seams, they took over the ninth floor of the building, in addition to the four floors above it that they already occupied. For it was on that famous ninth floor in what was then known as the U.S. Rubber building that, between 1940 and 1951, Leon enjoyed one of the several peak periods of his career. At this floor, the building's setback begins; the walls from here on up are set back some twenty-five feet, creating an attractive promenade that flanks all the outer offices of the firm. Bedecked with plants, small trees, and flowers, and with doors leading out onto it so that people could enjoy it outdoors in good weather, it was a rare beauty spot for an office to have. Justin Kaplan once said that it had it all over the deck of the *Queen Mary*, except that there were no lifeboats.

Shimkin was one of the half-dozen top executives who were blessed with a big corner office, out of two sides of which the view could be relished even in snowy weather. In the intervening years, the occupants of the floor had let the promenade decline to no more than

Dick Simon's corner office with outside garden promenade

a bare strip of roof, but efforts are going to be made to restore it to something like its former glory. Like all of us, Leon surely took pleasure in the old days in having the vista to gaze at in quiet moments—but then, Leon had scarcely had a quiet moment from the day he came, and the 1940s were positively noisy for him. Apart from his overwhelming concerns in seeing to the financial health of the company, Shimkin, though without editorial pretensions, had already acquired two spectacularly successful properties for Simon and Schuster in the latter 1930s, both of which will forever be associated with his name. The first, *How to Win Friends and Influence People*, by Dale Carnegie, is by far the biggest-selling book the house ever published, with well over a million copies sold in cloth-bound editions in this country and over 20 million worldwide in all editions.

After the Bible, *How to Win Friends* ranks high among the handful of all-time bestsellers. The book came about as the result of Shimkin's taking a fourteen-week course that Mr. Carnegie ran. Leon was so impressed that he urged Carnegie to expand his lectures into a book. Carnegie reacted coolly; Essandess had already turned down two of his book ideas, and why should he give away in a $2 book what he was successfully selling to thousands of people as a $75 lecture course? Shimkin turned out to be a good pupil: he won over Mr.

Dale Carnegie®

Carnegie as a friend and influenced him to go along with the book project. In 1937 the book was the clear Number One nonfiction bestseller in the country and, in that Depression year, earned a quarter of a million dollars for the author, and much more since.

There were times when Carnegie must have received less than top marks as a thoughtful friend. At the time that his book was selling at its peak rate and making him a fortune, he told everyone in the office who had anything to do with its publication that he was coming in the next week with a special present for each and all. There was considerable expectation, from bosses and editors to secretaries and the mailroom, as to what his or her present might turn out to be, and I would suspect there was widespread disappointment when virtually everyone received the same gift—a mechanical pencil that bore the legend "Dale Carnegie Course in Effective Speaking." Max Schuster got an ashtray, but Max didn't smoke. What is more, Carnegie had "M. W. Schuster" inscribed on it. M. Washington Schuster?

Leon Shimkin's other coup at the time was to inspire J. K. Lasser, an accountant who became one of his closest friends, to do a book addressed to the ordinary individual on how to prepare income-tax returns. That book, *Your Income Tax*, always published in the now familiar oversize yellow-cover paperback form, was so successful that it has been revised annually and each year sells one side or the other of a million copies, depending upon how much the income-tax laws change from year to year. In addition, the original concept and its success gave rise to a host of other Lasser books that also achieved very high sales figures—guides to business taxes, to saving on estate and gift taxes, and to Social Security and Medicare, plus tax diaries, appointment books, and heaven and the IRS knows what else.

There is an interesting story about J. K. ("Yoc") Lasser. At one point he became very ill and was hospitalized for some time. His wife sat by his bedside and read *Captain Horatio Hornblower* to him, and he fell completely in love with the book. When he recovered he bought the other Forester books about Hornblower to read himself, but he was an astonishingly fast reader and would go through each in something under an hour. He found that although he gleaned the entire story in so doing, he didn't enjoy the books anywhere nearly as much as he had when his wife had read the first one to him, obviously at a much slower pace. He thought he should slow down

J. K. Lasser

but had no idea of how to do it, so at Leon Shimkin's suggestion he enrolled in the NYU Reading Clinic to see if he could get help. The clinic people tested him and initially threw up their hands in despair. Yoc read accurately and perceptively at blinding speed, and they had never had to face this particular problem before. Eventually they did devise a way to shackle a too-speedy reader without hurting his reading appreciation but one wonders if they ever had occasion to employ the tactic on anyone else.

By 1940 Leon Shimkin's energies and goals were turning more and more to empire-building rather than to individual books. He had never tried to edge into any sort of editorial role and he became even less inclined to moonlight after this date, although it is true that he was responsible for one other commercial success in the mid 1940s, Joshua Loth Liebman's *Peace of Mind*. That inspirational book, which outlined a path for a reconciliation of psychiatry with religion, shot right up to the Number One position on nonfiction bestseller lists that year. Leon took justifiable pride in bringing Rabbi Liebman to the house, but by now he had other fish to fry. In the early 1940s, three major events took place at Simon and Schuster: the founding of Pocket Books, the founding of Golden Books, and the sale of the firm to Marshall Field Enterprises. Leon Shimkin was a prime mover on all three, but each was so vital a part of Essandess's history that they rate fuller coverage in subsequent chapters.

Joshua Loth Liebman

In the midst of all this exciting turmoil, Shimkin, almost as if he were doing it with his left hand, made an arrangement with the Sears Roebuck Company and the Consolidated Book Company to start a new book club, whose editorial office and control would be based at Simon and Schuster, but whose bills would be picked up by the other parties. Geared for a less sophisticated audience than the two major book clubs, the Book-of-the-Month Club and the Literary Guild, but hoping to be somewhat competitive, it was named the People's Book Club. After three years, in 1946 Leon sold the now established club to Sears for a substantial sum—a real coup, since S and S had spent virtually nothing in founding and running the club. No wonder he was dubbed "Our Little Golden Nugget."

Years after Marshall Field and Dick Simon and Max Schuster had all died, and Leon Shimkin had become the sole owner of the firm, he brought his son, Michael, into the business despite Michael's longstanding lack of enthusiasm for the idea. Michael, a talented musician and scholar, had no urge to be a businessman; after a comparatively brief term when Michael conscientiously tried to live up to Dad's hopes and expectations, it was agreed by all parties concerned that Michael would be better off pursuing a life more attractive to him. That experience brings to mind an interesting peripheral observation. In book publishing, among the old-line WASP houses, there are many cases of the passing along of the torch from father to son—the Scribners and the McGraws and the McRaes and the Doubledays are just a few examples. Yet the sprightly, second-generation American Jews who to a large extent took over both the intellectual and commercial flair in United States book publishing in the second quarter of this century almost invariably suffered some measure of disappointment in their hopes to pass the estate on to a son. Alfred Knopf's son, Alfred Junior or Pat, broke away from his parents' house after considerable friction to help found Atheneum. Bennett Cerf's son, Christopher, has been a prominent figure in publishing but he's never going to inherit Random House. Harold Guinzberg's son, Tom, did indeed head up Viking, but no longer and never again—he is now in an editorial role at Doubleday. Roger Straus is the principal of a most distinguished American firm, Farrar, Straus, and Giroux, but his accomplished livewire son, Roger III, left the firm some time ago for what he felt were greener pastures.

On the Simon and Schuster front, Dick Simon's only son, Peter, preferred Dick's hobby to his profession and became a professional photographer, and Dick and Andrea's three lovely daughters all pursued Dick's other passion, music. Max Schuster had no progeny himself but at one stage brought in Ralph Brendler, husband of one of Rae Schuster's daughters by a first marriage, to be his assistant at Essandess, but not in a way that ever even hinted at the possibility that Ralph could take over. That left Leon Shimkin as the only Essandess owner who might pass the torch along to his son, but that too went up in smoke. Even though Michael Shimkin had never been particularly keen about eventually stepping into Leon's shoes, one episode ignited the tinderbox that impelled him to leave.

Michael Shimkin had a friend who was his associate and to whom he was devoted. He was a man of extraordinary intellectual stature and, on the whole, a very nice and attractive young fellow as well; it was not hard to see why Michael counted him as his strong right hand. But he was also a hardheaded, driving businessman who could be arrogant, and on this occasion that was the characteristic that set

Michael Shimkin

Harold Robbins

things off. It happened at a party that was being thrown for Simon and Schuster's stellar commercial author, Harold Robbins, and everybody was there, including Paul Gitlin, Robbins's lawyer-agent. Perhaps the wine was flowing too freely and Michael's friend had had a glass too many, but at one point he collared Robbins, whom he had never met before, and confided to him that Michael and he were now taking over Simon and Schuster, that a new broom would sweep clean all the deadwood, and that no one who mattered in the firm would be any older than about thirty, and from now on all would be for the best in this best of all possible worlds.

Robbins, who had experienced years of friendship and success with Leon Shimkin and his devoted editor, Herb Alexander, both with Pocket Books and in hardcover publishing, looked at him with a fishy eye, turned on his heel, and went off to draw Paul Gitlin into a corner. Gitlin at the time was Simon and Schuster's pet agent and the house was his pet publisher. Besides Harold Robbins he represented the cream of the firm's crop of successful authors, including Cornelius Ryan and Irving Wallace. Connie Ryan had become the out-

Irving Wallace

Cornelius Ryan and Peter Schwed

standing popular historian of highlight events of World War II with his classics *The Longest Day* and *The Last Battle*, and had started research for *A Bridge Too Far*, which promised to be an equally distinguished and successful book. Irving Wallace was, of course, at the very top of notably thriving commercial fiction authors and one so productive that he delivered a winner almost every year. With three such stars under his agency banner, it is apparent why Simon & Schuster was likely to listen very attentively to anything Paul Gitlin happened to say.

A short discussion in the corner ensued, after which Robbins and Gitlin trapped Leon Shimkin where he was enjoying his martini and spoiled the drink quite as fully as if the bartender had used too much vermouth. "Either he goes," they said, indicating Michael's associate, "or we do."

No one can really blame Leon for the decision he was virtually forced to make under the circumstances. Robbins alone, let alone Gitlin's stable of best-selling authors, was much too important to shuffle off for a new employee, no matter how talented he might be or how much Michael esteemed him. Michael was told the bad news. After considering it, he made his own honorable decision, which may in some ways have been a relief to him. He handed in his own resignation. Leon, disappointed but finally reconciled to the fact that his son would never succeed him, decided that the time had come to rid himself of the problems and strains of ownership. He was nearing the age of sixty-five and felt he'd like to taper off, so he started to be more receptive to the feelers that often were floated out by people and corporations who were interested in buying or merging with Simon & Schuster.

The very first serious one that then came along very nearly came to a successful conclusion. Norton Simon, Inc., which among other holdings owned the *Ladies' Home Journal*, was by virtue of that magazine already in the publishing business and felt that an expansion into the book scene could work out beneficially for both parties. Shimkin and his most astute advisor Selig Levitan, his attorney and a director of S & S, thought the same and an oral agreement was made for Norton Simon to take over ownership in a stock exchange weighted heavily in S & S's favor. A short time later the Norton Simon people unexpectedly indicated that they'd rather pay cash, a change Leon gladly accepted. But then, even while office managers were drawing plans for the accommodation of the Essandess staff in the Norton Simon framework, the stock market took one of its precipitous drops. Norton Simon stock no longer had its former value but cash still did, and now the acquisition of S & S didn't seem as attractive to Norton Simon. With regrets on both sides, particularly Shimkin's, the apparently firm but unofficial offer was withdrawn.

Next came explorations from the Kinney System, Inc., the car-rental and car-park people, a conglomerate that also owned Warner Communications, Inc. Warner, in turn, owned a major mass-market paperback house, Popular Library, and the idea of merging that into Pocket Books seemed to open up the possibility of a firm that would dominate that market. However, this time extensive negotiations failed to satisfy Shimkin and he terminated them, unmoved by an extra inducement offered. Kinney also owned the Riverside Funeral Chapel on Seventy-sixth Street, and an unusual perquisite could be enjoyed by Simon & Schuster employees if the firm came under the Kinney wing: they could have a funeral service and be buried at bargain rates. Somehow Shimkin did not feel that tipped the scales.

The final flirtation before the one that eventually was consummated with Gulf & Western was one that initially seemed to make good sense. Simon & Schuster had a large and successful trade publishing business (nonacademic books for the general reader), but had never developed a textbook line. The firm of Harcourt Brace Jovanovich had a first-rate textbook division, but only a comparatively modest trade-book operation. A merger might well be a wonderful thing for both, and that is how Shimkin thought of the preliminary discussions—as leading toward a merger—even though in fact Harcourt Brace Jovanovich would be buying Essandess. The deal was near the point of being made when, in a newspaper interview about the matter, William Jovanovich said some extraordinary things for a man who apparently was sincerely interested in completing an amicable arrangement with a peer publisher. Whether it was simply injudicious or was calculated for reasons unknown, he implied that his firm was taking over Simon & Schuster lock, stock, and barrel, and one got the impression that Leon Shimkin would be fortunate if he got a job in the mailroom. Negotiations were terminated the day the newspaper story appeared.

Gulf & Western Industries came into the picture shortly thereafter. An agent who had met Charles Bluhdorn, G & W's head, had found him anxious to acquire a major publishing house that he could match up with Paramount Pictures, a subsidiary of the conglomerate, with the idea that each had access to properties that could bolster the other. Bluhdorn, the chairman, and David Judelson, the president, arranged for an exchange of stock that would enable Gulf & Western to take over Simon & Schuster and all its subsidiary publishing companies, including Pocket Books, but not before one very vital point was agreed upon. Throughout the proceedings Dick Snyder, who by then was Essandess's publisher and chief operating officer, had been busy impressing Bluhdorn and Judelson with his energy, imagination, and general know-how, and on a personal basis he and Judelson had become warm friends. So a condition had been insisted upon before G & W was willing to sign the final papers. It was a condition that Shimkin, now nearing seventy, was willing to accept. Richard Snyder was to be president of Simon & Schuster.

The fourth "S" of S & S had emerged.

# From "The Inner Sanctum" to Outer Space in Advertising 5

A LTHOUGH Simon & Schuster advertising in newspapers and magazines still stands out among the leaders in trade-book publishing, it is today more by virtue of spending lots of money on very big ads for the comparatively few books each season that have the greatest commercial promise. Even very good books which admittedly may have considerable sales potential are not too likely to get any newspaper advertisements at all, and stand or fall because of the effectiveness, or lack of it, of other selling techniques, such as publicity and selective marketing. This is a far cry from the philosophy that ruled at S and S through its first three decades or so, when "It Pays to Advertise" was the watchword, and the firm had the reputation in the industry of spending advertising money as if they printed it. In actual fact, Simon and Schuster did spend more than any other house, but even so the real reason people were so conscious of their ads was simply because they were unique and infinitely more engaging than anyone else's efforts.

The most intriguing S and S advertising was its famous "Inner Sanctum" column, which appeared regularly for the book trade in *Publishers Weekly* and for the public in the *New York Times*. The name "Inner Sanctum" was so inextricably tied into Simon and Schuster as to become the firm's nickname; it seems strange that no trace of the legend exists today, that the term is unknown to present employees, except possibly as the title of an old-time radio show. As a matter of fact, the radio producer bought the title from S & S, because the company's line of mystery novels, called Inner Sanctum Mysteries, dominated the field at that time. Don't ask who saw a way to capitalize on that—it was Leon Shimkin, of course. Yet Inner Sanctum Mysteries constituted only one fragment of what the term "Inner Sanctum" meant then, and probably the least important one. The famous little office that separated the big offices of the two founders, Richard L. Simon and M. Lincoln Schuster, was known as the Inner Sanctum; frequently the two men met each other there, on neutral ground, to discuss matters of state—which might well conclude with one of Max's classical dictums, "Give him a firm maybe!"

Most important of all, the name "Inner Sanctum" was applied to the delightfully written advertising columns, a feature that won the firm more friends and admiration than any comparable book advertising in history.

Sometimes it ran down a single column, sometimes it was more generously spread over two columns of the *Times* or filled a full page of the less expensive *Publishers Weekly*, but it was always completely recognizable. Each little paragraph, of the many that constituted every column, had three small sowers, the Essandess logo, as its lead. Also the column frequently ran small photos or drawings scattered down its length. One way or the other, it was instantly recognizable and, in those days when columnists like Heywood Broun and Alexander Woollcott and FPA were primary reasons why people bought newspapers, the Inner Sanctum column was a real rival, despite being an advertisement rather than a journalistic feature.

Originally written by Max Schuster for the general public, and by Richard Simon for the bookseller trade, it flourished and continued down through the years when others, notably Jack Goodman and Nina Bourne, took over with equal style and wit. They all held true to the original concept and rules for writing such a column, as dictated from the beginning by Max and Dick:

1. Be unblushingly specific in giving actual sales figures on any book discussed.
2. Discuss *Flops d'Estime, Successes de Fiasco*, as well as smash hits.
3. Shun the usual blurb-infested adjectives like the plague.
4. Don't be afraid to discuss and praise the books of other publishers.
5. Scorn not occasional hilarity nor the ancient serenities associated with quietly issuing a good book without much hope of profit.

Essandess received a regular flow of letters from readers of the columns who loved them, but once they ran a provocative full-page Inner Sanctum ad in *Publishers Weekly* that confounded readers. The ad told anyone interested that there was something phony and very intriguing about a forthcoming book that was soon to be published, *The Technique of a Love Affair,* and the ad offered to send anyone the juicy details. Simon and Schuster expected to get a lot of letters from people who were indeed interested: they got one (1).

Of the many conclusions that could have been drawn, Essandess admitted that the most valid one probably was that an Inner Sanctum ad in *Publishers Weekly* wasn't worth the $62.50 a page that it cost. They stated that conclusion in the lead paragraph of another ad run immediately afterwards in *Publishers Weekly,* bearing the headline: *And Yet Here We Are Again!* Then there followed:

Reasons:
1. The Big Idea is to sell books over the course of many years.
2. We've tried other ads in *PW* many times, and this is the first time that any evoked even one letter, so we've set a record this time.
3. We can get more words on a page in ads like this.
4. Being informal, this column doesn't have to clear its throat quite so often to make way for The Big Selling Message.
5. It gives us a chance to talk about books we've published in the past, sales of which at the present don't justify separate ads.

Simon and Schuster obviously had other reasons to continue them. The Inner Sanctum columns were economical because S and S often were able to discuss several books at one time, the ads were fun to write, and they were winning the firm admiration and affection, not only from the reading public but even from their publishing competitors, because now and then, when they were bowled over by what some rival house had issued, they said so. For example, an entire Inner Sanctum column was devoted to the three volumes that Harry N. Abrams, that unrivaled American art publisher, had just issued on Renoir, Van Gogh, and El Greco. Once, when asked why the Inner Sanctum so frequently talked about books other than Simon and Schuster ones, the answer given was "Why not?"

A more practical but equally unusual Inner Sanctum report quoted a major review of *Ripley's Believe It or Not* that said: "It is so marvelous and interesting a book that if it were priced at $100 a volume the reader would not regret its purchase." Essandess (as the Inner Sanctum column was always signed), responded: "Since this is true, your correspondent derived a sardonic delight in *reducing* the retail price last week (because of the economics effected by larger editions) from $2.50 to $2.00."

Often the Inner Sanctum column would make no attempt to plug any particular book or books at all, and simply chat informally about a topic the writer thought might be of interest to book readers. An example was the column that discussed the importance of one publication date as opposed to another. Essandess pointed out that September and October saw too many important books published, so any lesser work wasn't reviewed; spring was supposed to be the slowest time in retail stores; in summer the best reviewers and columnists were on vacation; and January and February posed the same problems as September and October. So any time was as good or as bad as any other, except perhaps the couple of weeks before Christmas.

Sometimes Essandess would wander off and write about something that had absolutely nothing to do with book publishing. I remember one column devoted to the art of flipping playing cards into a hat set on the floor, with the flipper sitting in a chair eight feet away from the hat. Jack Goodman was the uncrowned world's champion at this art—I bear witness to once having seen him pop in fifty-one out of the fifty-two cards in the pack. (Nobody's perfect.) There is a technique in doing well at this fascinating pursuit, and it is not the instinctive one of scaling the cards. If you try that, you will score anything from about a dozen back down to zero. Jack wrote a very entertaining, funny, and even instructive essay in that particular Inner Sanctum column, but why did he or anyone else concerned with an advertising budget think it was a good idea to have him do so? I think a major part of the answer was that embarking upon, and actually expending time and talent upon, trivial entertainment unrelated to the serious job was consonant with the personalities that combined to make the early Simon and Schuster firm such fun to work for. Whether by intent or happy serendipity, the regular appearances of delightful Inner Sanctum columns became an astonishingly successful piece of public relations for the firm. Almost invariably a publisher's imprint has an extremely small effect even on avid book readers. Ask most people who published their favorite books or current top bestsellers, and the general unawareness is widespread enough to keep any publisher's conceit within bounds. But in that second quarter of the century, when the Inner Sanctum advertising columns flourished, the house of Simon and Schuster was recognized as having its own unique personality as a result, and that was sustained through the years as new, brilliant copywriters, notably Jack Goodman and Nina Bourne, took over from Max Schuster and Dick Simon.

On the twenty-fifth anniversary of Simon and Schuster in 1949, the Inner Sanctum column, opining that the best way to plan the

Nina Bourne

future was to review the past, listed some statistics about the quarter-of-a-century of publishing:

| | | | |
|---|---|---|---|
| Manuscripts received | 62,636 | Bestsellers | 212★ |
| Books published | 1,028 | Intermediate sellers | 610 |
| Books still in print | 510 | Outright flops | 190 |

★These figures refer only to adult books. Virtually *all* Little Golden Books for children were multimillion copy bestsellers, and more expensive bigger Golden Books reached comparable plateaus in the hundreds of thousands.

Still, after pondering the figures, Essandess concluded that all the evidence did was to show that some good books won't sell, no matter what you do, and that other good books won't stop selling, no matter what you do or don't do! Which is what authors generally hear when they confer with publishers on the matter of disappointing royalty statements.

Nor, despite the Inner Sanctum's early first experience of eliciting only one response to a provocative offer, did the column stop trying. When Bertrand Russell turned up in 1953 with his first venture into fiction, a book entitled *Satan in the Suburbs*, Essandess offered a $5 prize to the person who could compose the most pleasing and elegant quatrain celebrating the event, with an additional 50¢ prize for anyone who managed to find a rhyme for "suburbs"! Ninety-three poems were submitted, many of them of quite high caliber, but the judges unanimously picked as the winner Mr. Arthur Everard Laing, of Chester, Connecticut, whose quatrain read:

> Unguarded, my garden's a bed of affliction;
> The busy moles burrow and grub herbs.
> Enhammocked, I care not; Earl Russell's in fiction
> And Satan's in style in the suburbs.

The Inner Sanctum duly sent Mr. Laing congratulations and a check for $5.50, explaining that it was in lieu of the "butt of Canary wine" which is traditionally a part of the standard wage of England's poet laureates.

The commemoration of the first twenty years

# January 1, 1924—Simon and Schuster, Publishers

*of what?*

**1924**
CROSS WORD PUZZLE BOOK, Series 1

**1925**
FRAULEIN ELSE
VERDI

**1926**
THE STORY OF PHILOSOPHY

**1927**
TRADER HORN

**1928**
BAMBI
THE ART OF THINKING

**1929**
TWELVE AGAINST THE GODS
BELIEVE IT OR NOT
WOLF SOLENT
CAUGHT SHORT

**1930**
BRING 'EM BACK ALIVE
CASANOVA'S HOMECOMING

**1931**
MEN OF ART
LIVING PHILOSOPHIES
HARD LINES
THE GERSHWIN SONG BOOK

**1932**
VAN LOON'S GEOGRAPHY
FUN IN BED
A NEW WAY TO BETTER GOLF
A HISTORY OF THE RUSSIAN REVOLUTION

**1933**
THE FIRST WORLD WAR
LITTLE MAN, WHAT NOW?

**1934**
NIJINSKY
NOW IN NOVEMBER
THE LIFE OF OUR LORD
THE VICTOR BOOK OF THE SYMPHONY
MODERN ART

**1935**
I WRITE AS I PLEASE
EYES ON THE WORLD
A TREASURY OF THE THEATRE
A MARRIAGE MANUAL
BEETHOVEN SONATAS

**1936**
THE BIBLE, Designed to be Read as Living Literature
WAKE UP AND LIVE
YOUR INCOME TAX
HOW TO WIN FRIENDS AND INFLUENCE PEOPLE

**1937**
THE ARTS
THE OUTWARD ROOM
OF MEN AND MUSIC
MINIATURE PHOTOGRAPHY

**1938**
WITH MALICE TOWARD SOME
WE SAW IT HAPPEN
THE EVOLUTION OF PHYSICS

**1939**
A TREASURY OF ART MASTERPIECES
THE LIFE OF GREECE
ADDRESS UNKNOWN
I BELIEVE

**1940**
KINGS ROW
HOW TO READ A BOOK
CROSS WORD PUZZLE BOOK, Series 50
AMERICAN WHITE PAPER
A TREASURY OF THE WORLD'S GREAT LETTERS

**1941**
MISSION TO MOSCOW
READING I'VE LIKED
A TREASURY OF GILBERT AND SULLIVAN
WALT DISNEY'S BAMBI
THE G-STRING MURDERS
LOW ON THE WAR

**1942**
VAN LOON'S LIVES
A TREASURY OF GREAT POEMS
VICTORY THROUGH AIR POWER
REPORT FROM TOKYO
The Inner Sanctum Edition of WAR AND PEACE
LITTLE GOLDEN BOOKS

**1943**
ONE WORLD
CARTOON CAVALCADE
ROUGHLY SPEAKING
THE FIRESIDE BOOK OF DOG STORIES
AN INVITATION TO SPANISH
THE TEN COMMANDMENTS

*January 1, 1944—Here's to the Next Twenty Years!*

At this point it seems only fair to allow the reader actually to see the complete copy of an Inner Sanctum advertisement, so the one that appeared in the February 23, 1955, issue of the *New York Times*, making "an apparently naive but actually devilishly canny free offer," is reproduced on the facing page.

It could be argued that the amount of executive talent and creativity that was expended upon Inner Sanctum columns for so many years was little more than self-indulgence, and that the effort and money couldn't possibly have been justified by bottom-line standards. That has certainly been the view now for some years and it may well be valid, but in a debate I'd be happy to speak for the other side. The Inner Sanctum not only won friends for the firm with readers and booksellers, but it also allowed S and S to carry out at least some small provocative advertising for books they cared for, but which didn't have the sales prospects to justify traditional advertisements. That won friends among authors.

Simon and Schuster's reputation as tops in book advertising in those early years didn't rest only upon the Inner Sanctum columns, by any means. In closer parallel to Richard Snyder's practice today, any time Max Schuster or Dick Simon sensed they had a real winner coming off the production line, they would shoot the works on huge and—at least for that time—unusual ads, overspending the normal budget allocation tenfold when they had the gut feeling that sales would eventually justify the expenditure. They were people of unusual talent who didn't delegate but carried through themselves on anything important. Unlike other publishing houses, Simon and Schuster wrote its own ads and used an advertising agency only for the mechanical preparation and placing of the ads. Max Schuster, an ardent proponent of the theory that making a difficult topic palatable for the ordinary lay reader was an irresistible formula, proved it early in the game. His enormously successful "windswept" advertisments—a term that conveyed unhibited expansiveness—may have aroused risibilities among sophisticates, but admiration and envy were the more likely emotions among rival publishers when they saw the results of a few of Max's ads for Will Durant, Hendrik Willem Van Loon, and Albert Einstein.

When Will Durant turned out the second volume of his *Story of from* THE INNER SANCTUM *of*

# SIMON *and* SCHUSTER

*Publishers* • Rockefeller Center • *New York*

*An apparently naive
but actually devilishly canny
free offer*

We address ourselves this morrow to Shining Youth, for whom we have gifts. Mature members of the audience, however awash with wisdom and charm, are not eligible and are requested to pass on to the financial pages.

O Youth, carefree and lyrical, trembling on the brink of a 9-to-5 job with one hour for lunch, you are about to begin the great adventure of Growing Up and Older. You will have your first kiss and know ecstasy. You will attend your first dance and know worldliness. You will be stood up on Saturday night and know tragedy.

And if you are lucky, you will discover the novels of P. G. WODEHOUSE (over which the older blokes have been purpling with laughter these many years) and learn the meaning of untrammeled hilarity.

By way of doing our bit to introduce WODEHOUSE to *la jeunesse*, we are going to Give Away 100 copies of his latest novel, *Bertie Wooster Sees It Through* (just published, $3.50) to qualified parties. More about qualifications in a sec.

Of this new WODEHOUSE novel *Punch* says:

*"The plot is as complex and adroitly manipulated as ever, the figures of speech as outrageous, the literary allusions as wildly misapplied. In comic invention, in sheer writing ability, it ranks with the author's best."*

Only a conscienceless worm would reveal the details of the demmed ingenious plot — a masterly structure built on the solid foundation of (1) Bertie Wooster's mustache, (2) Jeeves, the gentleman's gentleman, and (3) the giant conflicts these two fundamentally opposed elements engender.

Now, tads, Your Correspondents have 100 free copies of this book for those of you who meet the following requirements:

1. You must not be more than 26 years old.

2. You must not remember when Skeezix was a baby.

3. You must not have ever said "hotcha!", "voh-doh-dee-oh-doh!" or "wock-a-doo, wock-a-doo, wock-a-*doo!*"

4. You must have no recollection of seeing, hearing or shaking hands with Peaches Browning, Chandu the Magician, or Singing Sam the Barbasol Man.

If you fulfill these conditions and would like a free copy of the new WODEHOUSE novel, just write to us and ask for it. Send proof, however flimsy, of your age. Proof may be anything or anybody but must not exceed 11 x 14½ inches in size or weigh more than 32 pounds. (It is quite all right for you yourself to weigh more than 32 pounds.) Remember, neatness will get you nowhere. The important thing is to be among the best 100 petitioners. We are judge and jury, and there is no appeal. Write to Simon and Schuster, Dept. PG, 630 Fifth Avenue, New York 20, N. Y. Entries must be postmarked no later than Monday, February 28th.

You are not morally obliged to let us know what you thought of the book and why, on the handy form enclosed with each copy. However, if you feel that to remain silent would be an act of churlish ingratitude, send us your opinion.

We regret that oldsters get short shrift in this offer. All we can say to them is: hard cheese, old tops, we'll have something for you later — in the interim, hie to your bookseller's, buy *Bertie Wooster Sees It Through* by P. G. WODEHOUSE, and cheer up.

— ESSANDESS

*Civilization* series, Max Schuster's advertising copy began: "Tonight I will open to the first page of *The Life of Greece* and in my own armchair and under my own reading lamp I shall instantly be transported through thousands of years and miles to the glory that was Greece." And on and on in similar vein. In announcing Van Loon's *The Arts*, Max was similarly rhapsodic. "Today I explore the Arts with Hendrik Willem Van Loon and for the first time I find in a single volume *all* the arts, integrated and interpreted by one who is himself a great artist in the humanization of knowledge." Donald Culross Peattie's *Green Laurels* evoked this lead from Schuster: "This evening I open a book that leads me directly into the living world. With a turn of the page I quit the gray streets of the city and watch nature unfurl her green banners."

That was a little mild for Max, but he spread himself for Louis Untermeyer's *Treasury of Great Poems*. "This evening I shall look over Lord Byron's shoulder while he writes passionate stanzas about love and liberty. I shall sit under a palm tree with John Keats in the English countryside and listen with him to the nightingale. . . ." And in spinning off the copy for Walter Duranty's *I Write as I Please*, Max once again made plans for the evening hours: "Tonight I cover the biggest story of modern times with Walter Duranty. In my own home I will live twenty breathless years with the man who has been called the greatest reporter alive."

Windswept indeed, but those ads were marvelously effective. I do note that Max never seemed to do any reading until the sun had passed well over the yardarm—presumably he spent his daytime hours writing advertisements.

Schuster's admirable if flowery flair for writing long, inspirational copy was well suited to many of Essandess's biggest books, so he probably turned out the majority of the early ads, but Dick Simon too had the knack of dreaming up a provocative headline and lead for books that particularly interested him. One such was Thomas Craven's *Men of Art*, for which Dick's headline and following copy read:

## "VERY INTERESTING"

*Is that all you can say when standing before one of the world's greatest masterpieces?*

Max and Dick's advertising successors, Jack Goodman and Nina Bourne and, in more recent years, Strome Lamon, all were influenced by the early tradition but more inclined to introduce their own particular panache into ads that were often humorous and invariably provocative. The style changed somewhat, but Simon and Schuster advertising continued to stand out. When Herman Wouk's first book, *Aurora Dawn*, was published by S and S, Jack Goodman's full-page announcement ad began:

*Who—or What—Is*
WOUK?

and went on to inform the reader that the name was pronounced "Woke," which was a point worth clearing up right away because it was a name the reader would be hearing and using often from now on.

When Laura Z. Hobson wrote *Gentleman's Agreement*, the ad displayed a large picture of a man who was filling out an application form and who, on the line furnished for "Race," had written in "Episcopa . . ." and crossed it out and written "Jewish." That outspoken novel about social anti-Semitism in America was thought to be extremely provocative but doomed to failure. One of the country's top booksellers tabbed it "impossible to sell." Not quite right. It became the clear Number One fiction bestseller in the nation in 1947, and that advertisement, which was repeated again and again, was thought to have had a lot to do with its success.

Goodman and then Bourne used a combination of illustrations and spirited headlines and text that are still landmarks of American book advertising. They ranged from ads for humorous cartoon smash hits like Walt Kelly's *Pogo* and Al Capp's *The Shmoo*, through felicitous marriages of text and drawings such as Kay Thompson and Hilary Knight's *Eloise* and S. J. Perelman and Al Hirschfeld's *Westward, Ha!* to extremely solid volumes that lent themselves to the technique, like Roger Butterfield's *The American Past*. Jack Goodman set the pattern, and when he died, Nina Bourne carried on in similar fashion.

Some years later, after Nina left S & S to go and practice her magic for Alfred A. Knopf, Strome Lamon came over from Time Inc., to fill the Essandess advertising slot. Strome had the same sort of flair for improvising an arresting headline and writing catchy copy, but times and administrative attitudes about book advertising were changing, along with virtually everything else in the industry, so Strome accommodated his talents to meet circumstances. Whenever a special occasion arose that called for an old-time piece of charming brilliance in an advertisement, such as the publication of a new P. G. Wodehouse novel on Wodehouse's ninetieth birthday, Strome would knock off a little masterpiece quite worthy of the best of his predecessors. However, now the personal bond between publishers of books and readers of books was fading. The nature of communications had changed, and the sort of direct relationship that made the old Inner Sanctum columns memorable and which the *New Yorker* used so effectively for years in "The Talk of the Town" ("Our man Stanley was in Bloomingdale's the other day and overheard . . .") somehow had lost its appeal. Between television, cassettes, and the techniques of mass communications, the delicious small essay simply didn't appear to have sufficient punch to intrigue readers sufficiently

Strome Lamon

any more. The result is that, on the whole, book publishers' advertisements look more or less the same these days, even when there is an unusually creative advertising manager at the helm, such as Strome at S & S or Nina at Knopf. That's because it now appears that the effective ads require three elements and that's all: display of the book, favorable quotes from respected reviewers (not from the *Podunk Gazette*), and any special news that implies this is the book you've been waiting for all your life (your favorite celebrity wrote it, it's an immediate bestseller with three printings before publication and a major book-club choice, it's scandalous, it's sexy, it will make you a better, wiser, richer, or slimmer person, and so forth). That doesn't take the sort of exceptional talent that so distinguished the early S & S copywriters, but some advertising people still do it better than others.

To Strome the main challenge is to be sure that the thrust of the very first ad for a book is right, because advertising budgets are seldom big enough to allow a change of strategy in mid-campaign. He has to search out the most important thing and hit it hard. The audience for each Harold Robbins novel is so huge and so solid that the message need be no more than "The New and Best Harold Robbins," but usually Lamon has to work somewhat more energetically. Often he gets a handle to his ad by spotting a line in the book. Such a case occurred when he was mulling over the way to present a sales pitch for Dr. Laurence Morehouse and Leonard Gross's *Total Fitness in 30 Minutes a Week* and came across the sentence, "Even if you haven't exercised once in the last twenty years, you are just two hours away from good physical condition." (If that statement strikes you as belonging in the "or Not" section of Ripley's "Believe It or Not," pause before you condemn too quickly. Consider the title, which calls for three ten-minute sessions of exercises a week. The authors contend that anyone can attain at least pretty good physical condition after four weeks on the program—hence the claim that you are just two hours away from it. It's a claim that many thousands of people will swear to be valid, including this writer.) In any event, Strome knew that here he had everything he needed for a terrific mail-order advertisement, for what out-of-shape American could resist it? Apparently few did, because the book became the Number One nonfiction bestseller of 1975.

More and more, as space rates in newspapers and magazines have escalated so sharply, there is less of an impulse to divert much, if any, of a book's limited advertising budget in those directions, unless the book is a potential blockbuster. On most books there would be only enough money for one modest ad, and that won't get a book off the starting line. Accordingly book publishers try to get more realistic action for the money, and this can take a couple of forms. One is to use cooperative advertising with bookstores, preparing an ad for, let us say, B. Dalton and largely bearing the cost even though the ad doesn't seem to come from Simon & Schuster at all, but indicates that B. Dalton is the place to get this book. This approach has several advantages. The bookseller can buy space at his local rate, invariably less than the national rate; the costs are to some extent shared; and obviously the bookstore's energies are enlisted to push the book in any special way it can, sometimes including author's appearances in the store. Also, publishers are using radio advertising much more than ever in the past, finding that radio can often pinpoint a particular market better than any other medium. There are a great number of radio stations with a variety of special audience appeals—rock, classical, country music, news and talk about business, foreign affairs, and so on. Television can also be very effective, but it's infinitely more costly and isn't so likely to have a defined focus of listeners as radio. Publishers like S & S like to use TV commercials on occasion, and particularly in launching paperback lines and titles, but this is an area where the wise still tread gingerly.

Television and radio play a part in the book-publishing picture much more frequently, and often much more effectively, in an area that once was completely subordinate to space advertising but which in modern times is likely to surpass it. That is publicity, and in particular that aspect of it which sends an author on a tour, sectional or national, to plug a book as a guest on an established talk show. In such circumstances the publisher doesn't pay the television or radio station as he would have to do if buying a commercial ad, but at current costs for hotels and restaurants and travel, even a limited tour can run into money. Still, it's apt to be less than what visible space advertising would cost and, when the author is good, it can be much more fruitful. Many authors are unable to do much for their books, particularly fiction writers, and a tour may turn out to be little more than an ego trip or a way to satisfy a complaining author or agent. But when an author has written on a topic of real interest and is an articulate and attractive talker, money spent on publicity can be by far the best way to put a potentially big book across. Dan Green, who heads up the Trade book division of Simon & Schuster, made his reputation in publishing by being one of the best publicity directors in the field, and today his former assistant and successor, Julia Knickerbocker, plays a major role in S & S's marketing plans. Dan is very conscious of the importance of publicity and keeps a close eye on his first love, as does editor-in-chief Michael Korda, who is a wizard at it both for his authors and for himself.

Michael and Dan each has a story to tell about how Simon & Schuster learned to use publicity to best effect, but they will have to wait until I tell you about the first author who proved that a book could be sold spectacularly purely via guest television appearances. That was my own beloved Alexander King, who meant more to me personally than any author I ever handled, and whose first book of irreverent memoirs, *Mine Enemy Grows Older*, appeared in 1958. At that time publicity was handled conscientiously enough but routinely, with the department thought of as a sort of adjunct to the advertising department. Efforts were made to get authors appearances on shows if they didn't have to travel very far and could be home in their own bed by nightfall without incurring a hotel bill. If they enjoyed it and were grateful to the firm for having been able to arrange the exposure, fine and dandy. One could only hope that the whole thing might produce some actual sales because, short of a real boom in sales (which hadn't happened up to then as a result of television), there was no way of measuring any results. But Alexander King, in his first appearance on the Jack Paar Show, the equivalent of today's Johnny Carson Show, startled both Paar and his huge national audience with such a barrage of wickedly funny and unconventional comment on every untouchable subject from sex to religion that no one who heard him could get enough. He was invited back to the Paar show again and again, week after week, then also got his own television show with his wife, Margie, on PBS, and not only did *Mine Enemy Grows Older* become the Number One nonfiction bestseller of the year 1958, but so did his second book of memoirs, *May This House Be Safe from Tigers*, the very next year.

Remarkably enough—but then everything about Alex was remarkable—he went on to write two more volumes of memoirs, *I Should
Have Kissed Her More* and *Is There a Life after Birth?* Although neither
of them achieved Number One on the bestseller lists, both came
close. Alex was the most superb of storytellers and, unlike other
good ones, never repeated himself either in his books or in conversa-
tional evenings. Through the sheer force of his unmatchable cha-
risma on the tube, he captured the nation's imagination, and since his
books delivered with equal impact, they all were wildly successful.
Alexander King was the man who taught the entire book industry
that the right author, with the right topics and the right flair, could
sell books via television better than any other way books could be

Alexander King

sold. The lesson was well worth learning, and many others have profited from it to a greater or lesser extent, but there was only one Alexander King. A decade went by before Simon & Schuster benefited again so handsomely by virtue of an author's genius at publicity, and when it happened it was of a very different nature.

Jacqueline Susann had written a sensational and whopping bestselling novel, which Bernard Geis Associates had published, *The Valley of the Dolls*. Despite its success she appeared to have reasons why she wanted to leave Geis, so the publication rights to her next novel, *The Love Machine*, were put up at auction to several other houses, including S & S. Against stiff competition, Essandess paid what, at the time, was an enormous amount of money to get a book on which the probabilities of earning such a sum back seemed highly dubious. Today, in an extremely competitive era where almost every big property is sold by agents using the multiple-submission technique, this act wouldn't be extraordinary, but back in the late 1960s, when S & S went all out to secure *The Love Machine*, it was a most risky gamble for the house and struck some as insane. Why did the firm do it? It was because the new team that was taking over the running of Simon & Schuster, Dick Snyder and Michael Korda, wanted to show the world (and particularly authors and agents) that S & S could be more than a leader in nonfiction bestsellers, which had been their chief stock in trade. They intended from then on to publish commercial fiction as well and as successfully as anyone in the business. Up to that time, that had not been a top priority in the firm's editorial pursuits except during the golden years when the brilliant Robert Gottlieb had forged an impressive fiction list for Essandess. But Gottlieb had left to head up Knopf, taking most of his novelists with him; fiction bestsellers were now more likely to come to S & S through personal acquaintance with authors than via literary agents, who handled virtually all of the "hot" properties. Despite having published some extremely successful fiction in the past, even before Gottlieb, such as Henry Morton Robinson's *Cardinal*, Eric Hodgins's *Mr. Blandings Builds His Dream House*, Henry Bellamann's *Kings Row*, Laura Z. Hobson's *Gentleman's Agreement*, and several bestselling novels by Irving Wallace, agents didn't really think of S & S as a fiction house. Michael Korda was keen to change that image, and Dick Snyder willing to back him up.

Jacqueline Susann and Irving Mansfield, with "Josephine"

Seldom has publishing risk money been spent more wisely. Jackie Susann and her publicity expert, her husband, Irving Mansfield, were calculating and inventive ballyhooers who worked unceasingly at the game, and the S & S people, quick learners, picked up tricks and techniques that they've used on other books up to the present moment. Jackie's publicity impact was planned and executed with definite goals.

The first thing the Mansfields came up with was the creation of a symbol—almost a trademark—for the book. It was the ankh, the Egyptian cross that is identified with love and life. Gold-plated ankhs in the form of necklaces were made up in the hundreds to be sent to major bookstore people. Leatherbound diaries with golden ankhs stamped onto the binding followed, and Irving Mansfield appeared all over every major city in person and on television resplendent in a blue blazer with a large gold ankh emblazoned on the breast pocket. Jackie, wearing at least one ankh on her person in the form of jewelry, was the hostess of elaborate parties at which the guest list was certain to include every gossip writer or columnist in that particular city, and if it was in New York the recounting of some Max Schuster bon mot was absolutely certain to appear the next day (slightly mangled) in Leonard Lyons's column along with the latest dirt on Jacqueline Susann and *The Love Machine*. When the time came to prepare a jacket for the book, an area which by contract is the publisher's responsibility and one in which authors with suggestions are generally told by the art director what they can do with their suggestions, there was no restraining Jackie and Irving. Shown a four-color photograph of a woman's hand with an ankh bracelet on her wrist, which was intended for the front of the jacket, Irving hit the roof. "What an ugly woman's hand!" he roared. Michael Korda, speaking up for Frank Metz, the art director, who had turned purple with fury, replied, "Irving, that is the hand of the Number One hand model in the United States." Mansfield pondered for a moment and then bellowed, "Get me Number Two!"

Even when, out of courtesy or intimidation, authors are permitted to express opinions and make jacket suggestions, usually it can be done within the confines of an office. Not so with Jackie, who was not satisfied with the jacket for *The Love Machine* until, prior to the Johnny Carson Show, she could see a film of herself holding the book up and be sure that the title registered boldly enough on the small screen to have an impact. She kept a card file on bookstore clerks, knew them by their first names, jumped from table to table at booksellers' dinners so that she could sit for a while with each old or new pal. The Mansfields really taught Simon & Schuster the tricks of a modern, show-business publicity campaign, and Simon & Schuster never forgot the invaluable training.

In more recent times, a dozen years after the Susann era, Simon & Schuster had another phenomenal success where credit for huge sales went to publicity rather than space advertising. That was *Jane Fonda's Workout Book*. Other S & S books in the interim had sold very well chiefly because of effective publicity work, but the Fonda book was by far the most spectacular.

Jane Fonda and her successful book are toasted by Fred Hills, who was her editor, Frank Metz, and Dan Green.

The literary agent for Miss Fonda, Georges Borchardt, offered the book to several publishers simultaneously, looking essentially for an auction among them that would produce the highest offer, which is the factor that usually settles such matters. The S & S editorial board was eager to obtain the book, as well as a proposed second book to follow about physical workouts for pregnant women, and made an extremely substantial bid for a two-book package. The thinking was that the basic workout book would have very big sales immediately, in view of Jane Fonda's screen fame and her well-known devotion to her exercise salons, and that the pregnancy book would do nicely too at the outset and then settle down to being a long-life staple on the backlist. However, the handsome Simon & Schuster bid turned out not to be handsome enough, for Random House made an even better offer. As is the practice on auctions, Borchardt came back to see if S & S wanted to go further, but the editorial board decided it had already gone far enough. S & S was prepared to bow out.

But Dick Snyder, never a man to give up as long as there are some vital signs left, had a joint discussion with the publishers of two S & S collateral trade-book houses, Joni Evans of Linden Books and Dan Green, then the publisher of the now-dissolved Kenan Press. They both screamed to high heaven about how Dick simply *had* to buy the books for some S & S imprint, Joni on the basis of the fortune that was sure to be gleaned out of the sale of subsidiary rights both here and abroad—knowledge in this area is one of Joni's specialties—and Dan on the basis of how well S & S in general, and he in particular, knew how to make such books work, all the way from design and format to publicity and marketing. Dan had excellent credentials to support his plea, having been the editor-sponsor of Arnold Schwarzenegger's *Body Shaping for Women*, which sold 170,000 copies in hardback despite being a much harder book than Fonda's for women to accept and adopt. It required using weights, while Fonda's book was based on much more ordinary and approachable techniques like exercise and isometrics. Also, said Dan, let's face it. Arnold Schwarzenegger was an attractive figure to be the author of such a book, but he wasn't really up to Jane Fonda for credibility in telling women how to combine feminine beauty and physical fitness.

Arnold Schwarzenegger

Impressed by Joni and Dan's persuasiveness, Snyder put in another bid that topped all rivals, and S & S won the auction. The proposal had originally been sent by Borchardt to Nan Talese, who was then a senior editor and a member of the S & S Editorial Board, and she was to edit the book, with Dan Green cooperating on packaging and marketing, but before things got underway Nan left S & S to become head of the Houghton Mifflin editorial office in New York, and Dan Green became Jane Fonda's sole sponsor.

A suitable book was produced, crammed with splendid and practical illustrations, and the plan was to underprice it somewhat at $15.95, because the marketing strategy was to put 85,000 books into the stores by publication date, and a higher list price would have made that difficult. Advertising budgets and promotion schemes had not yet been determined, when the motion picture of *On Golden Pond* was released, featuring Henry Fonda and Katharine Hepburn and containing some exquisite shots of Jane Fonda and her superb body. That film was a huge popular success in the theaters and won virtually every Oscar a movie can win, so Dan Green, now the publisher, decided to go with his initial instinct—not to run any space advertising at all, but to rely upon Jane Fonda's image and her promise to carry out an extensive promotion campaign. She did indeed carry out her end of it magnificently, appearing in city after city from coast to coast talking about fitness and her book. And so, with no advertising at all except for one mail-order ad in a women's magazine and one brief TV commercial, well over a million copies of the book have been sold; it is still going strong at its current price of $19.95. The book's continuing vitality is astonishing: it sold just about as many copies in the first few months of 1983, more than a year after it was published, as it did in a similar stretch of time in 1982.

The performance of the second book, *Jane Fonda's Workout Book for Pregnancy, Birth, and Recovery*, targeted for a much smaller audience, has had comparably gratifying results as to both quantity of sales and continuing ones. Over 200,000 copies have been sold at this writing in late 1983, with sales actually higher than the same months in 1982, and once again it has all been achieved through publicity rather than advertising.

I don't mean to imply that space advertising can no longer be used to good effect. If that were the case you would not see full-page ads, a great many of them featuring Simon & Schuster books, appearing each Sunday in the *New York Times Book Review*, and big ones frequently in the daily paper as well. Many books continue to need and profit from generous space advertising, but publishers have to choose the titles on which they decide to plunge with infinitely more care than they once did, because of the enormously escalating costs today in preparing advertisements and buying space. There was a day when just about every book considered worth publishing automatically got at least one respectable ad to help launch it, but currently that policy simply isn't justified in economic terms. An author understandably bemoans a situation where a major publisher has accepted and published his or her book and then doesn't run even one advertisement, but from the publisher's standpoint, and the bottom-line pressures that have descended upon the industry, it makes sense. An almost certain best-selling book by a distinguished author like Graham Greene, or a very popular one like Harold Robbins, or a celebrity like Phil Donahue, justifies generous space advertising expenditures. They act on such books like the effect on a snowball that has been formed and is solidly packed when you start rolling it down a hill. With each revolution it picks up lots of additional snow and becomes much bigger. That is how lavish space advertising can be a catalyst for sales on a book that has something solid going for it from the beginning. If a book doesn't have that, money spent on advertising might well be spent better on other marketing techniques, or tucked back into one's pocket.

The theory that advertising alone can sell a book has been proved a fallacy time and again over the years, as when a motion-picture company, trying to hype a forthcoming film based upon an unknown author's soon-to-be-published book, decides that a sum like $100,000, which is a fabulous amount to spend on advertising one book, is just a drop in the bucket out of their total production budget for the movie. They have been known either to give the book publisher the money to spend, or to have the advertising for the book done themselves. In either case it never works, at least not on hardcover books to any extent that would come near to justifying the expenditure. When a book already has a big reputation and is being made into an important film at the same time as a paperback edition of the book is planned, as was the case with *The World According to Garp*, an advertising tie-in can be spectacularly effective.

I doubt if any book ever proved the futility of trying to achieve colossal sales by pouring unlimited money into advertising than a book published by S & S in 1981 and reprinted by Pocket Books in paperback the following year. That was a volume entitled *A Remarkable Medicine Has Been Overlooked*, written by Jack Dreyfus, the multimillionaire founder of the renowned Dreyfus Mutual Fund. A scratch golfer who won the Montgomery, Alabama, city championship when he was eighteen, Dreyfus switched to tennis in his later years and won the National Senior Grass Court Doubles Championship with Gardner Mulloy when he was in his sixties. A tournament contract bridge player, he has been rated the best gin-rummy player in the country. He has also been the breeder of outstanding thoroughbred horses and has twice been chairman of the New York State Racing Association. His hugely successful business operations made him one of the richest men in the nation. Dreyfus was not a man, one would think, who would be likely to be overwhelmed by severe depression when he was approaching fifty years of age, but that is what happened to him. Then, by chance or intuition, he got the idea that the drug universally accepted as the effective anticonvulsant in the treatment of epilepsy, DPH, or Dilantin, might help him. His doctor, knowing that Dilantin was a solidly established drug for epilepsy, also knew it had very few and not serious side effects, and saw no harm in Dreyfus trying it. The results and Dreyfus's improvement were so immediate and so dramatically successful that Dreyfus felt an obligation to spread the word.

Once Jack sets his mind to do something, he knows no half measures. He established a nonprofit medical foundation for the sole purpose of looking into what he felt the broad range of DPH might be, and over the next fifteen years spent over $20 million of his own money amassing and distributing volumes of clinical evidence, culled from doctors' reports all over the world, about its effectiveness in benefiting sufferers of many problems, from cardiac arrhythmias through migraine headaches to excessive anger and fear. There were approximately two dozen conditions where the evidence seemed to show considerable therapeutic response to treatment with DPH, but despite Dreyfus's efforts—and he had very good connections in government and prestigious support from some of them—the Food and Drug Administration continued to recognize Dilantin as the specific for the treatment of epilepsy—and nothing else.

Yet Dreyfus pursued his mission of bringing to light the other benefits he perceived in DPH with the fervor of a knight errant seeking the Holy Grail. He spent his years and his millions furnishing evidence to the medical profession, to the governmental regulatory commissions, to people in the highest places both in this country and abroad, and he did make some dents in very rigid armor. DPH is indeed used today by a number of doctors both here and abroad to regulate excessive bioelectrical activity and to stabilize excitable nerve cell and nerve tissue, but he never got past first base in what he was really trying to achieve—a universal acceptance of DPH's virtues as a benign medicine over and above its recognized one as an anticonvulsant.

So after his fifteen years had gone by and his $20 million had been spent, Jack decided to plunge one last, big time. He wrote *A Remarkable Medicine Has Been Overlooked* and, because Dreyfus is a talented man in carrying out everything he undertakes, it was a persuasive book. He prefaced it with an open letter of personal appeal to President Reagan to read it, and then proposed arrangements with Simon

Jack Dreyfus

& Schuster to bring the book out and distribute it in a massive way. His proposal was such an extraordinary no-lose arrangement for the publisher that it was virtually impossible to decline. S & S was to perform its customary mechanics of editing the manuscript, producing and paying for the manufacture of finished books, and then marketing them through its sales force to the country's bookstores. Dreyfus himself didn't want any money at all, neither royalties nor any other earnings that might develop out of publication of the book. What is more he would pay all advertising and promotion expenses and guaranteed that he would spend at least $1 million to launch the hardcover edition. (Actually, the amount he finally did put out for full-page ads, run several times in almost every major publication all over the United States, came nearer to $1.5 million.) In the end S & S printed 50,000 books and sold most of them, but no more. That would be a very gratifying sale for most hardcover books, but it's one for which an advertising expenditure of something closer to $25,000 would have been all a normal budget could stand. Simon & Schuster came out nicely as far as its profit on the book was concerned, but Dreyfus—even though it was his intention and he did it with his eyes open, not caring about the money—had added another $1.5 million to the $20 million that had already been run up to spread his gospel.

Nor was that the end. Although the hardcover S & S edition had borne the low retail price of $9.95 due to its being endowed in this fashion, Jack now felt that many more people could have the message reach them if a still-lower-priced paperback edition would be published. Accordingly he made the same sort of arrangement with S & S's sister company, Pocket Books, and spent *another* $1.5 million to publicize the edition! The result was that another 150,000 people bought the book in that format and, while that too is by no means a bad performance for a paperback, it would have been a catastrophic performance if the advertising money had been accounted on a routine Profit-and-Loss worksheet.

What is the moral of this story? Remember that this was a good book with an intriguing topic, whether you believe the author was off his trolley or not. (I was his editor and I didn't.) It was a well-written book with a dramatic and often spellbinding quality. It was on the side of the angels and the book received many more good reviews, both in general publications and in medical ones, than it did indifferent or dubious or poor ones. The distribution by the two publishers' very efficient and well-respected sales forces blanketed the bookstores of the country with piles of books on display shelves and in windows. Everything was perfect—except the original snow-ball never had the packing or momentum needed for even such a fabulous amount of advertising money to get it rolling lustily down the hill. About $3 million of Dreyfus's money was spent to reach a total of about 200,000 readers—that comes to $15 per book!

Simon & Schuster didn't really learn anything it didn't already know. The Dreyfus experience simply solidified a general rule that is likely to table early discussions about advertising for forthcoming books, which is to make the item HFQ, which means "Hold for Quotes." If the quotes come along reasonably quickly (which means before the bookstores start returning copies), then indeed the ad or ads may be authorized. If they don't, the chances are they won't, for it is generally futile for a publisher alone to try to tell the world how wonderful a book is: he needs other and unprejudiced authorities, like major book reviewers, to say so.

Book publishers are realistic enough to know that, on the whole, book buyers and readers neither know nor care much about which firm issued a book. That is true of other products too—quick, can you tell me which companies produce Shredded Wheat? Some few firms have enough distinction to use their name effectively as part of the title on a book that they are proud of, as for example *The Oxford Book of Verse*, put out by Oxford University Press. But back in 1949 Dick Simon had an idea for promoting Simon and Schuster books as S and S books (this was in the pre-ampersand era), which was in-spired by what the eminent British publisher, Victor Gollancz, had done with apparent success.

Victor used no jackets for any of his books other than a solid yellow one with simple black and red lettering. No graphics or art work at all. The technique certainly saved Gollancz money and it certainly made Gollancz books stand out in the bookstores. Whether it was as effective, book by book, in selling a title as a more am-bitious jacket is moot: one might infer that it was not from the fact

Victor Gollancz

that after Victor's death the house of Gollancz stopped the idea and
began turning out display-type jackets just like everybody else.
However in 1949 Gollancz and his yellow dustcovers seemed to be
making out splendidly.

Dick Simon wasn't rash enough to think that something like the
bare, unadorned Gollancz jacket would work in this country, but he
was bemused by the idea of doing *something* with his books that
would scream out "This is a Simon and Schuster book!" So in the
spring of that year he saw to it that each new title had an element
added to its jacket, regardless of what sort of beautifully planned
jacket the art director had conceived. Nine horizontal half-inch
bands, alternating black and yellow, with one piled atop another,
made a striped column like a flag that totaled a bit more than four

inches in height, and this was placed on the bottom of the spine of each jacket. Since most books are eight or nine inches tall, this meant that just about the bottom half of the spine looked like a yellow-and-black barber's pole, and "Simon and Schuster" was printed on the bottom yellow stripe. Artistic it may not have been, but visible it was. You could spot a Simon and Schuster book from the second balcony.

It happened that the one and only list on which Dick Simon tried this experiment was a weak one. The outstanding result of it all was that the nation's booksellers, seeing all those yellow-and-black-striped unsold books on their shelves, were inclined to reach for them first when they were looking over their stock to decide on which books to return! Victor Gollancz had had no such problem. In those days British publishers didn't have a return policy.

# Fun and Games

# in the Classless Society     6

HUMOR, as a commercial commodity in the book-publishing world, is at its lowest ebb in the century. That's true of the other forms of entertainment too, with rare exceptions such as the columns of Russell Baker, Art Buchwald, and Erma Bombeck. Woody Allen's movies do a lot for the cinema, but when delightful comedies like *It Happened One Night*, made in 1934, are shown on late-night television these days, the cryptic one-line review in the newspaper program says—quite truthfully—something like: "Catch it. They don't make them like this anymore." A young audience of book readers along with a new breed of younger book publishers all were born and matured under the ever-present threat of an atomic cloud, so perhaps it's little wonder that they no longer feel that casual fun constitutes an important portion of life the way we elders once did. What humor continues to exist is invariably black humor or is woven into contemporary life and problems.

That certainly wasn't the case in earlier years at Simon and Schuster, where anything from the wry gag to the riotous belly laugh were high points of the day. The business of publishing was undertaken just as seriously as it is now, but the atmosphere was constantly punctuated with the pause that refreshes, the merry quip, and very nearly everybody working in the office at that time had an astonishing flair for carrying it off. From bosses to secretaries and mailroom clerks, almost everyone was on a first-name basis, and tasteful glee even at someone's expense was no respector of rank. Max Schuster was probably the target of more buffoonery for his unusual traits than anyone else, but no one took it better or more readily gave back as good as or better than he received. The humor wasn't mean and the aura of innocent if meaningless fun lent itself to S & S's active pursuit and profitable publishing of funny books. To cite a few, there was Frank Scully's *Fun in Bed*, Eddie Cantor's *Caught Short*, Bob Hope's *I Never Left Home*, Al Capp's *Li'l Abner* and *The Shmoo*, George Baker's *Sad Sack*, Bennett Cerf's *Try and Stop Me*, Shepherd Mead's *How to Succeed in Business without Really Trying*, Eric Hodgins's *Mr. Blandings Builds His Dream House*, the cartoon collections of Peter Arno and Charles Addams, and Max Eastman's *Enjoyment of Laughter*, among many others. Three giants of comic writing joined S & S ranks along about the end of this period and they con-

S. J. Perelman

P. G. Wodehouse
and Peter Schwed

tinued to be published by the house regularly through later, more sober years, but then what publisher would not have welcomed regular new books by S. J. Perelman, P. G. Wodehouse, and Sam Levenson during any climate? Sadly, all three are dead now, and in an era when the "funny book" is more likely to slip on a banana peel than not, S & S isn't so interested in encouraging any Diogenes with a lamp looking for a new court jester. If a real comic does happen to come along, he or she is more likely to be published as an original paperback, as was the case with Bruce Feirstein's extremely successful *Real Men Don't Eat Quiche*. The answer seems to be that people will still pay what a paperback costs for a book whose only aim is to amuse, but resist hardcover prices.

Sam Levenson

Nor do the halls in the modern S & S offices echo with laughter as they once did. It isn't that there aren't even now extremely humorous people employed, but on the whole they are funny on their own time. Justice demands a number of explanations other than changes in management attitude. Book publishing has become a much more competitive and important Business with a capital B, and the volume and pressures are enormously greater than they were in the days when one bestseller was an occasion for parties, love affairs, and a successful season. If Richard Snyder is to continue to supply better working conditions, higher salaries, better benefits, and the continued recognition that even in bad times for the industry S & S has been something of a miracle among trade-book publishers—all of which he has done—then his staff had better work long and essentially serious hours. But let's look back to the sorts of episodes that made S & S such fun Once upon a Time.

There were the Jones Beach parties. Each summer the entire organization, then something less than a hundred people, piled into buses early on a weekday morning and were driven out to Robert Moses's best contribution to New York life. The office was closed for the day and everyone came, from Simon and Schuster and Shimkin down through the ranks to the mailroom boy hired the previous week. The notion that a Jones Beach office party was a corny way to spend a gloriously sunny summer day never occurred to even the most sophisticated. Those who owned cars did not use them because the idea was for the Essandess family to mingle. The Big Wheels made a point of not sitting together nor did personnel in the same department bunch up in clusters: pairings usually were dictated by personal and sexual preferences rather than professional. The buses were merry with chatter, music, and the playing of games. Editor Maria Leiper recalls that the single thing Max Schuster ever did that impressed her most was, when Twenty Questions was being played on one trip Max needed only three questions to identify the person about whom the questions were being asked as Hamilcar Barca—who, as I'm sure all my readers know, was the Carthaginian general who eventually made peace with Rome, thus ending the First Punic War.

At the beach a crisp bill was handed out to each person, more than enough to pay for a bathhouse locker, lunch, and admission to those sports such as Pitch-and-Putt Golf or Paddle Tennis that charged a fee. A softball game between the uptown executive office personnel and the downtown stockroom employees was a regular feature, usually won by the latter despite the valiant efforts of Maria, a remarkable athlete. She was counterbalanced, however, by the athletic ineptitude of editor Jerome Weidman, who was so inexperienced at sports that he was consigned to right field, a position where it was hoped by the uptown group a ball would never be hit. Eventually however one was, and Jerry stood transfixed and watched a soft fly hit the ground five feet in front of him and roll between his legs. Then, realizing his great responsibility, he tore back after it, picked it up, and saw that what should have been an easy out or at worst a single was turning into a home run; desperately he drew back and flung the ball with all his might in the general direction of home plate. The fact that his throw didn't reach the infield is of little importance; what mattered is that Jerry broke his arm in two places making the attempt.

At the end of the long day everyone piled back into the buses and made for a Long Island roadhouse that had been reserved for an evening of dinner and dancing. The last bus didn't pull out until the small hours, but all were back at their jobs the next morning, with no worse aftereffects than some cases of severe sunburn and half a dozen new love affairs.

Then there was the Barney Greengrass file, perhaps the most elaborate jape ever perpetrated by supposedly serious people engaged in a supposedly serious business office, but publishers are sometimes inclined that way. It was a fictitious editorial folder looking just like the ones that exist on every book, containing everything pertaining to a project from inception through publication. Inspired and carried out by a number of gifted wags—notably Nina Bourne, the advertising copywriter; Helen Barrow, the production chief; and Jerry Weidman—the file began with a short memorandum from Sam Meyerson, the mail-order director, to Max Schuster. It said that for a long time he had been interested in fish and suggested that there might be a book in Barney Greengrass, the Sturgeon King, whose splendid establishment was (and still is) on Amsterdam Avenue just above Eighty-sixth Street. From then on the file was expanded as a flood of documents was added, all bearing the style and individual characteristics of the people supposed to have written them, with each signature or scribbled initials beautifully forged. The elaborateness of the jest included obtaining Schuster's own highly identifiable embossed stationery, which he used to write to dignitaries, and sheets of the bright canary-colored bond paper on which his interoffice communications were typed, along with the green-ink pen he always used to sign or initial anything. Maria Leiper's memorandums were always typed on pink paper, and she used a straight pin to secure more than a one-page memo, rather than a paper clip, so the entries to the file that were credited to her featured pink paper and pins. And so it went, with everyone's personal quirks and manners of expression shamelessly satirized.

The Barney Greengrass file ran to some thirty documents, and, while it was consistently hilarious for anyone who worked at S & S at the time, much of it can be appreciated only by insiders who knew the characters. But a brief summary may convey the idea.

On the heels of Sam Meyerson's original diffident suggestion, Max Schuster instantly congratulated him on "fine spade work" and offered his vast hoard of clippings on fish "to help Greengrass integrate, implement, and activate this unique, need-filling, and statesmanlike project." Maria thought it might have the Byronic sweep and gusto found in other Schuster projects, provided one question could be answered—who is Barney Greengrass? Quincy Howe offered to have the project mentioned with anticipation once a week on his radio broadcasts. Jack Goodman said he liked the idea but it would need rewriting and offered the services of Agnes Rumsey (his wife) or Adeline Marx (his sister-in-law) or Gladys Benmosche (his mother); from the advertising standpoint he thought it was a whale of an idea.

Meanwhile Max Schuster was writing exquisitely phrased ambassadorial letters to Greengrass and receiving six-word replies from Barney, scribbled in pencil on brown paper bags. Albert Leventhal noted that he was working to prepare a color brochure and a prepublication offering for the time the book would be ready, but panic ensued when Dick Simon had to report that he had lost the manuscript. (A while later Dick's favorite photography shop sent him a letter asking if they could dispose of the batch of paper he had left on the counter at the time of his last visit along with his overcoat.) Leon

Shimkin wrote that in view of Schuster's making available to the author his vast research material, wouldn't it be fair to suggest to Greengrass that he do the book on a small flat-fee basis rather than royalties? Max proposed that the title be changed to *How Greengrass Is My Valley.* Lee Wright, Dick Simon's editorial assistant at the time, asked by him to review the project and write a report, merely typed a line saying this was the most loathsome book idea she had seen in her entire life. Tom Bevans, the production manager, sent a memo to Simon saying that a Western Union boy had delivered a large man- uscript from Dick's photography shop and that he had sent it out to get prices on typesetting. Schuster solicited Clifton Fadiman's expert opinion despite the fact that he no longer was working for S & S and received a terse reply—"This is crap"—accompanied by a bill for $100 as his fee for an outside reading. The agent, Alan Collins of Curtis Brown, wrote to Simon that he now represented Greengrass and that he was tired of waiting to hear S & S's proposed terms so he had submitted another copy of the manuscript to Doubleday, who had accepted the book, and that contracts had just been signed. Si- mon dashed off a letter to Doubleday: "Dear Nelson: An awful thing has happened. You've probably had a similar experience in your organization. . . . the unfortunate thing is that we have already printed 17,000 copies of the book and in good faith have submitted it to Doubleday's book club, the Literary Guild. I have two sugges- tions: (1) Make the Guild take it. (2) Special discount to all Double- day book shops. And finally, how about a merger?" To which Nelson Doubleday replied that Essandess might keep the Greengrass book provided that Doubleday took over *A Treasury of Masterpieces* and the reprint rights to it.

Max Schuster now dropped a short query to his assistant of the moment, Jerome Weidman, reading: "What is new with the Green- grass matter? Has anyone read the manuscript?" The top salesman on the road wired in that he'd been able to sell only one copy, and that only because the bookstore had a customer named Greengrass and thought he might go for it. Another brown bag with penciled writ- ing arrived from Amsterdam Avenue addressed to Mr. Schuster: "I am sending you herewith a Nova Scotia salmon and four pickled herrings. How is our book doing? Will there be much advertising? Sincerely, Barney Greengrass, Fish." The next item came from Albert

Leventhal in a note to the head of the biggest remainder house in the industry to the effect that S & S was willing to let him have approximately 17,000 copies of *The Life of Barney Greengrass* for 14¢ a copy rather than the somewhat higher price quoted a few days earlier. In the final document in the folder we hear again for the first time since the original suggestion from Sam Meyerson. He penned a new memorandum to Max Schuster: "Was there ever any action taken on that Greengrass book idea that I proposed some time ago?"

The mischievous élan that characterized the firm to the extent of a number of key people spending so much of their time and imagination for no good reason except enjoyment sometimes was extended to embrace relationships from the outside world. One of Dick Simon's and Max Schuster's closest British connections was with Hamish Hamilton, whose nickname was "Jamie." He came to the Essandess offices one year on an editorial scouting trip, and Dick and Max offered him the exclusive opportunity to secure British rights on a particular pet book of theirs, one in which they both had unbounded confidence and pride. To their amazement and chagrin Jamie turned it down flat, saying that he thought it fell between two stools. Soon afterward, Hamilton boarded the *Queen Mary* to return to England and went to his stateroom. Opening the door he found in the center of his cabin two footstools, each with a large ribbon tied into a bow surmounting its seat, along with a card that read: "Dear Jamie. Fall between these. Bon Voyage. Max and Dick."

No offense was taken. Max and Dick knew that Jamie too liked a good joke.

So outstanding was Essandess's reputation for publishing humor at this middle period of its history than an extraordinary number of submissions of a comic nature came its way, and two of them won such affection and success that each became for a time a substitute for or an embellishment to the Simon and Schuster colophon of the Sower. They were Walt Kelly's *Pogo* books and Kay Thompson and Hilary Knight's *Eloise*. Here is a sampling of how Essandess adapted the first of its two pet characters for use on books, stationery, Christmas cards, sales letters, and ads, which was a good idea because there have been mighty few cartoon characters so universally beloved as Pogo. Eloise was another, and you'll learn about her a few pages on.

The first collection of *Pogo* comic strips burst upon the world in 1951 as the result of Jack Goodman's insistence that there should be such a book for those who could not afford a daily newspaper, particularly since it was the only thing in the newspapers worth reading. As Walt Kelly wrote in a reissue of the original book in 1963, according to wall scratchings in the caves of Simon and Schuster, the daily strip in 1951 had 205 newspapers and 26,000,000 readers; subsequently those figures tripled or quadrupled, and over the years Essandess issued about thirty more *Pogo* books. *Pogo* was *the* comic strip of the nation and the many books that were published before Walt died each sold in the hundreds of thousands of copies. Several of them are still going strong, although of course not to that extent. *Pogo*, through the 1950s and 1960s, had the sort of unstinted popularity with fanatics that *Peanuts* enjoys today.

*Pogo* was more than a funny comic strip, and Walt Kelly was much more than a brilliant cartoonist. He was an engaging writer as well, and both in accompanying text and in the words in the balloons that issued from the lips of Pogo Possum—and the other denizens of the Okefenokee swamp, Albert Alligator, Howlan' Owl, Churchy Turtle, and others—Kelly turned out some of the most biting and effective satire against political evil of anyone in the nation. Senator Joseph McCarthy and Richard M. Nixon were particular targets, and readers, while constantly laughing at the humor, were at the same time getting punchy social commentary. Kelly had a powerful effect upon the entire nation but, since we all knew him so well on almost a daily basis, he had a particularly strong one on his worshippers at Simon and Schuster. He was the only author whose advertising copy for his own books was so marvelous that the S & S professionals took the day off.

When Pogo was out on the swamp in his flatboat, Walt would letter a pal's name on the side of the boat, thus immortalizing that person in several hundred newspapers. It is one of my proudest publishing boasts that he did that twice with me in his full-color Sunday strips, and a black-and-white reproduction of one of them appears on the next spread page.

A collateral effect that *Pogo* worked upon millions of Americans ranging from schoolchildren to stockbrokers took place each Christ-

10-4

One of the author's foremost claims to immortality

Walt Kelly, self-portrait

mas in homes all over the country, when the words to the traditional carol, "Deck the Hall with Boughs of Holly," suffered a deep sea change. People instead were singing the lyrics that the *Pogo* ensemble was chanting on those occasions, "Deck Us All with Boston Charlie." They didn't have the slightest idea of what the apparently nonsensical words meant either in that first line or the following ones, like "Nora's freezin' on the trolley," or why strange towns like Kalamazoo, Walla Walla, Pensacola, and Louisville suddenly popped up in a verse, but they didn't care. The parody was fun to sing, forming a sort of brotherhood for *Pogo* fans among the carolers.

Walt Kelly went for years without ever revealing the secret of what inspired his catchy but incomprehensible lyrics. Now, in what is probably the biggest news scoop in this book, I am privileged to unveil it. Wilbur Crane Eveland, who along with Bill Vaughan of the *Kansas City Star* was probably Walt's closest friend, had been saving it for a biography of Kelly that he had planned to write, but since he has now discarded that idea, he has graciously given me the story to use.

At one time Walt held something of a record for making speeches all over what *Pogo* fans know as the U. S. and A. He made no distinctions with respect to his audiences: the staff of the Harvard *Crimson* was no more attractive to him than an assemblage of convicts. It was for those convicts, for many of whom he had sympathy, that Kelly wrote "Deck Us All with Boston Charlie." There is an explanation for every unfathomable reference, but just a few are all that are needed here.

Walla Walla, Kalamazoo, Pensacola, and Louisville are the sites of state prisons. "Boston Charlie" was the name given to all guards in prisons—you can look up "Charlie" in Eric Partridge's *Dictionary of Slang* and you will find that he is the man with the stick, the prison guard. Why "Boston"? A throwback, in all probability, to the days of the original Colonies.

Why is Nora "freezin' on the trolley"? "Nora" is the cognomen given to sexual partners of male prison inmates, and the answer to her/his cold condition comes in two parts. The trolley is the wire that inmates string between cells for use in passing notes to one another. Thus, Nora was not communicating via the trolley. The second aspect of the line is that a person in the "freezer" is in solitary confinement, so Nora was not only not communicating, he/she had been slapped into solitary.

You may wonder why Kelly, a law-abiding citizen, had enough empathy for his convict audiences to write a special, secret Christmas song for them. I suspect it was because that good man felt, along with Pogo, that we are all God's Screechers.

Moving along to the other publication whose charm and fabulous success impelled Simon and Schuster to adopt its character as a sort of trademark, we encounter Kay Thompson and Hilary Knight's *Eloise*. Kay Thompson was a well-known nightclub chanteuse and comedienne, and she conceived the character of Eloise, a little girl who lived at the Plaza Hotel in New York and who knew *everything* about the Plaza, in particular Room Service. Although she is likely to drive everybody crazy from the hotel manager and the bell captain to the English nanny who takes care of her, she is the life of the Plaza, and the hotel could hardly carry on without her. As the flap copy for the book puts it, Henry James would want to study her, Queen Victoria would recognize her as an equal, the New York Jets would want to have her on *their* side, and Lewis Carroll would love her once he got over the initial shock.

A superb book for precocious grownups, in other words, but one which demanded illustrations worthy of its text. Simon and Schuster found the perfect artist to do justice to Kay Thompson's creation, a young man named Hilary Knight, and his delightful drawings contributed as much to Eloise's success as the story itself. It was as blessed a marriage of talents as Gilbert and Sullivan even though, like that celebrated collaboration, sometimes there were blowups of temperament that threatened to put paid to the partnership. It didn't happen, however, and the immense success of *Eloise* gave rise to two subsequent books, *Eloise in Paris* and *Eloise in Moscow*; but the real gem continued to be the original *Eloise* at the Plaza.

Not only did Simon and Schuster use the character in a number of imaginative public relations ways, as they had done on Pogo, but so did the Plaza Hotel. Hilary Knight executed a huge portrait of Eloise, which was framed and hung on a wall of the lobby of the hotel; today, if you walk into that great hotel and circle the tea drinkers in the Palm Court, you can still see it displayed on the wall.★

---

★The reader may be puzzled by the omission of any drawing of Eloise when she was such an important figure in Simon and Schuster's history, but permission to use such a drawing could not be obtained. I regret that the charming logo of Eloise being the Sower, or the striking portrait of her that Hilary Knight painted for the Plaza Hotel, cannot be reproduced here, but you will be able to see the one if you buy a copy of the very much still-in-print book, *Eloise* (which is an excellent suggestion), and the other if you go to tea at the Plaza (which is a good idea too).

Hilary Knight and Kay Thompson at the Plaza Hotel

Perhaps it is not completely appropriate to bring up the name of Alexander King in juxtaposition with those of Walt Kelly and Kay Thompson, for his works were of a very different nature. However, King's book, replete with drama and romance and sentiment and philosophy, were also riots of merriment on virtually every page. Actually, if his four volumes of memoirs had not dealt so thoroughly with his own career, he would rate an entire long biography of his own rather than what can be recorded here, for I esteem Alex King as the most interesting man I ever met.

Until 1958 only a few hundred privileged insiders in the world of books, art, and the theater were the sole beneficiaries of a secret formula for regaining the zest of living when life became flat and stale. The procedure was to corral a man named Alexander King and get him to talk about practically anything—preferably his own fantastic safari through the world of books, art, and theater, as well as the larger world of love and trouble. But with the publication that year of his first book, *Mine Enemy Grows Older*, this unfair monopoly was happily broken. The book was greeted with an instantaneous shower of praise, and the incomparable Alex, with his zest for life despite having to operate on one-half of one kidney, became the property of the nation, the beloved gadfly whose childlike insistence on reality never spared anyone the truth about the emperor's new clothes.

Sid Perelman, one of King's oldest and best friends, was the man who brought Alex and his manuscript to me at Simon and Schuster. A long first meeting, even before the joy that evening of reading his unputdownable manuscript, convinced me that he was the greatest raconteur of our age. He loved to startle, to launch verbal Roman candles and watch his audience draw in its breath, first with shock and then with pleasure. The reading public responded simply and directly. They fell in love with him and, as I've reported earlier, made each of his four volumes of memoirs enormous bestsellers. The critics cheered and the letters from his readers poured in—letters that were not only admiring and adoring but each, in its own idiom, full of the expressiveness and openness that exposure to King invariably evoked.

Even Jack Paar, who presided with controlled calm over his nightly extravaganza of spontaneous interviews, was bowled over by this uninhibited guest. With the exuberance of an *enfant terrible* among loving family, King captivated Paar, who kept inviting Alex back on the program week after week. All over the country people descended upon the bookstores and cleared out every last copy of *Mine Enemy Grows Older*. They found it good, cried out for more, and as book followed book in rapid succession, swooped them up by the hundreds of thousands.

King led a hundred lives. He knew the giants of our times and the midgets (including the twenty-one-inch midget whose photograph he realized could be published *full size* over a spread in *Life* magazine when, as one of the first editors of that publication, he was looking for something unusual to run). He spoke freely—about his marriages, about how a famous author once sat quietly on shore watching him, King, drown, and why. About the time when an advertising agency gave a sumptuous party in honor of nine "prominent artists" responsible for the success of a big campaign—all nine of whom were King, painting in different styles under nine different names and gracefully invented past histories. About his battle with drug addiction, the detectives who pursued him, the "doctors" who supplied him, the hospitals that helped him, the fellow addicts whose tragedies he shared, and his final triumph. Somehow he managed to make any anecdote, no matter how serious or tragic or condemnatory, a gem that on the few occasions when it didn't inspire unrepressed gales of laughter would be deeply moving. He lashed out at what he termed "creative stupidity" wherever he found it.

Alex had three separate professional careers—artist, editor, and writer—and he reached the top ranks in each.

# On Shaky Ground

7

AN ENGLISH WRITER named Ethelreda Lewis was living in South Africa in the early 1920s when she met a drunken and garrulous old soak named Smith who had long tales of trading in ivory and rubber on the west coast of Africa. Miss Lewis was after all a writer, and regardless of how else she may have felt about Smith, his stories intrigued and enchanted her and aroused her muse. She wrote a long manuscript about his adventures, dubbing him "Trader Horn" and sharing the author's by-line with him. Four American publishers were shown the manuscript and turned it down before Clifton Fadiman, then a working editor at Simon and Schuster, read it and told Max Schuster and Dick Simon that they had to take it on. The original oil gusher of crossword puzzle books was running thin by then, and since Fadiman's judgment was already highly respected, the rights to *Trader Horn* were purchased. Dick Simon, even then the master promoter, seeing pictures of the old boy with his long beard trailing to the waist, brought him over to the United States and put him up at his own father's house on West Eighty-ninth Street. There was no television in those days, of course—this was 1927—but there was radio, and there were a slew of newspapers and magazines. Alfred Aloysius Horn, the name that had now supplanted the modest name of Smith, became an instant national celebrity. Many reviews decided that Trader Horn himself was a fraud and the book a hoax, but an unabashed advertising and promotion campaign put the book over with such wild success that a second volume was published with

Trader Horn flanked by Dick Simon and Max Schuster

equal fanfare and equally good results the next year. Despite considerable suspicion about how genuine Trader Horn and his exploits
were, no one ever proved them phony. And the publication of the
books worked no substantial harm to Essandess's reputation, while
doing a lot of good to its profit picture in those early, uncertain years
of the firm's life.

Then, in 1929, lightning struck again when Simon and Schuster
spawned another top bestseller whose authenticity was even more
widely questioned than Trader Horn's. This was Joan Lowell's *Cradle
of the Deep*, a first-person story of her nautical career, involving sev-
enteen years as the only woman on board a four-masted schooner
captained by her father. She described in lurid detail the exotic scenes

Joan Lowell

she had witnessed in the South Seas, and how she swam ashore after the ship caught fire and sank off the coast of Australia, carrying a kitten on each shoulder! She even boasted that she could spit a curve into the wind.

There were doubters from the very first, and a lot of factual evidence was dug up to prove that Miss Lowell and the book were both fraudulent. The author didn't help matters on a publicity tour by declining to exhibit her skill at spitting a curve into the wind. Some booksellers placed copies under the "Fiction" section rather than "Nonfiction," but in any case an amazing number of copies were sold, regardless of the location of the piled-up stacks. At the height of the critical furor, both Essandess and the Book-of-the-Month Club, which had made the title a selection, offered to refund the price of the book to any customers who felt they had been bamboozled, but virtually no one took them up on it. However, the experience of publishing the Joan Lowell book so soon after *Trader Horn* did indeed reflect badly upon Simon and Schuster's reputation as responsible book publishers. Yet I'd venture to say that there isn't a major publisher in the world who hasn't had to face comparable embarrassments from time to time.

Thirty years later, I myself wanted to risk publishing another dubious project on one of my scouting trips to London in the late 1950s, when I came across a manuscript shown me by Frederic Warburg, head of the estimable house of Secker and Warburg. It too was a whopping good yarn, told in the first person by T. Lobsang Rampa, and entitled *The Third Eye*. I can scarcely begin to recount what Rampa's experiences had been as related in the book, but they included expansion of his inner consciousness and vision by means of a technique, taught him by Eastern mystics, wherein a sliver of wood was implanted into the center of his brow, which enabled him to have "the third eye." This in turn set him free, and not only spiritually—it enabled him in actuality to soar over the chasms of the high Himalayas on a huge kite. This was before anyone ever heard of hang-gliding, so Rampa's story, although gripping adventure reading, seemed quite suspect.

Fred Warburg had taken the book on for the British territory, and had salved his editorial conscience to his own satisfaction. He had written a Publisher's Foreword in which he stated frankly that he could not be certain of the veracity of Rampa's tale, that he tended to believe it was true, but regardless of that it was a wonderful and enjoyable story. That seemed to me a sensible way to go about matters. I did not buy American rights from Warburg on the spot, but simply paid him a modest sum for a month's option. I wanted Max Schuster to read the book and share the responsibility if we decided to go ahead.

I didn't have to wait long for an answer. A few days after Max received the manuscript I had airmailed him from London I got a telegram. It read: "We need this book like a hole in the head!"

The story has two aftermaths. The first is that *The Third Eye* was a tremendous success in foreign editions all over the world, as well as for Secker & Warburg in England. It was less so with the original American publisher, Doubleday, which got cold feet and "privished" it rather than publishing it, but later more than one paperback house in this country took it on with considerable success. The second aftermath is that T. Lobsang Rampa turned out to be a Lancashire plumber turned author, who had never been out of England.

So Essandess did avoid publishing another questionable book. I can't recall any other quite comparable circumstance at Essandess except for some suspicions when a mysterious genius named Carlos Castañeda swam into the firm's ken. Castañeda's strange and almost unbelievable adventures and training in the use of peyote that he was taught by "Don Juan" had the surface appearance of a hoax to many, but Castañeda's editor, Michael Korda, one of the few people who has ever seen or talked intimately to the author, vouches very strongly for Castañeda's credibility. In any event, all five of the Carlos Castañeda books have been enormous successes, and a huge cult of devoted readers would testify to the books' influence on their lives.

Down through the years, in areas quite apart from authors' shaky credentials, Essandess has had its own share of treading on shaky ground. A good example is what happened to Dick Simon in 1930 after half a dozen years of publishing with great pride the works of one of his European acquisitions, Arthur Schnitzler. Dick had taken on all of Schnitzler's delightful Viennese novelettes in 1925 and had issued about one a year from then on, starting with *Fräulein Else* and including such classics as *None But the Brave* and *Daybreak*. In 1930, it was *Casanova's Homecoming*'s turn to be published, but that was the year in which the New York Society for the Suppression of Vice was flourishing, and the Supreme Judicial Court of Massachusetts had affirmed the conviction of a bookseller for selling Theodore Dreiser's *American Tragedy*, holding to be "lewd and obscene."★

*Casanova's Homecoming*, like all of Schnitzler's works, could best be described as nostalgic and charming. There were passages that depicted sexual activity, but certainly by today's standards there was no attempt on the author's part "to deprave or corrupt minds." Those were the words in Great Britain's Obscene Publications Act, a bill that had great influence in the United States as well. Dick Simon received a summons to appear in court in connection with his publication of *Casanova's Homecoming*, and for quite some time it appeared that his comparatively innocent little volume would be in hot water. Somehow the summons was quashed, however, and Dick never did have to appear in court. He and his wife, Andrea, had the notice of relief framed and hung it in the guest washroom of their Riverdale home.

Then there was the time in 1962 when Simon and Schuster issued a small humorous novel that had been published successfully in England a while earlier, *The Passion Flower Hotel*. Supposedly written by a teenage girl named Rosalind Erskine, although rumor had it that its actual author was a well-known British satirist writing under a pseudonym, it took the form of a narrative by a high-spirited, somewhat bawdy-minded, but essentially innocent fifteen-year-old girl in an upper-class girls' boarding school who, along with four other fifth-formers, organized a syndicate that offered its services (for a cash consideration) to the young boys at a nearby male boarding school. "The Syndicate Will Meet Your Needs" read its slogan on flyers covertly smuggled to the other school; "Actions Speak Louder than Words." A schedule of offerings and charges was developed, starting with "Vision Only, above Waist Only, 5 Shillings." A saucy

★The fight to assure free speech and a free press went on for more than another quarter of a century after that. It was finally won, largely through the effective pleadings of Charles Rembar before the Supreme Court, as is so rivetingly recounted in his book, *The End of Obscenity*, so that today the issue is settled. Appeal to sexual interest does not create obscenity, was the thrust of his brief for *Lady Chatterley's Lover*, and literary merit was the consideration by which a book must be judged. Rembar won the day on this later occasion and for all time, but back in 1930 the issue was very controversial, and a large segment of the population was very much on the side of the Victorian-minded censors.

# Court of General Sessions of the Peace

COUNTY OF NEW YORK

Clerk's Office, *Nov. 3rd* 192*3*

THE PEOPLE OF THE STATE OF
NEW YORK

against

*Richard L. Simon*

ON COMPLAINT FOR *publishing an obscene book*

Dated, *October 23* . 192*3*

I DO CERTIFY that it appears from an examination of the Record
of Complaints on file in this office that the above complaint was
dismissed by the Grand Jury, at the *October* term, 192*3*
~~and~~ the said *Richard L. Simon* .

~~and his surety~~

~~were severally discharged from their Undertaking to Answer.~~

*Edward R Carroll*
Clerk of Court.

The exhibit in the Simon guest washroom

little book, yes, but it would take a stretch of sensibilities to term it a pornographic one; no sexual consummations ever took place. When the novel was published it was reviewed admiringly as a delightful comic novel both in England and in the United States. For example, in Jessica Mitford's *New York Times* review she wrote: "Miss Erskine is a true original, her style unconnected with any contemporaneous school of humorous or satirical writing. If anything her unique talent seems to derive (albeit in a flying leap) from E. Nesbit, beloved English children's writer of the nineteenth century."

In the month or two after American publication, Simon and Schuster ran several very funny lighthearted advertisements for the book, with headlines like "Au Revoir *Bonjour Tristesse*—Make Room for the Funniest Book Ever Written about Sex," and the book was selling well. However by then the firm's primary interest had turned to the necessary preparatory work for books that were to be published in the following season, a major feature of which was the semiannual sales conference. That year it was being held in a large private room of a prestigious New York hotel. Sales conferences bring in all the travelers who sell a company's books throughout the country to listen to the presentations of the books on the forthcoming list, as delivered from a dais by the major editors.

I happened to be the editor making the usual impassioned presentation of what I confidently, but probably incorrectly, claimed would be the next season's top smash hit when a tall man, dressed in flowing clerical raiments with a wide-brimmed black hat surmounting his dead-white face, burst into the room and stalked up to the dais. He carried a large prayerbook or Bible in his hand and I, guessing that this visitation was in response to an advertisement which S & S had run for *The Passion Flower Hotel* the week before, broke off my speech. That ad had reproduced the "List of Charges" from the book's jacket, and this, some of us knew, had been abhorrent to the Reverend Morton A. Hill, a zealous prosecutor against pornographers. He was now in our midst, for this certainly must be the one who had both written to Max Schuster about it and tried telephoning him several times. Failing to reach Max, he had been transferred to me, and had promised me that Simon and Schuster "would burn in Hell."

Most of the group in the room were taken by complete surprise and watched in stunned alarm, frozen in their seats, as the minister thundered in a harsh voice that shook with rage, "Which of you is Mr. Schuster?" Max, seated at the center of the presenters' table, identified himself and the minister addressed him.

"I have demanded from you a letter and an advertisement retracting—and apologizing for—the one you ran. I have received nothing from you. I am here to tell you that if I do not have on my desk this afternoon by two o'clock a letter from you and a copy of a retracting advertisement, I will do the following four things."

He raised his hand dramatically in the air and his voice rose another decibel or two.

"One. I will this evening address a gathering of parents of teen-age children that will start a national movement against your company.

"Two. There is in preparation an article in a national magazine that will tell what you are doing to the morals of this country and denounce you.

"Three. The mothers of teen-age daughters will march on your company and tell you what they think of you.

"Four. I will wipe the dust from my shoes on your face."

Then he merely spun on his heels and departed from the room in a furious manner worthy of Tomás de Torquemada.

Well, Doomsday never did arrive either at two o'clock that afternoon or later, and we heard no more about the matter. In fact, two years later Simon and Schuster published a sequel, *Passion Flowers in Italy*. It may have offered some consolation to the Reverend Hill that it suffered the same unfortunate commercial fate that most sequels do.

In the portion of the previous chapter given over to the Barney Greengrass prank, you will recall that it was Dick Simon's leaving the manuscript in his photography store that set off the tragic final act. That, like the rest of the Greengrass satire, was fiction solidly inspired by fact. With all his talents Dick, like his idol Albert Einstein, was constantly mislaying everything from his appointment calendar to his tennis racquet. His outstanding performance came one day when he received a manuscript, read it, and was not particularly impressed, but before he got around to returning it with a rejection letter he discovered that he had lost it. Today it is an accepted rule of the game that publishers take no responsibility if such a disaster occurs, and the stationery of many firms actually states that right at the bottom of the page; the assumption is that any professional author makes sure to have another copy tucked away safely. However, in those earlier days Dick Simon, burdened with an excess of the Judeo-Christian ethic in which he had been brought up, saw no honorable recourse except, after apologizing to the author profusely, to promise her he would publish her book if she would sit down and write it all over again! She did so, and he did so. It would be nice to report that it became a sensation but it would not be the truth. However, Dick's honor was preserved.

A footnote to this story is that four years later Dick's wife, Andrea, doing a rare bit of housecleaning in the vestibule of the Simon country house, found the original manuscript at the bottom of the umbrella stand.

Probably the most publicized embarrassment that S & S ever suffered occurred in the early 1960s as the aftermath to one of the most successful books the firm ever published. That was a diet book brought in to the house by a vice-president, Dick Grossman. It did not follow traditional medical thinking, which held that the only relationship that meant anything in one's effort to lose weight was to ingest fewer calories than you expended. A decade earlier Essandess had published the diet book which decreed exactly that and which the entire medical fraternity applauded so solidly that it is still regarded as being more or less the bible in the field, Dr. Norman Jolliffe's *Reduce and Stay Reduced on the Prudent Diet*. So the firm knew how successful a diet book could be. But Simon and Schuster, having what was recognized as the classic, had not taken on any further books of that nature.

The manuscript that came to Grossman, written by Dr. Herman Taller, embodied a concept that seemed to be completely new and absolutely irresistible—if it worked! Using it, an obese person could eat himself or herself silly so long as he or she stuck completely to certain hearty protein and fat foods—steak, fish, butter, cheese, and such—and sedulously avoided most carbohydrate foods that a real trencherman wouldn't find too hard to resist in any case—fruits, vegetables, and the like. The concept was more involved than that simple summary, but it was clear that on Taller's diet no one would ever be hungry. A person might be glutted with heavy food or bored by its monotony, but hunger pangs couldn't possibly pose any problem. An additional aspect to the diet was that it should be accompanied by a couple of tablespoons of safflower oil a day, that being a method of holding down the cholesterol level that such a diet would be likely to produce.

Dr. Taller had many testimonials to offer from happy weight-losers, and a few overweight people in the S & S office and their friends had a stab at trying out the diet and found that it worked. The manuscript was accepted despite the fact that it was poorly written. So, as is often done in such cases, the firm turned it over to an experienced and very good nonfiction writer to put into shape. He not only did so but came up with an inspired title, *Calories Don't Count*.

The book was published in late 1961, accompanied by extremely lavish advertising and promotion efforts and, before it came to its sad end, more than a million copies were sold in hardback. It is claimed that it was the fastest and most popular bestseller over a brief period in publishing history—300,000 copies were sold in the first three months. Then the eggs (and incidentally you could eat as many eggs as you desired on Taller's diet) hit the fan. George Larrick, commissioner of the federal Food and Drug Administration, not only asserted that the diet was no good and even harmful, but also charged that one of the main purposes of the book's publication was to promote the sale of CDC capsules. Others in the medical world and crusading journalists picked up the accusation and made a considerable issue of it and of S & S's morality standards.

CDC capsules? What were they? Practically no one at Simon and Schuster had the faintest idea, even when told they were Calories Don't Count capsules, but gradually the story emerged. It appeared that in the midst of the intense prepublication excitement over the book, at the stage when it was in galleys, Dr. Taller himself made arrangements with a pharmaceutical company to produce capsules containing safflower oil and call the product CDC. Having done so, he telephoned Dick Grossman's secretary and instructed her to insert a sentence or two into the galleys near the end of his opus to the effect that if taking two tablespoons of safflower oil daily was dis-

tasteful or burdensome, capsules were available from Cove Phar-
maceuticals, New York. To the secretary's innocent mind that
seemed a routine request and she duly carried it out, so that when the
actual books were printed the notation appeared in them.

No one at S & S, including Grossman, was at all aware of this
last-minute insertion by Taller until Commissioner Larrick came out
swinging, which was some time after publication and when the book
was at the crest of its success. Apart from the widespread airing given
to this attack upon the bestselling book in the country, the FDA
ordained that many department stores that carried both the book and
the pills—and displayed them together with a large notice that
screamed, "We've got the book, we've got the capsules!"—had to
cease and desist. The legal explanation was that this was "false label-
ing" and that, regardless of the merits or demerits of either the book
or the capsules, the one had to be carried in the book department and
the other in the drug section, and there must be no overt connection.
Despite all this unfavorable publicity, the demand for the book continued to be very strong, since, although Larrick and others criticized
the thesis of the book severely, it really wasn't under fire. The capsules were.

I have indicated that no one at S & S knew about the insertion in
the book referring to capsules, but there were two people in the firm
who knew about Dr. Taller's arrangement to have capsules produced.
As the two directly concerned with the marketing of the book, Dick
Grossman and another S & S sales executive whom Taller knew were
offered personal shares in the Cove CDC Corporation, and both had
purchased a few. When Grossman came to the realization that in
doing so he had at the very least acted imprudently, he immediately
terminated his interest and launched an inquiry into Dr. Taller, which
included making him slice CDC capsules in half and pour out the
contents of each one until the equivalent of two tablespoons of oil
were reached. It turned out that it took some eighty capsules to
produce this result, so no matter what might have been right or
wrong, in recommending that a couple of capsules could be taken in
place of the two tablespoons, Dr. Taller had certainly allowed opportunistic values to override medical ethics.

Although Essandess obviously had come to consider Dr. Taller an
albatross around its neck, everyone continued to feel that the book

itself (minus the capsule reference, of course) was a valid and effective treatise about losing weight, and in response to the criticisms, both Max Schuster and I, then the publisher, wrote strong rebuttals that were published prominently. The case we tried to make for the book rested chiefly upon two facts. The first was that our mailroom was flooded each day with hundreds, mounting to thousands, of letters from people who had never lost weight before with conventional diets, but now had succeeded under the Taller regime. They almost universally blessed both the author and the publisher. Very few letters had been received as a result of the "money-back" guarantee offered in case the buyer of the book found the diet ineffective, and virtually no letters at all claiming that the diet had physical ill-effects. This impressive audience of public backing and acceptance gave Max and me ammunition, but as invariably is the case when people under attack write rebuttals, the effect carries no such weight as the original condemnation. So there is no blinking the fact that the publication of *Calories Don't Count*, even though it made 1961 and 1962 banner years in sales figures, gave Simon and Schuster a black eye in publishing.

Suits and countersuits were brought by and against all parties and in the end Simon and Schuster was adjudged guiltless by the court, while Dr. Taller and the owners of the Cove Corporation were indicted and convicted. What is more, a number of diet books embodying the basic concept of the Taller book—high protein and fat and virtually no carbohydrates—were published in subsequent years very successfully by other firms, with no repercussions—books like *The Air Force Diet* and *The Drinking Man's Diet*. Today the pendulum of weight-loss theory has swung just the other way, and carbohydrates are in, while proteins and fats are more or less taboo, but diet books go in cycles and what is apparently new and convincing rides a crest for some years.

Another hugely successful book, which after a skyrocketing climb on all bestseller lists died out with a whimper instead of a bang, did so simply as a result of bad luck. Two extremely bright young journalists, Jack Shepherd and Christopher S. Wren, in the middle of the Vietnam War came up with a viciously satirical parody of the book that had become the bible of the Peoples' Republic of China, *Quotations of Chairman Mao*, that small red-covered paperbound volume that countless millions of Chinese carried religiously in their pockets every day. Shepherd and Wren's book was entitled "Quotations from LBJ" and divided into "inspirational" chapters. It consisted of direct short passages taken from the speeches, musings, and digressions of the then President of the United States, Lyndon Baines Johnson. Presented with a completely straight face, their substance added up to being a vitriolic condemnation of this country's part in the Vietnam War.

It's probable that I had more to do with the packaging of that book than any other on which I was the editor. First I had Helen Barrow design an unusual very small format, as close to the dimensions of the Mao book as possible, a bright red paperbound book that measured a tiny 3½ inches by 5 inches. I added a word to Shepherd and Wren's title so that it became *Quotations from Chairman LBJ* and engaged an artist to play with the portrait of a benevolently smiling Johnson that was used on the front cover so that his Western business suit, shirt, and tie were brushed out and a Mao jacket painted in.

Simon and Schuster then published the little volume and there was no way that the presses could operate fast enough to keep up with the demand. The book got vast favorable coverage from virtually every newspaper and magazine in the nation, for by 1968, most people had become very disillusioned about the Vietnam War. Print orders as large as 50,000 copies at a shot kept rolling off the presses and all copies were snapped up; for some weeks it looked as if this book might well smash all previous sales records. And then, with some 100,000 new copies in the warehouse ready to be shipped, and no qualms about our ability to sell them, something happened. Completely unexpectedly, President Johnson announced that in November he was not going to be a candidate for reelection! The sales of *Quotations from Chairman LBJ* came to an instant and complete stop, for people obviously felt it was now whipping a dead horse, and Simon and Schuster had to eat those last 100,000 copies. They couldn't even command a few pennies each in the remainder market.

Sometimes a publisher's problems are attributable to certain authors who, irrespective of how well they write, are unable to stop writing at some point and as a result turn out manuscripts so lengthy that they can't possibly be published for any sort of retail price per volume that can work. The earliest case of this sort on record at Essandess came in 1929 when Max Schuster fell in love with novelist

John Cowper Powys's work and, as a result, gave him a contract for one of the very first books the house ever acquired in England. When that book, *Wolf Solent*, finally arrived here in manuscript form in the hold of an ocean liner, it was found to be tightly packed into a huge and completely filled trunk. Had an attempt been made to print and publish the novel in its original form, it would have had to be issued in ten volumes. Never a man to be discouraged, Schuster set about cutting the manuscript himself. Finally he acknowledged that his brilliant young editor, Kip Fadiman, could probably do it better and much faster. Approximately 80 percent of the book was eventually hacked away and the balance issued in two volumes. There is no entry in *The Guinness Book of Records* for the most massive job of cutting a book, but surely *Wolf Solent* would have a good claim.

Another possible entry for record recognition might have been James R. Newman's extraordinary anthology, *The World of Mathematics*. Newman, a remarkable man who was writer, scientist, and lawyer, had previously collaborated in 1940 with a Columbia University professor of mathematics, Edward Kasner, to write a delightful and very successful book entitled *Mathematics and the Imagination*. Those were the days when anthologies were popular, so, in 1941, it seemed to Jack Goodman a good idea for Newman, with his impeccable taste in these matters, to collect some intriguing mathematical writings, by men from Bertrand Russell and Alfred North Whitehead to Sir James Jeans and Oswald Spengler, and to work up a nice volume to be called *The World of Mathematics*. It wasn't thought of as any big deal, and the contract called for an advance of $1,000 with a delivery date set for a year from then. But with that sort of small money and no one really following up on Newman or the project, the whole thing lay dormant as the years went by. Then, one day fourteen years later, a huge package arrived at S & S containing the incredibly expanded project that Jim Newman had quietly been working at, off and on, all that time! All of it, including Newman's long and consistently intriguing prefaces to each piece, was so wonderful that S & S decided to go all the way and publish the entire work in four clothbound volumes, boxed. It seemed to many a ludicrously impractical project but a positive influence that led to not trying to whittle Newman's book down to size was the delight readers in the office, even those not particularly mathematics-minded, had in reading the pieces Jim had unearthed. There were "The Ability of Birds to Count," by O. Koehler; J. B. S. Haldane's classic essay on "The Importance of Being the Right Size"; "Probability and the Laws of Chance," by John Maynard Keynes; "Can a Machine Think?" by A. M. Turing; Russell Maloney's riotously funny *New Yorker* story, "Inflexible Logic," about how six chimpanzees set to work pounding six typewriters at random would in a million years turn out all the books in the British Museum; "What the Tortoise Said to Achilles and Other Riddles," by Lewis Carroll; and "Mathematics for Golfers," by Stephen Leacock. Every page, both the profound and the lighthearted, turned out to be so irresistible that Essandess bit the

James R. Newman (and, as a bonus, a photo of another S & S author, Albert Einstein, in the background) (*Copyright by Philippe Halsman*)

bullet, published the four-volume boxed set in the fall of 1956 at the then very fancy price of $25.00, and held its collective breath. *The World of Mathematics* became the publishing sensation of that and the following year, selling almost 125,000 hardbound sets before being issued in paperback, being used by three major book clubs, and having foreign rights sold to ten nations. An element that bolstered its continuing big sales in 1957 was the successful launching of Sputnik and the space rivalry with Russia, which involved great mathematical interest and inspired a surge in science and math in schools and colleges.

It is likely that the people known as the production department who oversee the manufacturing of the physical book encounter more problems than anyone else in a publishing office. It goes without saying that everyone encounters problems with top management, so that needn't be considered, and top management has tremendous major problems such as cash flow and meeting the payroll and staff problems as well, but management is in a position to take care of much of its grief by virtue of simple fiat. Editors have problems with authors and agents. The sales department has problems with bookstores, particularly those that are bad credit risks. Publicity has problems with reviewers, newspapers and magazines, television and radio stations, and authors, but their problems are pretty much of one nature, courting cooperation. Subsidiary-rights people have a major but essentially direct problem, to sell a lot of rights for maximum money. But everybody listed above is likely to have problems which involve throwing some of them on the production department's shoulders.

When I joined Simon and Schuster's ranks in late 1945, at the close of my army service in World War II, the production manager was my close friend, Tom Bevans, who had inherited the job from Philip Van Doren Stern. Phil had been such a legend in the field that he had been drafted by the government to head up the production of all the Armed Services editions, books of all publishers put out in a horizontal paperback form that made it easy to slip into the pocket of a uniform. The Armed Services books were a godsend for people overseas during the war, like myself, and they had to be produced in the millions of copies. Stern therefore had plenty to do without worrying any longer about Essandess books, so Bevans took his place, solidly aided by two assistants, the Barrow sisters, Helen and Roz. Some years later, when Tom retired, Helen became the production manager and ran the department with utmost competence: after her retirement she set up her own freelance production service and is busier than ever. Roz eventually was offered a bigger job at Harper and Row than the one she held at S & S and moved to that firm.

This trio ran the production department right through World War II, for although Tom was a sergeant in the air force, working on that service's publication, he was based in New York City and had sufficient free time to keep his hand on Simon and Schuster matters, even if Helen took the brunt of the day-to-day burdens. And World War II, with its shortages in everything from manpower to paper, and its government restrictions, made life in production particularly arduous. A unique example occurred when the house obtained official governmental permission and cooperation in the publishing of General George C. Marshall's *The Winning of the War in Europe and the Pacific* at the close of hostilities in 1945.

There were good things and bad things about securing this obvious bonanza of a publishing property. Clearly it was going to be a bestseller, dealing triumphantly with the subject uppermost in everybody's mind and heart and written by the military man most revered by the cognoscenti. Also, since it had been prepared for the government, it, like other official publications, would be in the public domain and no royalties need be paid. (As a matter of fact Simon and Schuster did pay a royalty on every copy sold, but it was a voluntary donation to the Army Emergency Relief Fund and a comparatively small royalty.) Finally, it would be a patriotic piece of publishing that any house would feel privileged to undertake. Those were the good things.

The bad things devolved specifically upon the production department. Despite the fact that this book had the blessing of the United States government, continuing wartime restrictions on paper meant that every trick, every favor that could be wangled legitimately with suppliers had to be exercised. The detailed maps in full color that comprised an essential part of the book demanded not only outsize dimensions of the page but also a paper quality that could take the color reproductions faithfully. There was only one printing concern at the time that had the seven-color presses required, the Jersey City

Printing Company, which not only had much of its time occupied by a regular contract to print *Fortune* magazine, but had been drafted on a twenty-four-hour-a-day assignment by the military to print the war maps used in combat. The company was muscled into squeezing in General Marshall's book both by governmental plea and by Richard Simon, but its early performance on a book where time was of the essence failed to satisfy Dick. He called the president of the printing company and demanded forcibly that he come to town and discuss matters.

When the president appeared and explained the realistic facts of life to Dick in even more forceful manner than Dick had used, Simon cooled off. However those who were present say that while his rebuttal to Simon's complaints was valid and undoubtedly had some effect, the major reason for Dick's swallowing his rancor was that, for the first time in his business career, he could no longer look down on someone to whom he was talking. Simon was 6 foot 4 inches tall, but the Jersey City president towered over him by a good four or five inches. Dick retired from the scene. Helen Barrow poured oil on troubled waters and saw the project through successfully and in time to satisfy the crash scheduling that Dick wanted.

Sometimes authors have valid complaints about the way the people in production or copy-editing, an area so closely tied to production that it can be included in this connection, have handled their books. Often the complaints are less valid, but in any case it is the obligation and the burden of publishers to cater to an author's wishes within reason—even past reason.

When Eric Hodgins wrote his delightful novel *Mr. Blandings Builds His Dream House*, he delivered a beautifully typed, perfect manuscript that needed almost no copy-editing. But Hodgins was fond of the serial comma, which separates parts of a series and precedes the conjunction in a sentence, and was accustomed to use it in his regular work at *Time* and *Fortune*. Unfortunately in those days at Simon and Schuster the house style was *not* to use the serial comma: it's quite acceptable to use it or not and Essandess didn't. So a conscientious copy-editor faithfully removed every one before sending the manuscript on to production to have type set, and complete proofs were printed that way. When Hodgins saw them, that essentially courtly and gentle man hit the roof. The serial commas had to be restored, damn it all, and since the problem came up on virtually every page that meant in effect that the entire book had to be reset. Adding to the horror and expense of it all was the fact that *Mr. Blandings* had been chosen by the Book-of-the-Month Club and announced in its mailings as that month's choice, so there simply could not be any delay there. When a catastrophe of such nature looms there's no one who can achieve the impossible except the people in the production department. Somehow they usually do.

A somewhat similar story concerns the second volume of memoirs by Alexander King. After Alex had astounded the literary world, the television world, Simon and Schuster, me, and possibly himself by the fantastic Number One bestseller results obtained by his first book, *Mine Enemy Grows Older*, his follow-up book, *May This House Be Safe from Tigers*, often employed in print a technique that he had proven effective on television. Using punctuation marks in a cockeyed and startling way that no English teacher or copy-editor could countenance, he gave the page something of the same startling and emphatic punch that he brought to his television delivery. This meant a lot of italicized words and occasionally a series of exclamation points, sometimes mixed; on one page I've turned to at random the line reads: "*Four dollars*?!?!?! Who in heaven's name wants four dollars worth of wool?" Of course the plodding copy-editor of that era removed what he or she considered the author's unjustified and nonsensical hyperbole and left only the simple question mark at the end. Alex, not as gentle a man as Eric Hodgins, didn't hit the roof—he went right through it. Luckily this sort of thing occurred only now and then in the manuscript and only a few pages had to be reset rather than the entire book.

These stories might make it appear that I am contemptuous of the conscientious, play-it-by-the-book stance of copy-editors. Not on your life! They rescue the often sloppy performances of both authors and editors a hundred times for every once when going by the style rules conflicts with a personal predilection. In my judgment Sophie Sorkin, these many years the S & S copy chief, comes close to topping my list to get the Most Valued Employee Award, if there were such a thing.

Henry Morton Robinson was an experienced author and magazine editor when he wrote his tremendously successful novel of 1950,

*The Cardinal*. So it seems almost inconceivable to learn what he did when S & S sent him the galleys of that very long book for his review and corrections. At that stage Rondo, as he was called, decided to change the entire sequence in which scenes had been written. That was his right so long as he paid for excessive author's alterations, as is called for in all contracts. So Rondo, using a pair of scissors with abandon, cut up all the long galley sheets as he saw fit and then, having arranged everything in the new order he now wanted, pasted the bits and pieces together. What he neglected to do was to indicate on each bit or piece the number of the galley from which he had snipped it! That meant that Helen Barrow had two choices when this monumental mishmash was returned to her. One was to put an army of drones to work searching out which sections came from where, so that at least most of the type could be switched and reused; the other was to have the entire book set again in Rondo's new order. Whichever decision was made, a very hefty unnecessary expenditure had to be incurred, and whether Robinson got billed for it—which he should have—or it was decided he was too important an author to dun is one of those questions that history hasn't recorded.

Another person who used a cutting implement on galleys in a manner to drive both the editor of the book, Joseph Barnes, and the production department crazy was the widow of Harold L. Ickes, the Secretary of the Interior under Franklin D. Roosevelt. Two volumes of the very outspoken and often cantankerous author's memoirs, *The Secret Diary of Harold L. Ickes*, had been published successfully, and the manuscript for the third and final volume was complete when Ickes died. That was sad, but at least the book was done and ready to go, and it was just as strong, informative, and gossipy as the first two, so Joe did his editing and passed it along to production to be set. When galleys came back, in lieu of sending them to the author for approval and any corrections, he was obliged to send them to Mrs. Ickes, who had been appointed literary executor. He thought it was no more than a courtesy, not dreaming that the widow would want to tamper with what her famous husband wrote or, since she knew Barnes as the impressive editor he was, with his editing.

However this third volume obviously covered the more recent events and personages in Ickes's career, and that blunt author had no more pulled his punches in discussing people than he had in the previous books. The problem for Mrs. Ickes was that many of the people in this final volume were still around in Washington, and so was she. They met socially, even dined together, and having this book come out the way it was written was likely to be extremely embarrassing for her. So she sat down with a razor-blade cutting tool and carefully excised every word or phrase or paragraph in the galleys that threatened to make her uncomfortable in Washington society. When the galleys came back to Tom Bevans and Helen Barrow, every sheet was shot full of small, medium, and large rectangular holes! Some sheets were so crammed with holes that the effect was positively lacy. Short of going to court on the matter, almost never a good idea and in this case a distasteful one, S & S had no alternative but to have Joe Barnes negotiate what compromises he could and then reset new galleys and publish the book.

Joseph Heller's *Catch-22* featured an entire cast of military figures, and Heller's technique, clearly calculated to produce part of the zany

Joseph Heller

effect that gorgeous novel evoked, was almost invariably to use both an officer's full rank and his name over and over again, such as Major Major, Colonel Cathcart, and General Dreedle, even when using one or the other would have been the more usual practice. However now and then, in spots where he didn't want that effect, he did indeed simply use the man's rank in referring to him. The S & S house style called for a military rank to be capitalized, so in those cases "the Major" or "the Captain" or "the General" were set that way. Not for long. Joe insisted, and he didn't want any rebuttals, that whenever he had written about a character using only his rank without his name, the word must be set lower case, viz., "the major," "the captain," "the general." Joe got his way, but once again the production department had suffered an unexpected sneak punch.

All of this sounds as if production's problems always arise out of authors' peccadilloes or paranoias, but publishers can perpetrate their own stumbles as well that cause panic in the streets. Two extremely simple ones that I recall each had to do with only one letter. In the first case, William Holly Whyte's distinguished sociological work, *The Organization Man*, came out with the author's name spelled "White," an understandable but ghastly goof not spotted by a number of people in the house who had a good chance to do so. In the second, even though Essandess had been publishing a book a year by P. G. Wodehouse for some fifteen years at the time, his 1964 novel, *Biffen's Millions*, bore a large "P. J. Wodehouse" on its spine in the first few copies that came up from the bindery and were shipped to the stores. The error was spotted and corrected before the rest of the first printing was bound, but those faulty copies exist somewhere. Let us hope that some good came of it, and that purchasers of those copies are the owners of a rarity that may have extra value, like a postage stamp that bears a considerable premium because it was printed incorrectly.

The shortages of materials during World War II posed a number of problems for Helen Barrow. Perhaps the most involved one had to do with the production of a beloved children's classic, *Pat the Bunny*,

The young models are Mary Seligman, Elizabeth Simon's daughter, and Joanna Simon, Dick Simon's daughter. Great friends at the time *Pat the Bunny* was published, they still were twenty years later (see next page).

# PORTRAIT OF A COUPLE OF BOOK REVIEWERS

THEY never heard of the word "significant". They're a couple of hedonists interested in just one thing: having fun. That's what's causing all the excitement over their new book.

It's called Pat the Bunny. It's a simple story, but that's not what's responsible for the *oohs*, the *ahs*, and the giggles. Pat the Bunny is a book you can press and it will squeak. You can put your finger through a page and have a ring on your finger. You can look at another page (the page with the mirror) and see your own funny face. You can run your finger over the picture of daddy and really feel his beard. To these book reviewers, Pat the Bunny *does* "live and breathe"! (And it also squeaks!!)

Mary and Joanna still at it

by Dorothy Kunhardt. That book has delighted generations of children for four decades and it sold like the proverbial hotcakes from the second it was issued, but at that time, obtaining the quantities of the elements that had to go into it was often virtually impossible and Helen had to improvise with reasonable facsimiles. She had to get something small and flat that squeaked, a metal ring, a steel mirror, a piece of sandpaper, and so forth for each of the avalanche of books that was being ordered. (For a quick explanation of why these items were required, see the copy in the advertisement for the book which is on the preceding page). Somehow she managed to collar what was needed effectively enough that, while the book had to be "out of stock" for short periods of time, it never had to be "out of print."

Helen Barrow came to the firm as a very young girl in 1938 and retired in 1973, but never did anyone retire so actively. As a freelance expert in production, she is so in demand that each new potential customer is likely to have to wait in line for weeks. She was always the vital woman she continues to be, and on one occasion, many years before the nation began to wake up to the inequities that women suffered in business, she left an indelible mark on the publishing industry. Back then a most important printer and binder of books was the H. Wolff Company, and each year it hosted the biggest and most lavish Christmas party in the publishing business. It was held at Gallagher's steak house and the only thing that surpassed the sumptuousness of the food was the imposing array of booze. Ob-

Helen Barrow

viously all of Wolff's customers, from the various production department bosses of firms plus their assistants, the heads of houses, down to minor executives and even friends, were invited. There must have been a couple of hundred guests, and they shared one common characteristic. They were all male.

Now Helen happened to be the only woman in the business at that time who headed up a production department, and Simon and Schuster was one of Wolff's top customers. On her own recognizance, Helen authorized millions of dollars of Essandess money to be spent with Wolff, but she was never asked to the Christmas party, despite dropping some not very subtle hints over the years. Finally she took the bit in her teeth one December and had a giant sandwich-board lettered "H. Wolff Is Unfair to Helen Barrow," flung it over her shoulders, and picketed Gallagher's at noontime on that memorable day. Long before we ever heard of Betty Friedan or Kate Millett, Helen Barrow carried the banner for women. She was promptly asked in to join the crowd, was the belle of the ball, and from that time the Gallagher affairs were reborn as mixed doubles.

An interesting legal opinion about a publisher's sensible steps to avoid shaky ground was put forth along about that same time by Joseph Iseman, a partner at Paul, Weiss, Wharton, Rifkind, and Garrison. That law firm represented the Marshall Field Enterprises, then the owners of Simon and Schuster, so Joe was an active advisor and consultant. It was his practice to warn editors not to include an index in nonfiction books they were sponsoring if they could possibly avoid doing so. Admittedly a scholarly or even semiacademic volume demanded one, not only for its necessary reference value but also because the absence of an index would probably be the chief point that reviewers would home in upon when blasting the book.

However, Joe maintained that the almost invariable practice of preparing an index for any nonfiction book was a dangerous one when characters in it were still alive. An index can act like a red cape acts on a bull. Anybody who thinks he is likely to be in a book, but doesn't intend actually to read it, is likely to scan the index to see if there are any references to him. If the author has written something false, or damaging, or even annoying, the end result can be anything from the destruction of a beautiful friendship to a lawsuit. Indexes present more perils than rewards.

Nevertheless, Joe, with due respect and appreciation for what may have been good free legal advice, I think I must disregard your counsel now. For one thing I grew up at Simon and Schuster under Dick Simon, who as you will recall coined a motto for his firm: "Give the Reader a Break." A major item in that injunction was to see to it that a book that would benefit readers by having an index got one. Furthermore, there are no villains in this book. So it does contain an index. Besides, if worst comes to worst, my older son is a lawyer and my younger one soon will be.

# The Tails That Wagged

# the Dog                                          8

ALMOST on the eve of the new decade of the 1940s a man named Robert Fair de Graff, an experienced hardcover reprint publisher, thought that the time had come when mass-production and mass-distribution methods might make the publishing of inexpensive paperbound reprint books work in the United States, even though that had been tried unsuccessfully in the past. De Graff had observed how well the new Penguin Books firm in England had been making out and felt that if he could find enthusiastic and talented and monied partners, the same sort of success could be put across in this country. Despite the fact that most people were dubious about the project and advised against it, Dick Simon and Max Schuster and Leon Shimkin agreed to put up 49 percent of the capital that de Graff said he needed, and they came through with $30,000. De Graff himself went for the balance, and Pocket Books' first small office was installed in the tiny Inner Sanctum chamber in the Essandess office.

The four partners announced that they would be printing ten titles, reprints of bestsellers and of classics, on their first list and would be charging 25¢ per copy for each paperbound book under the imprint of "Pocket Books," a name de Graff coined. Their own doubts about how well the project would fare was reflected in the temperate phrase used at the head of the first advertisement, which with unaccustomed modesty for Essandess merely stated that this new line "*may* revolutionize book publishing in America," even though the ad didn't italicize the word "may."

At the outset Bob de Graff bought reprint rights from the hard-cover publishers for a $500 advance, to be applied against a royalty of 4 percent of the 25¢ cover price on copies sold, or a penny a copy, which meant that 50,000 copies of a title had to be sold before the advance would be earned out, before the publisher and author, who split any income, could earn more. Since it was Shimkin's original idea that first printings of 10,000 copies were risky enough, it seemed that $500 was probably all that a reprint lease was likely to toss off. But most publishers and authors were very willing to accept the sum as unexpected "found money"; since Pocket Books would probably die aborning, it wouldn't hurt anything else. The first ten titles selected were: *Lost Horizon*, by James Hilton; *Wake Up and Live*, by Dorothea Brande; *Five Great Tragedies*, by William Shakespeare; *Topper*, by Thorne Smith; *The Murder of Roger Ackroyd*, by Agatha Christie; *Enough Rope*, by Dorothy Parker; *Wuthering Heights*, by Emily Brontë; *The Way of All Flesh*, by Samuel Butler; *The Bridge of San Luis Rey*, by Thornton Wilder; and *Bambi*, by Felix Salten. *The Good Earth*, by Pearl S. Buck, was added as a trial balloon.

Test copies of Pearl S. Buck's *The Good Earth* were printed and displayed to the stores, and a direct-mail campaign, largely directed to the New York City area, solicited questions from respondents about their buying habits with respect to books, their price, and what sort of titles they'd like to see if Pocket Books priced them at 25¢ a copy. A colophon featuring a kangaroo was devised by one of the cover artists and dubbed "Gertrude"; Gertrude still exists, even though, like the Essandess Sower, she has undergone several changes over the years. An advertising space salesman for the *New York Herald Tribune* named Wallis E. Howe, Jr., was engaged to try to sell the new line to book accounts in New York. He managed to place a number of books with Macy's and the Liggett Drug chain, but not enough to make Leon Shimkin feel that more than 10,000 copies of each of the first ten titles should be printed initially.

When the first day of publication rolled around, the scene became as frenzied as back in the crossword puzzle era. Pocket Books only had one telephone, but reorders from stores that had cautiously stocked the list, and orders from those who had only just heard about it, so jammed the line that it was clear that another publishing phenomenon was taking place. In his travels Howe, whom everybody

Robert de Graff, Leon Shimkin, Pete Howe, and James Jacobson, surrounding "Gertrude"

called Pete, happened to drop into a bar in Denver and struck up a conversation with the man on the next stool. He turned out to be Joe Morton, manager of the Rocky Mountain News Company—and Morton, an important wholesaler, fell in love with the entire idea and the titles in the line itself. He had such success with it in Denver that very soon Pocket Books had more than 600 independent wholesalers across the country distributing its books through 100,000 newsstands, bookstores, stationery stores, food stores, terminals, and other outlets. Leon Shimkin authorized full steam ahead.

The nation and the whole world wanted Pocket Books, and despite the fact that these were the war years and paper rationing was imposed after Pearl Harbor, Shimkin was successful in making arrangements to take over the quotas of other publishers who were not fully utilizing theirs. The various wartime agencies alone shipped 25 million Pocket Books overseas, and the sales in the United States to civilians mounted to numbers never before approached. The biggest bestseller of all, *Dr. Benjamin Spock's Baby and Child Care*, is certainly among the top half-dozen sellers of all time, and there are some statistical historians who maintain it is second only to the Bible. Whether that is true or not, in all editions worldwide it has sold nearly 30 million copies, and a great number of other Pocket Books have been in the healthy millions.

There is no doubt that Pocket Books did indeed revolutionize book publishing in the United States, and as the paperback explosion built up over the years it held unrivaled sway as the leader in the field, despite the emergence of many competitors. After some time, other paperback firms were successful in challenging and then surpassing Pocket Books' results, notably Bantam Books, and for a while Pocket Books fell to being no higher than one of half a dozen major paperback reprinters, but in recent years, under the shrewd guidance of its present president, Ron Busch, it has forged upwards again and has regained a position at or near the top. The full story of Pocket Books would constitute a volume in itself but it doesn't belong here. That is because this is a book about Simon and Schuster, and, although it is a firm that Essandess founded with de Graff and is today a division of the huge overall company of Simon & Schuster, Pocket Books has always been a separate, arm's-length organization, allied to S & S but more a close relative than a member of the immediate family. With the exception of the two heads of the house, Leon Shimkin for the first thirty years and Dick Snyder for the past ten, no Simon and Schuster people have had much or anything to do with Pocket Books, which has its own editors, publicity and advertising staff, art department, and sales force. I myself never played any part in Pocket Books affairs and so am not equipped to write very knowledgeably about that company beyond what I've recorded above, so I doff my cap with respect to the many good people who made Pocket Books a firm that Simon and Schuster has been proud to have as a sister company and apologize to all who might well feel that they are receiving short shrift in this narrative.

The story of Golden Books, however, certainly does mesh closely into that of Simon and Schuster, for it was truly part of it, with the same people performing functions in both areas. Albert Leventhal was the outstanding example of this: at the same time that he was the chief operating executive at Simon and Schuster he was immersed in planning and building the other "tail that wagged the dog," the division of the firm called Golden Books, which revolutionized the publishing of books for children every bit as much as Pocket Books had done for adult reading.

Surely it was largely because he had sniffed the heady air of what mass distribution could offer in the case of Pocket Books that, soon afterward, Leon Shimkin turned a very attentive ear when a charming Frenchman named Georges Duplaix approached him with the concept of issuing "real" full-color books for children at a modest retail price. Duplaix was at the time a major figure in the publishing of millions of copies of cheap comic-strip books put out by Western Printing and Lithographing Company, and he had more elegant and more ambitious ideas about the sorts of books that might be made available for children. Shimkin's subsequent part in what developed into one of the greatest triumphs in Simon and Schuster's history, Golden Books, was minimal, but his initial reception of Duplaix was the springboard from which it took off. Not only was he very enthusiastic about the basic idea but he told Georges, who was thinking of children's books that would carry a retail price of something like a dollar a copy, that every effort should be made to put out books for 25¢ a copy, as Pocket Books did. At that time most juvenile books containing color cost about $2.50 and Leon had heard Albert Leventhal's rueful story of what happened when he took one home to his three-year-old daughter. Less than ten minutes later the book had been taken into the bathtub for companionship, and it didn't weather the test. "H'mmm," Albert had thought, "it wouldn't have mattered so much if the book had only cost a quarter."

Georges Duplaix threw up his hands when he heard Shimkin's dictum. "A twenty-five-cent book printed on good stock paper in four colors? To be able to do that we'd have to print and sell each book in the hundreds of thousands of copies, even the millions!" Leon replied, "Exactly my idea of how it should be done."

The first twelve Little Golden Books, a name proposed by Tom Bevans, rolled off Western Printing's presses in the fall of 1942, for the project had been set up with Simon and Schuster carrying out the creative editorial, art, and sales part of it, and Western the production and manufacturing end, with the two firms partners in the enterprise. Albert Leventhal wrote an article in 1957 about what happened in those first fifteen years and I am grateful to his widow, Janis, for unearthing it and giving her blessing to me to use it as I saw fit. What

Georges Duplaix and his best Golden Books customer, his daughter

follows is a condensation of Albert's review; since Simon and Schuster sold its half interest to Western the following year, in 1958, and retired temporarily from juvenile publishing, it really tells the entire tale of Golden Books under the Essandess aegis:

"In the initial letter to the trade the publishers pointed out the tremendous gamble that was being taken—50,000 copies per title—saying, 'It is our belief that as many as 1,000,000 copies of these little books can be sold each year.' A Company Oracle at that time who could more accurately have predicted the future would have been hooted right out of the office. Nevertheless, fifteen years later . . . close to 400,000,000 Little Golden Books had been sold to the nation's small fry. Of the first 250 titles published, more than 100 sold more than a million copies apiece, 16 others sold over 2 million, and six others sold between 3 and 5 million copies each.

"The number of outlets for these unassuming little quarter books broadened from the original 800 book and department stores to the incredible total of 120,000 national points of sale! Little Golden Books were also published with equally startling success in England, France, Australia, Germany, Norway, Sweden, Mexico, the Argentine, Saudi-Arabia—indeed virtually everywhere in the world except the Soviet Union, where Poky Little Puppies are apparently regarded as tools of the Capitalistic Overlords.

"Golden Books, together with their cousins from other publishing houses who took up the challenge of competing—Wonder Books, Jolly Books, Bonnie Books, Elf Books, Cozy Corner Books—grew to an annual sales total of 100,000,000 units. Since the total market [in 1957] consists of only about 18 million small boys and girls, this makes close to six books per year for each and every pre-school child in the nation.

"What accounts for the success of these 25¢ books? First, of course, is the price. Parents, no matter how rigidly the family budget is controlled, do not mind plunking down a quarter for a book. It is partly a pacifier, partly an educational instrument, partly a gift. Were the price of the book $1.00, things would be different. Yet there are other reasons for the success of Little Golden Books. They are well made and more durable than most higher-priced books. They are more colorful, with color on every page. They offer all the Big Names in the Little People field—Disney characters, Lassie, Rin Tin

Tin, Annie Oakley, Roy Rogers and a host of others in Golden Books; Ding Dong School and Raggedy Ann from Rand McNally; and many other appealing characters from other publishing houses.

"As already indicated, Little Golden Books began in the book and department stores. There was no way to keep them from spreading. First they crept into the syndicates where Woolworth, Kress, Grant, and the others found that the dollar turnover per square foot of store space was gratifying. Then into toy stores, drug stores, stationery stores, newsstands, and infants' wear shops. Finally they crashed into the biggest outlet of all—the supermarkets, where perhaps 30 percent of the total is sold. Interestingly enough, sales haven't dropped off too sharply in the original outlets, the book and department stores, considering the tremendous expansion elsewhere. Many thousands of units per month continue to be turned over by stores like Macy's, Marshall Field, Famous Barr, Higbee, and others.

"It takes a vast amount of intestinal fortitude to keep publishing good 25¢ books for children. Plate costs are high and the printings, by the very nature of the enterprise, must be enormous. First printing runs of 500,000 are considered modest for a new Little Golden Book, and many are astronomical. It is our opinion that the near future will see a period of overproduction and overexpansion in the industry, followed by the inevitable shake-out."

The principals at Simon and Schuster must have given heed to Leventhal's warnings, or else they were enticed by the huge payment Western Printing was willing to make to purchase Essandess's half interest and take over the entire thing themselves. In any case the sale was effected in 1958, and while Golden Books still survives with Western, in view of widespread competition, it's nothing like its former self. Nor, of course, is the 25¢ book at all remotely possible. Perhaps Simon and Schuster and Shimkin and Duplaix got out when the getting out was good.

There was more to Golden Books than Little Golden Books, as a matter of fact. After it was clear that the line not only was enormously successful but had built itself a reputation for quality, a parallel series of Big Golden Books, Giant Golden Books, and even a Golden Encyclopaedia were produced at substantially higher retail prices. Obviously these books couldn't produce the sort of skyrocketing sales that the 25¢ books did, but they too were fantastically successful, chiefly in book and department stores, and many sold hundreds of thousands of copies. Then Golden Books inspired the creation of still another division, Little Golden Records, which flourished for quite a considerable period of time under the supervision of Leon Shimkin's nephew, Arthur Shimkin, a man experienced in the recording field. Among the several top artists who made a Golden Record was Bing Crosby, and to get Der Bingle's voice on a well-recorded, very inexpensive record singing a current children's hit like "In Every Family . . . There's Got to Be . . . One Rich Brother!" was more than almost any parent could resist.

Arthur's chief sidekick in the Simon and Schuster office, who, in addition to being one of Albert Leventhal's aides in sales, had the job of marketing Golden Records, was a very tall, rawboned, freckled, extremely engaging young man named Robert Bernstein. Albert had hired him away from a job he held at radio station WNEW simply

Robert L. Bernstein

because he liked his looks and his apparent energy—and Bob certainly was energetic. He typed labels, he sent out posters and giant display cards, and once when Albert, for some reason or another, came into the office at 7:30 in the morning, he found Bernstein already there working at his desk. Bob looked up at his boss, the man who was then really running the firm, and said: "I'm ambitious. What's your excuse for being here at this unearthly hour?"

The day came when Golden Records started slipping to the point where Essandess decided they had had enough of a good thing and decided to quit while they were ahead. There were many in the S and S organization who hated the idea of letting Bernstein go and thought that another job should be found for him, but Leon Shimkin had made up his mind to cut overhead, and that included firing Bob. It's certainly an apocryphal jest made up by people who deplored Leon's practice of breaking bad news cheerily, but it's been claimed that he told Bernstein about his imminent departure with the words: "Congratulations! You're in a lower tax bracket!"

Bob didn't mind in any case. He had won the confidence and heart of Kay Thompson, whose *Eloise* had been such a smashing success as a book that an entire industry of Eloise dolls, dresses, and the like had sprouted, and a businessman was needed to supervise and run it. Bob took that on for a comparatively brief period until Bennett Cerf at Random House, who had heard extremely good things about Bernstein and his career at Essandess, offered him a position at Random House. The rest is publishing history. The friendly, freckled kid grew through the years to be one of the finest minds in book publishing, a generous and distinguished statesman not only for that estimable house but for the entire industry.

There is one anecdote about what was probably the most successful of all Little Golden Books that should be put on the permanent record. It has to do with *Doctor Dan, the Bandage Man*, whose hero was a doctor who fixed the wounds and injuries of children, pets, or any other creature around who was scratched or bleeding or in pain—including, of course, dolls and tin soldiers. How? Don't ask a silly question—by bandaging them, of course. Essandess came up with the happy thought that, if it were economically possible, it would be fabulous if each copy of *Doctor Dan* contained a few small Band-Aids affixed to an interior page so that a child could detach them and use them. The firm had unbounded confidence in this charming story and had set a first printing tentatively of a million copies, so a highly placed sales representative hied himself over to New Brunswick in New Jersey, home of the Johnson & Johnson people, to discuss the possibility of getting quite a lot of Band-Aids.

Say a few million.

Johnson & Johnson didn't take very long to see the enormous publicity appeal of the *Doctor Dan* book and how effectively a tie-in could boom their product. The details of what was worked out that day in New Brunswick are lost, but whatever S and S was charged—and it may well have been nothing at all*—it fitted into the budget for the book. Having secured this plum of a premium, S & S decided to increase the first printing from the planned 1 million copies to 1,750,000. That was the biggest first printing of any Little Golden Book, but in the end it wasn't nearly enough, for *Doctor Dan* is one of those books that sold between 3 and 5 million copies, and it is to be presumed that Johnson & Johnson kept a steady flow of Band-Aids coming as long as was necessary.

---

*If the reader is puzzled by some lack of detailed statistical information here, it's because as far as historical data is concerned both at S & S and at Western, the unwritten motto seems to be "Never mind what happened yesterday. What have you done for me today?" If records are kept, they are stored away in a warehouse in Outer Mongolia or somewhere.

# Gulliver Captured by

# the Lilliputians

9

T HE STORY is that Marshall Field, the millionaire liberal publisher and business tycoon from Chicago, was no
more aware of Simon and Schuster than he was of any
other book publisher until one day, in the early 1940s, he
was passing through Grand Central Station in New York City and
spotted a display of Pocket Books. Browsing through them, he asked
the newsstand proprietor behind the display how long this had been
going on. Along with the answer that Pocket Books was a couple of
years old, he was given the information that the line was a division of
Simon and Schuster.

That rang a bell, because Field had met Richard Simon and had
even played contract bridge with him. Field was interested in expanding his media network to the East, and for some time had been
intrigued by the idea of becoming associated with a book company.
Although originally his chief interest was in Pocket Books, upon
hearing that any major operation involving that firm would have to
include Simon and Schuster as well, Field was even more eager to
arrange something. A believer in diversification, the idea of a combination of an established and successful hardback house with this
new, appealing paperback line seemed to Field exactly what he was
seeking, and he got in touch with Dick Simon to sound him out
about the possibilities.

Simon reported this interest to his associates, Max Schuster, Leon
Shimkin, and Bob de Graff, and there was a general consensus that
the proposal should be pursued. He also talked about it to his wife,

Marshall Field

Andrea, who felt with no little fervor that Simon and Schuster was an intimate and personal family and the idea of selling out to anyone, no matter how noble and solid and well-heeled he might be, was unthinkable. "Would you sell Joanna?" was her argument, referring to their first-born and only child at the time. Andrea's opposition had great effect upon Dick, and he put up considerable resistance against the affirmative instincts of his partners, but with so solid a front in favor of negotiating with the Field people, he had little choice but to go along, and Leon Shimkin began a series of meetings with the Field attorneys. Finally, in 1944, Simon and Schuster and Pocket Books were sold to Field for about $3 million, but the money, although providing a welcome base of stability, was in a way less important than the other aspects of the deal which Shimkin managed to include. All the partners were sympathetic to Dick's personal feelings about the firm even if they were outbalanced by the opportunity to ease financial problems, so a number of agreements were reached. Not only would the companies operate with complete autonomy and no editorial interference, with the principals receiving long-term management contracts and bonuses keyed to profits, but also it was tacitly understood that they would have first opportunity to reaquire the firms if Marshall Field decided to dispose of them, or died. It turned out to be a truly splendid deal for the Essandess group and quite a dubious one for Field financially, but in compensation he appeared to enjoy every minute of the relationship. Marshall was a real lover of books and reveled in the contacts his peripheral position afforded him, and he never took any advantage. Once every few months he would come to New York, lunch or dine with the Essandess people, and attend an editorial board meeting. He neither ventured an opinion nor suggested anything different than the board members were leaning towards, unless asked. It scarcely seemed of any importance to him that Field Enterprises didn't ever profit much from its ownership. When Marshall died in 1957, Simon and Schuster and Pocket Books were reacquired for considerably less than they were worth at the time. It was a clear case of benevolent absentee ownership, and was described by one Essandess wit as being a situation where Gulliver was taken over by the Lilliputians.

As a matter of fact, except for his association with these previously successful book-publishing companies, which never added anything much to his fortune, Marshall Field didn't have much luck in extending his communications empire to the East Coast. He founded a liberal evening newspaper in New York, *PM*; when it folded he founded another, the *Star*, which suffered the same fate, despite the valiant efforts of two Simon and Schuster people who were solidly involved, Leon Shimkin on the business side and Joseph Barnes as the editor. Joe Barnes had been foreign editor of the *New*

Joseph Barnes

Wendell L. Willkie
*(Copyright by Philippe Halsman)*

*York Herald Tribune* before coming to Simon and Schuster as an outstanding book editor. He kept a low profile at Essandess, not only because he was a modest and gentle man, but undoubtedly because as an articulate liberal in an era when any prominent leftist was likely to be a target of Senator Joseph McCarthy's smear tactics, he had been prominent on McCarthy's blacklist. As a result, when Barnes was hired, Dick Simon received a number of letters of protest from McCarthy adherents who called themselves 100 percent Americans. He responded to them all simply by writing that any man who was good enough for Wendell Willkie and Dwight Eisenhower was good enough for him. (Barnes accompanied Willkie on his famous "One World" around-the-globe trip, and helped in the writing of the celebrated book of the same title. Later he wrote the official biography of Willkie, and he also worked with Eisenhower on his memoirs.) So Joe, although he had the talent and personality to rate a high editorial title, never aspired to be more than a senior editor at S and S. In that role, his great coup was nursing William Shirer and his monumental classic, *The Rise and Fall of the Third Reich*, through years of preparation to eventual publication. It was a herculean task, almost comparable to the one invariably cited as an American editor's Oscar-winning marathon performance on a book, Scribner editor Maxwell Perkins's labors over Thomas Wolfe's opus.

During the Marshall Field period, the Simon and Schuster list grew and thrived. In the entire time there was no year in which several titles didn't make the annual bestseller tabulations, and the catholicity of the list was extraordinary. Ever among the most eclectic of publishers, S and S during World War II brought out books of a number of citizen-statesmen: Willkie, General Marshall, Alexander de Seversky, Joseph E. Davies, Joseph C. Grew. Fiction successes included *Gentleman's Agreement*, by Laura Z. Hobson; *The Cardinal*, by Henry Morton Robinson; *The Blackboard Jungle*, by Evan Hunter; *Father of the Bride*, by Edward Streeter; annual novels by P. G. Wodehouse; *Compulsion*, by Meyer Levin; *The Man in the Gray Flannel Suit*, by Sloan Wilson; and several bestsellers by Irving Wallace. Humor was represented by Bob Hope's books, cartoon books by Charles Addams, Al Capp, Herblock, and Walt Kelly, and books by S. J. Perelman, James Thurber, and Kay Thompson, among a flock of others. Charles Goren's contract-bridge books, John Scarne's guides to gambling, Tommy Armour's golf books, and then Jack Nicklaus's dominated their respective fields. Many successful books came out of collaborations with magazines such as *Life*, the *Saturday Evening Post*, *House and Garden*, *Scientific American*, *American Heritage*, as well as occasional tie-ins with major commercial industries. An outstanding one of these produced the remarkable *Mobil Travel Guides*, the first real American equivalent of the classic French Michelin Guides. Among the notable entries on the list were Bertrand Russell's *History of Western Philosophy*, Roger Butterfield's *American Past*, Cornelius Ryan's *Longest Day*, Edward R. Murrow's *This I Believe*, Vannevar Bush's *Modern Arms and Free Men*, Max Lerner's *America as a Civilization*, Robert Oppenheimer's *Science and the Common Understanding*, William H. Whyte's *Organization Man*, Ernest K. Gann's *Fate Is the Hunter*, essays by A. J. Liebling. It was all business as usual, with no negative effects felt as the result of being part of Field Enterprises.

After Marshall Field died, his son, Marshall Field, Jr., had little interest in anything except the Chicago elements of the Field media group; and the original idea of the Estate, honoring intentions expressed in Field's will, was to pass ownership of Simon and Schuster and Pocket Books to a nonprofit foundation. Not only was this a concept that Leon Shimkin found distasteful, but from the outset it

Bertrand Russell

had been agreed that Simon and Schuster would have the opportunity to reacquire the firm if circumstances permitted. The Field trustees concurred with that viewpoint when they were reminded of it, so Shimkin and Simon and Schuster bought back the hardcover firm of Simon and Schuster. At Pocket Books, de Graff had retired some years previously and the other principal in that firm, apart from Shimkin, now was James M. Jacobson, whom you may recall as the unsurpassed Ping-Pong champion back in the old Fourth Avenue days. In the intervening years Jimmy had been affiliated solely with Pocket Books and had risen to become executive vice-president, so Leon and he joined forces and raised the money—a reported $5 million dollars—to reacquire that colossal company, which had become the largest book publisher in the world, with over 700 million books sold in its eighteen years of existence. So for the time being Simon and Schuster and Pocket Books became even more separate entities than they had ever been before, but not for long.

In 1957, the year of Marshall Field's death, Dick Simon retired after some difficult years of declining health. In 1960 he died, and Max Schuster and Leon Shimkin acted upon a long-standing agreement that if ever one of the three partners died, the other two would buy his stock. Thus they became equal partners in Simon and Schuster.

Jack Goodman had also died and Albert Leventhal had resigned to go over to Western Printing, so the top active operating officers who would have continued to serve under Max and Leon at Essandess were gone. I was appointed publisher of trade books and Herbert Alexander, who had similar tenure with Pocket Books, became that firm's publisher. Soon afterward I named Robert Gottlieb the Essandess editor-in-chief and Anthony Schulte the marketing director, but that is all part of another story that comes later. Seymour Turk, a

*Reading from bottom to top:* Leon Shimkin, Emil Staral, and Albert Leventhal

Seymour Turk

trustworthy and valued Leon Shimkin protégé, took over the post of executive vice-president and treasurer, succeeding a nice but somewhat unflamboyant man named Emil Staral, who had diligently performed those thankless tasks previously.

When Sy Turk first got his job, he would lunch every Monday at the Rockefeller Center Luncheon Club with Max Schuster and report on the previous week's activities and sales; then they would talk about anything else that occurred to one or the other. Very informal. But in 1966 Leon persuaded Max to sell out to him and retire. That made Shimkin the sole owner of Essandess; he immediately merged the firm with Pocket Books and created a new public-issue company, Simon & Schuster, Inc. (putting the ampersand firmly in place at last). Once Leon had the reins exclusively in his hands, Seymour continued to lunch every Monday at the Rockefeller Center Luncheon Club, but now with Shimkin, and Leon always brought along an extensive agenda so that the hour wouldn't be frittered away with small chitchat. A few years later Shimkin elevated the ever-reliable Turk to the presidency of S & S, but his tenure was comparatively short, for the sale of the firm to Gulf & Western was not far off and the hot breath of Richard Snyder, the man who would take over control of Simon & Schuster, was blowing hard on both Leon's neck and Sy's.

In addition to Joe Barnes, there were two other excellent male editors who performed their roles so quietly among their peer group of flashy extroverts that a historian of the house could unjustly overlook them. They were Quincy Howe and Wallace Brockway, both men of learning and integrity.

Quincy Howe was engaged by Essandess on Clifton Fadiman's strong recommendation. The descendant of a long line of distinguished New England Yankees, after his graduation from Harvard and a year at Cambridge he plunged into a career marked by his dedicated opposition to censorship and social injustice. At one time he was the editor of *Living Age*, a small but influential magazine that analyzed international news, and he was also a director of the American Civil Liberties Union. Although he was Simon and Schuster's chief book editor for half a dozen years, and despite his intellectual attainments, Quincy was a little bit a fish out of water among all those ebullient characters who surrounded him. He became a strong and articulate Anglophobe and wrote a very controversial book in the late 1930s, *England Expects Every American to Do His Duty*, but with the outbreak of World War II his views changed and he swung

Quincy Howe

Max Schuster, Will Durant, Dr. Abraham Stone, Leon Shimkin, and
Wallace Brockway

to full support of England and the Allies. It was then and shortly
afterward that his entire life truly changed, when he began to broadcast news and comment, first on the radio and then on television. His
radio stint was with WQXR, where he was widely praised for low-
keyed and fair reporting, and he carried those characteristics over to
television and soon became the ace CBS newscaster. Later he moved
to ABC with equal success. Howe had been a highly respected editor
during his S and S years, but it wasn't his natural bailiwick, and he
will be better remembered as the fine newscaster and political analyst
that he became.

Wallace Brockway was almost certainly the storehouse of more
erudition than could be believed, but his aspirations were never to be
more than an ivory-tower editor. He was a walking encyclopedia
and, being an expert in many fields, a regular contributor of *Britan-
nica* articles. Wallace and his close friend Herbert Weinstock attended
the University of Chicago when one of the most famous criminal
cases of the century took place there, the murder of young Bobby

Franks by Leopold and Loeb, and they knew all the protagonists in the affair very well. When Meyer Levin wrote his gripping novel *Compulsion*, based upon the case and Clarence Darrow's memorable defense of Leopold and Loeb, Wallace was a valuable source for Levin's research, although it was a part of his life that Wallace would gladly have swept from his memory. One of Wallace's own several books, written in collaboration with Weinstock, was *Men of Music*, a bestseller in its day that then became an outstanding perennial backlist title.

The roster of S and S people who wrote books on the side or even turned to authorship as a career is impressively long. Undoubtedly the flame of authorship was sparked by the heady atmosphere of the book world, but that atmosphere was shared by any member of a staff in any publisher's office, and I doubt that many book publishers can claim so many employees who wrote books. The reason, I believe, is that from the firm's beginnings S and S was geared to conceive ideas for books, and Dick Simon, Max Schuster, and Jack Goodman in particular were likely to stimulate anyone, from a partner to a secretary, by tossing out a fragmentary concept for a book and saying, "Why don't you write it? You could." Probably the most exceptional example was Dick Simon's prodding of Margaret Halsey to write *With Malice Toward Some*, about which you've already read, but here is an alphabetical list of Essandess staff members who also wrote books; I have little doubt that I may have overlooked or forgotten a few, for which I can only apologize:

Joseph Barnes, Alexis Bespaloff, Sonia Bleeker, Wallace Brockway, William Cole, Julia Colmore, Don Congdon, Jonathan Dolger, Clifton Fadiman, Margaret Farrar, Evelyn Gendel, Vicki Goldberg, Jack Goodman, Ronald Gross, Richard Grossman, Margaret Halsey, Diane Harris, Raymond J. Healy, Quincy Howe, Paul Jensen, Justin Kaplan, Richard Kluger, Michael Korda, Robert Kraus, Maria Leiper, Albert Leventhal, M. Lincoln Schuster, Peter Schwed, Henry Simon, Richard L. Simon, Sophie Sorkin, William Steinkraus, Philip Van Doren Stern, Scott Sullivan, John E. Walsh, Jerome Weidman, and Patricia White. In addition the pioneer bigwigs in the office encouraged, solicited, and bludgeoned books out of their doctors, lawyers, and even—believe it or not—an Indian chief. They were equally persuasive with their accountants, bridge partners, lovers,

Ray and Max Schuster

parents, children, and distant relatives, and it's quite remarkable how many interesting and viable books emerged out of it all.

In sheer numbers there have always been a heavy proportion of women employed in book publishing, and I believe rather especially so at Simon and Schuster. But it wasn't until comparatively recent years that many of them were more than secretaries or clerks or, at best, executive assistants. There were a few fine women editors, yes; but they were working editors rather than occupying any top roles. There were a great number of particularly talented and energetic women who became such dominant figures in important departments—sales, advertising, promotion, production, art, subsidiary rights—that they rose to head up their special areas. However, they got paid substantially less than a man would holding down the same position. An exception to this generalization was in mass-market paperback publishing, where for quite a long time women have been among the principal figures in the industry. But in trade hardback publishing they were few and far between. One thinks of Blanche Knopf and Helen Wolff and then it is hard to recall anyone else, at least in editorial ranks, until late last year, when Phyllis Grann, an Essandess alumna, became president of G. P. Putnam's. Max Schuster used to credit his wife, Ray, with contributing considerable editorial input, but Ray's active role was essentially a social one. The

Schusters entertained lavishly and Ray did have a capacity to form a rapport with eminent figures that may well have played a part in Max's acquisition of certain books, such as the memoirs of the Aga Khan and *Rumor and Reflection*, by Bernard Berenson.

But for decades the realistic story of women at Essandess was largely limited to those who got jobs as underlings and proved so good that they became department heads. They stopped abruptly there, at comparatively low salaries, no matter how good they were. At least in this respect to some extent the world has changed for the better, and Simon and Schuster has changed with it. There still are very few women at the actual top in publishing, but there are a few; and those at a level just below Mr. Big command infinitely more respect, power, and money than women once ever could aspire to win.

Let's look back at some ancient and middle history. Maria Leiper, Lee Wright, and Charlotte Seitlin were editors as talented as any of their male peers and quite possibly more so than some men who rose to executive posts, but they always were in the position of having to go, hat in hand, to people over them to accomplish the smallest things for their authors, their books, or themselves. In this last respect, the most they ever did win was a minor raise in salary now and then, nor was any of them even remotely considered for a major editorial position that would permit them to have anything more impressive than "Editor" on their business card or stationery. Other splendid women editors subsequently worked for the firm without much more recognition. It wasn't until the 1970s, when Dick Snyder hired Phyllis Grann, a lady who turned out to have a great deal of clout and a flair for acquiring big commercial novels and then doing a good job publishing them, and Nan Talese, a topnotch literary editor, that a woman became a recognized star among the editors. Phyllis was so successful that she was enticed away some years ago to become the top editor and publisher and then the president of the trade-books division of G. P. Putnam's Sons, and Nan left for a more prestigious job with Houghton Mifflin, but Snyder sprang into action again immediately. He engaged Joni Evans, a highly respected senior editor at William Morrow, to come over to S & S, not primarily to be an editor but to fill the vital post of director of subsidiary rights, which had been vacated when the seemingly irreplaceable

Milly Marmur had left to go to Random House. Just how Dick sensed that Joni had the personality and competence to be able to succeed so well in a role that was completely new to her is a trifle mysterious, but she did possess everything that was needed to make her a worthy successor to Milly. After a while, however, it was clear that Joni's other publishing gifts were too widespread to confine her to that one departmental operation, and Joni was able to turn over subsidiary rights to another while still keeping an eye on things there, and move back to her real love, editing and general publishing operations. Snyder was clearly impressed with everything about Joni—not much later she became his wife, and when the new trade-books imprint of Linden Press was inaugurated, she became its president. Some cynical comments were made about the importance of her relationship to Dick with respect to that appointment, but as a person who was on the ground and witnessed Joni's performance, I can attest that she earned the spot by virtue of her flair and faculties, just the way James H. Silberman, former editor-in-chief of Random

Joni Evans (© *1978 Helen Marcus*)

James H. Silberman (© *1983 Helen Marcus*)

House, who was lured away by Snyder to head up the other new trade-books imprint, Summit Books, had clearly already earned his.

Two other strong women editors also added to the Essandess editorial board by Snyder were Alice Mayhew and Patricia Soliman. Alice, a specialist in serious nonfiction, has become the firm's guru for almost all its political and sociological books, and it is she who is accorded deserved major credit for her editorial work on the several fabulously successful Washington-based books that led off with *All the President's Men* and were followed up by *The Final Days*, *Blind Ambition*, and *The Brethren*. Pat Soliman is more a low-key Phyllis Grann type of editor, with a taste for commercial fiction and a good touch in acquiring and editing such books.

Moving along to publishing domains other than editorial, three of the outstanding women in Simon and Schuster's earlier years, each of whom was completely capable of filling in or replacing her respective boss, were Helen Barrow in production, Elinor Green in sales promotion, and Nina Bourne in advertising. Helen finally did attain boss status in production at S and S; the other two went on to bigger and better things elsewhere—Elinor in politics and government and

Mildred Marmur

Nina at Alfred A. Knopf, where she is vice-president and advertising manager. They all look back on Essandess days as having been a lot of fun, but they didn't really attain the recognition or financial rewards that their talents would have earned them if they had worn pants. But to be fair, that was then, and the men who ran S and S were no different from other male bosses of the time.

Now we might turn to that area of publishing, subsidiary rights, where women finally came into their rightful own and practically took over, and to the heroine who was among the first of a new breed, Mildred Marmur. Milly came to Simon and Schuster fresh out of Brooklyn College, an intellectual behind a bouncy facade. I took her on as my assistant when I was the director of subsidiary rights, and it may well be that I never did anything more astute in publishing than hiring Milly. When I moved up to become publisher of the trade-books division and left Milly in charge of subsidiary rights, she spread her wings and really flew.

Up to that time subsidiary rights, as an aspect of general book publishing, had received a certain lip service as being the difference annually between profits and loss, but it really was a kind of stepsister in company thinking, and for the most part, men didn't covet the job. Two things, one of her own making and one by chance, made Milly different from her predecessors. The first was that she was not at all content to sit at her desk and telephone, or go out to a long lunch to try to sell rights to a book. She was a gadfly in seeing to it that many of the functions in standard operating procedures that were supposed to be the burden of others got carried out, by getting involved in everything. Besides that she was a tough and persuasive salesperson.

The other factor, which was Milly's luck in being the right place at the right time, was that book publishing changed to a large extent just then and the mass-market paperback industry really took over as far as commerce was concerned. Suddenly the paperback rights to a successful book that formerly would have been fortunate to squeeze out a $35,000 or $50,000 advance were fetching a quarter of a million dollars or more—that is, if Milly was conducting an auction among the paperback houses, which she did often with the telephone nestled between her shoulder and one ear while she was carrying out a myriad of other publishing matters with her free hands. Milly was the Founding Mother of a considerable number of other women who have followed her lead with comparable skill.

# A Last Brave Fling

# 10

WHEN Marshall Field Enterprises took over Simon and Schuster in the mid-1940s, Richard Simon was at the peak of his career and powers, and no one antici- pated what was to follow in the next few years. Of course Dick had never really been happy about selling the firm, and the fact that Leon Shimkin, who had been the prime factor in engi- neering the operation, had strengthened his position and was calling more of the shots than in the past didn't help. For although the three partners usually worked in concert for the general good health of the firm, there were certainly more disagreements in ideas and tempera- ment between Leon and Dick than between either of them and Max. Lee Wright, who was Simon's secretary in 1939 when Geoffrey Hellman wrote his long, three-part *New Yorker* Profile of Essandess's first fifteen years, recalls Shimkin's bitter resentment of the almost slighting mention he received in it, which he ascribed to Simon, Hellman's chief source in his interviewing. For his part Simon, though he had early recognized Shimkin as "Our Little Golden Nug- get," had very different personal values, and Leon's growing impor- tance exacerbated underlying friction for him when they disagreed.

But what was not generally known then or even much later to people who were not very close to him was that Dick's health was on a sharp decline. By the mid-1950s, even those who had always ad- mired him felt he was unaccountably losing his grip. Among those was his old friend and associate, Bennett Cerf, who after Dick's death in 1960 wrote a glowing tribute to him in the *Saturday Review* but implied in the final paragraph that he had become difficult and al-most psychotic in his later years. Simon's sister, Elizabeth Seligman, tried to set the record straight in a letter to Bennett, and a portion of that letter follows.

"You may not know that during the last few years, in addition to two heart attacks, Dick had a series of little strokes. Laboratory tests and neurological examinations showed that there was physical dam-age to his brain caused by hardening of the arteries. This resulted in an impaired memory for recent events and a decrease in his energy and ability to concentrate.

"He was by no means psychotic.

"His circulation was poor and he was extremely sensitive to cold and drafts. He did turn radiators up and close windows, but none of us ever saw him wear an overcoat indoors. As far back as any of us can remember, he was a locker of front doors, but he never locked himself into a room. None of us feels [*as Cerf implied*] that there was any question of his trying to shut out death.

"I wish you had seen more of him recently. Except for tiring easily and becoming confused by new faces and events, he was very much the Dick you knew. He had no delusions. He never lost his familiar humor, warmth, gentle disposition and extraordinary mem-ory for the more distant past. He spent the evening before he died with his family and gave some clear-headed, valuable advice to a young friend who was facing a change in his publishing career.

"The family has heard of occasional misinterpretations of his ill-ness and I've written this letter to you only because we are distressed that an old friend of Dick's should have this misconception of him."

Putting aside my knowledge that Elizabeth was a passionately devoted and loyal sister, it is completely easy for me to accept her explanations of Dick's erratic behavior in his late years as solid fact. I saw Dick regularly in the office during that period, and, while he wasn't the old Dick Simon, his changes appeared to be no more than those of someone who was suffering the plague of aging somewhat prematurely. Still, for whatever reasons, he was not the tower of strength he had once been, and he needed a person to be his support and stand in for him, and that brings us to Richard Grossman.

Dick Grossman was one of the most gifted and impressive people who ever dwelt in the non-ivied halls of Simon and Schuster. He had been a grassroots advertising copywriter in Canton, Ohio, with an additional flair for photography, and the combination of these two talents, so dear to Dick Simon's heart, impelled him to seek out Grossman for what turned into an eleven-hour interview and concluded with one Dick hiring another. Grossman initially had not been too keen about a New York job, but even when Simon's health was on the decline he could be a persuasive man. One particular lure finally enticed Grossman. It appeared that after Essandess's success with its new edition of *War and Peace*, the next similar project on the drawing board was to get Vladimir Nabokov to do a new translation of *Anna Karenina*, and Grossman was to be involved, along with

Richard Grossman

editor Wallace Brockway, in enticing Nabokov to undertake the assignment. The attraction of becoming an important factor in this marriage of his favorite author with his favorite novel was too much for Grossman to resist. Act I portrays Dick coming to work for S and S. Act II reveals the unhappy fact that the Nabokov *Anna* never came to pass.

Still, once ensconced not only as a Dick Simon protégé but also as an obviously effective all-around publishing newcomer, Grossman found plenty to do. Simon had come up with three spectacular photographic-book projects that were pretty overwhelming, coming as close together as they did, and even had he been in the best of shape he would have welcomed help. He was still glowing with pride at having recently published Henri Cartier-Bresson's classic book of photograpy, *The Decisive Moment*, and he had on tap another such gem, Werner Bischof's *Japan*. Then he was planning to issue a popular-priced but lavish edition of *The Family of Man*, the work of Edward Steichen, which Jerry Mason's Ridge Press had published earlier in hardcover at a price beyond the reach of the ordinary book buyer. Dick Grossman was the man who could solve the myriad problems that invariably accompany the publishing and promotion of complicated photography books. And he would really have to do it more or less alone, because just about at this time it had been agreed that Dick Simon's books should be separated editorially from the regular publishing program of the firm. Simon was allocated a separate budget to create his own private undertakings, to be called New Ventures. Essandess's service departments would be available, of course, for such things as warehousing, marketing and billing, and extra rights exploitations, but essentially the two Dicks had to make New Ventures work on their own. All the talent up and down the halls would be engaged in producing the regular house list and couldn't be diverted by a sideshow. And it was rather a sideshow, for many of Simon's New Ventures were projects unlike traditional book publishing.

One of Simon's first dreams was to corral the finest photographers and produce a line of postcards of such superb quality that they would put to shame any existing cards. The trouble with that idea was that Dick was innocent about the sordid details of the established picture-postcard business, and his concept went down the drain after considerable preliminary work and excitement, when he was made aware of two realistic facts that spelled ruin to his hopes. The first was that the discount offered to retailers by postcard producers was so big—well in excess of anything book publishers give to book-sellers—that there could be no profit on the sort of expensive cards Dick envisaged. The second was that, on the whole, purchasers of such cards in hotels or on vacation couldn't care less about beautiful or imaginative pictures if a card cost much more than ones alongside it. One could scribble "Having wonderful time—wish you were here" on any card.

Simon also wanted to start a humor book club, but this time he did enough preliminary research to be convinced that the idea wasn't viable.

So in the end New Ventures turned into simply an arm of Essand-ess's normal publishing, and Simon and Grossman largely shelved Dick Simon's more Utopian prospects and settled down to publishing regular books. Some stunning ones came out during the short life of New Ventures. Two of the very first, one the novel by Sloan Wilson titled *The Man in the Gray Flannel Suit*, and the other the nonfiction work by William Holly Whyte, *The Organization Man*, achieved such prominence that their respective titles became part of the language as depicting the up-and-coming young executive. When Dick Simon first read the manuscript of Sloan Wilson's book he felt immediately that he was onto a very good thing indeed. A motion-picture company was simultaneously committing itself to produce a film from the script that would star Gregory Peck, but nobody was very happy about the tentative title, *A Candle at Midnight*. Wilson was talking to Simon and Grossman about how the book idea had first occurred to him: "I went crazy on that commuters' train each morning, seeing all those guys in gray flannel suits—" He was interrupted by Dick Simon's shout of jubilation: "That's it!" Some book titles are born, some are achieved, and some are thrust upon us, and *The Man in the Gray Flannel Suit* falls into the third category.

Knowing that Gregory Peck would be featured in the movie, it seemed a good idea to try to convey a connection with him on the jacket of the book. Of course paperback books brought out to tie in with a movie invariably display a photograph of the star on the cover, but that isn't usually done with hardbacks: the feeling is that it hasn't sufficient dignity. Still there would be obvious benefits for all concerned if the novel, almost certain to be a bestseller, could help create an image that the movie company could exploit on posters and billboards as a sort of trademark for the film. Reciprocally, of course, it wouldn't do the Simon and Schuster book any harm to be identified with so popular a movie idol as Gregory Peck.

It was decided to shoot a photograph of a man who, though it would be only a solid gray silhouette, would convey an impression of Gregory Peck. He would be wearing a felt hat—this was in the mid-1950s, before President Kennedy destroyed most of the men's hat industry by not wearing one, and a gray-flanneled commuter would no sooner have stepped onto the New York train hatless than pantless. To take such a undetailed and nonspecific image, it certainly wasn't necessary for the eminent photographer selected to fly West, or for Peck to come East to pose. All that was required was a tall, slim, rather elegant young man with a good physical bearing, and there he was in Dick Simon's office. Dick Grossman could fit the role perfectly, but Grossman, ever a man ahead of the times, never wore a hat and didn't own one. Simon pulled out his wallet, extracted a couple of $20 bills, and told Grossman to run over to Brooks Brothers or Tripler's and buy himself one. The photographic assignment was carried out handsomely and soon thereafter Dick Grossman's silhouette figure was being displayed on something like a hundred thousand copies of *The Man in the Gray Flannel Suit* in stores all over the country. Not much later, similar huge renditions of the shadowy Grossman were dotting the countryside on billboards announcing the movie. When one considers the sorts of fees male models receive these days, Dick's reward doesn't seem very generous. He did get a good hat out of it, but he was never seen wearing it again.

Dick Simon's gratification at having secured and made huge successes of two such books as *The Man in the Gray Flannel Suit* and *The Organization Man* must have been considerable, but it didn't stop him from being wistful about publishing another photography book. A decade earlier he had met a world-famous photographer who didn't simply aim a camera and click the shutter, but was chockful of creative ideas for unusual and frequently playful pictures. His name was Philippe Halsman, and Dick and he became fast friends. Back in

1949, intrigued by the zany sense of humor that had led Philippe to shoot a series of photos of the French movie star Fernandel clowning it up, Simon had been inspired to publish a little book called *The Frenchman*. Fernandel was able to register every emotion by manipulating his engaging, rubbery countenance, and the book had each of Fernandel's expressions reply to an American interviewer's question. The effects were as riotously funny as the questions were imaginative. One gem, shown below, was the Frenchman's response to "We hope that you have been able to sample our California champagne?"

(*Copyright by Philippe Halsman*)

*The Frenchman*, a tremendous seller, prompted a number of similar books from both Essandess and other houses. The most notable was Constance Bannister's *The Baby*, happily a Simon and Schuster publication, which sold hundreds of thousands of copies.

In the years following *The Frenchman*, Halsman had become a solid member of the Essandess family. He produced two lesser picture books—*Piccoli*, a children's book, and *Dali's Moustache*, and he was commissioned to take portraits of the authors of most major S & S books, for use in promotion and on the jackets. The personal relationship of Halsman and Simon deepened through the years, and Dick became a frequent visitor to Philippe's studio; camera buff that he was, that was a real treat. So it came about, in the midst of this New Ventures era, that Dick learned how Phillippe put his photo subjects at ease before taking formal portraits.

Philippe Halsman *(Copyright by Irene Halsman Rosenberg)*

He took photos of people jumping up in the air. Halsman had a psychological theory that everyone wears armor and hides behind a mask, which get in the way of the photographer's attempt to capture true personality. To try to overcome this before taking portraits, he first asked his subjects to jump and let him snap some shots in full flight. He felt that the subject could not simultaneously control both facial expressions and limb muscles, so the mask falls and the subject's real self becomes visible. Whether Philippe's theory was actually valid or not hardly matters: He and his celebrated subjects had great fun experimenting with what Halsman termed "jumpology," and he piled up a great number of interesting and amusing photographs on a shelf. The moment Simon saw them, he wanted to do a *Philippe Halsman Jump Book*. If you can ever find a copy in a second-hand or rare book shop (extremely doubtful; I've tried), latch onto it. There wasn't one in Essandess's library, which isn't zealously guarded, and I managed to secure one only by borrowing it from Philippe's widow, Yvonne. There are fantastic jumping shots in the volume of everybody from the eighty-seven-year-old Judge Learned Hand, through a variety of such notables as Grace Kelly, Thomas E. Dewey, Richard Nixon, Adlai Stevenson, Walter Winchell, Jack Dempsey, Bennett Cerf, John Steinbeck, Aldous Huxley, Ben Hecht, Robert Oppenheimer, Marc Chagall, Walter Gropius, Salvador Dali, Victor Borge, Bob Hope, Jackie Gleason, Dinah Shore, Carol Channing, Sophia Loren, Audrey Hepburn, Eddie Cantor, Maurice Chevalier, Groucho Marx, Lena Horne, Benny Goodman, Marian Anderson, and Liberace, as well as dozens of others of comparable fame. Simply to give you a taste of it all, here are three of my favorites on the facing page.

Max Schuster and Dick Simon became two of the jumpers too, once the book had been decided upon, because Halsman wanted to include them. Somewhat surprisingly, Max jumped as high as Dick did—both well above the average, although of course well below the heights attained by people like Ray Bolger and Maria Tallchief!

The *Jump Book*, published in 1959, was Dick Simon's last hurrah, and he died the following year, attended by his adoring family. That was no more than just, because Dick himself had very strong family feelings, which even extended to his quite tyrannical father. During the Depression of the 1930s, when his father, Leo, and his uncle were

Duke and Duchess of Windsor
(*Copyright by Philippe Halsman*)

Peter Ustinov
(*Copyright by Philippe Halsman*)

Marilyn Monroe
(*Copyright by Philippe Halsman*)

suffering financial catastrophe in their feather business, Dick and Jerry Weidman often would go to the old Seventh Avenue garment center, especially right after New Year's Day, to spend several hours with the brothers. Jerry accompanied Dick because he had worked in the area and knew his way about it: his first great success, *I Can Get It for You Wholesale*, came out of that period of his life. Also he was a much better man with figures than Dick—and the purpose of the call was not only to pay a solicitous visit but to help the old men go over the books for the preceding year. Jerry added up the monumental red figures and subtracted the modest black ones to arrive at the yearly thousands of dollars that the enterprise had lost. The Simons had once been important New York merchants who dominated the feather business, but feathers had been out of style for a quarter of a century. Everybody knew there was absolutely no hope of recovery, but after all, this was the old boys' entire life. So at the end of the day's visit, Dick wrote out a check to cover the year's loss, so that the brothers Simon could continue to fail at trying to re-popularize and sell feathers to the ladies. Alas—Lillian Russell was long dead and gone.

# Damon and Pythias

# II

B Y 1933 the firm was almost ten years old, clearly no fly-by-
night enterprise, and Dick Simon and Max Schuster, now in
their midthirties, felt that new young blood was needed in
case they were nearing senility. Dick was the one who could
best ferret out some talent, and he started by hiring a twenty-four-
year-old named Jack Goodman to try his hand at writing jacket and
advertising copy. The salary was around the standard $20 a week that
fledglings, lucky to find a job at all in the Depression, were paid.
(One friend of mine, running into an acquaintance who asked how
he was making out, replied: "Fine. My salary runs into four figures
and stops abruptly." For the benefit of my non-mathematically-
minded readers, 52 times $20 is $1,040.)

Goodman so impressed Simon from the very outset that soon
afterwards he decided to splurge another $20 a week and take on
another youngster whom Jack recommended without reserve, Albert
Leventhal. Albert had been a cub reporter for a Brooklyn paper and
wrote a contract-bridge column for it, and Simon took him on as his
assistant in the sales department. It's hard to think anyone ever employed two novices almost simultaneously to better effect, for Goodman and Leventhal were to become the backbone of Essandess in the
years to come. They virtually ran the show during the decade before
Jack's death in 1957 and Albert's resignation the following year.

It is recounted that Simon wasn't exactly bowled over by Goodman's presentation of himself in his first interview for a job, but after
it was over they went down together in the same elevator and onto

the street. Dick, a cautious man with his own pocket money as most people were then, stood waiting for a bus but Jack hailed a cab and said, "Coming my way?" Dick was indeed headed in that direction so he stepped in, although a little taken aback by the way this young man, who had seemed so eager to secure a low-paying job, would casually commandeer a taxi. He asked where Jack was going, and Jack replied that he was off to play in a contract-bridge tournament at the Cavendish Club. Excellent bridge player that Simon was, he wasn't quite in that class and he was impressed. Jack was hired the next day. When it later turned out that Leventhal was Jack's partner and a player of equal caliber, Dick needed no further recommendation, for by this time Jack was established in Simon's esteem, not only for his copywriting accomplishments but also for his cocky and humorous personality. Jack had not been at work more than a month

Jack Goodman

or two when, just before the holidays, Dick walked through the office handing out gold pieces (still legal tender at that time) as Christmas bonuses. Reaching Jack's desk he said, "Merry Christmas, Jack," and handed him a shiny, new $20 gold piece. You should understand that Goodman had no money other than his salary at the time, but he looked up at his boss, grinned, and said, "Toss you, double or nothing."

The careers of Albert Leventhal and Jack Goodman at S and S rose extremely rapidly and always virtually equally, although they worked primarily in different areas. They became officers of the firm at the same time, were made directors at the same time, and jointly pretty well took over the daily operations of the company from Dick Simon and Max Schuster after a while, the founders being glad by then to disburden themselves. Leon Shimkin by this date had moved

Albert R. Leventhal

his offices and most of his energies to Pocket Books, so except in ownership matters, he didn't concern himself with Essandess. Albert became executive vice-president and chief operating officer, Jack was editor-in-chief and advertising director, and no one who ever worked at S and S in those days can ever think of Goodman and Leventhal except as a team.

What few people ever knew was how very closely they chose to link themselves in their interests and activities outside of the office. Naturally they had the sort of daily masculine camaraderie that good friends who are working associates often enjoy, golfing and tennis

Al Leventhal, Jack Goodman, Max Schuster, and Dick Simon on Ambassador Joseph E. Davies's yacht

and poker and summer vacations together, contract bridge partners in friendly and tournament competition, and at one point—but not concurrently—attracted to the same woman. But the exceptional aspect of their relationship was the financial bond they chose with which to link their fortunes together and which, regardless of circumstances that tipped the scales in favor of one or the other, they never severed.

At the time both were vice-presidents, earning identical salaries and appearing to have comparable futures ahead at Essandess, so they decided not to have their respective incomes from the company a factor in the arrangement. They formed a partnership corporation in which each would share fifty-fifty in any extra earnings either one made. (Poker and bridge and other gambling winnings or losses were excluded.) The impulse that inspired Albert and Jack to adopt this unusual course was twofold. First, these were the years of the Great Depression and no one knew what turns it might take or how long it would last. Then there was each man's trust and confidence in the other's abilities in fields other than his own. That gave them the idea, so similar to the practice of mutual funds, of spreading their investments. They wanted to hedge whatever fortune might bring to either one by having a substantial stake in each other.

In the years that followed, among less profitable items such as writing an occasional book, Jack became Eastern story editor for Columbia Pictures, a job which not only didn't conflict with his Simon and Schuster editorial role but actually supplemented and helped it, in that he had early access to movie properties that might be converted into literary ones. Jack also collaborated with my brother, Fred, in writing a monthly humorous column for *Cosmopolitan* magazine. Both sideline jobs paid Goodman handsomely— but 50 percent of everything he made that way went into Leventhal's pocket.

Albert also had some book-writing income, but his huge bonanza came when he became a focal figure in the creation, production, and exploitation of the biggest new enterprise in the S and S organization—Golden Books. That separate division was so successful that as its manager Albert earned really big money over and above his regular S and S salary, and Jack Goodman, who had absolutely nothing to do with Golden Books, got half of it.

Did any of the emotions arise out of all this that one would think might have arisen? Natural reactions under such circumstances such as regret or envy? Actions that could have flared up, such as fights between themselves or their respective wives, recriminations, a parting of the ways, lawsuits? Even a temporary cooling of their Damon-and-Pythias relationship? The answer is no. Both men continued to live happily under the arrangement until Jack's death. It's a story which Robert Ripley might well have included in "Believe It or Not"; I know it is a fact, and you can believe it. And if any reader harbors a cynical thought about the relationship, be assured that Albert and Jack never lived together and both were solidly heterosexual.

From my close to forty years of working at Essandess, three people stand out in my affectionate memories: Jack Goodman, Albert Leventhal, and Tom Bevans, the last the only one still alive although he's been retired these many years. There were others who, had they been my age, might have won comparable affection; but people of different generations are less likely to grow close. You will read more about Jack and Albert before this chapter ends, but let's turn to Tom for the moment. Since he's still thriving and playing a good game of tennis in West Cornwall, Connecticut, he's not yet ripe for the sort of eulogy I will give the other two.

One of Will Rogers's most quoted remarks was that he never met a man he didn't like. I take that with several grains of salt—even a saint must have more discimination—but I have never met a person who didn't like Tom Bevans. Tom was the production manager during the Leventhal-Goodman era and although he wasn't a part of their unique financial partnership, they included him in just about every move they made upward. Later, after World War II, when I joined the firm, I was fortunate enough to have the same personal and business affections and advantages extended to me, and the foursome of Albert, Jack, Tom, and me became more tightly knit than the Three Musketeers.

Although Bevans married one of Carl and Irita Van Doren's lovely daughters, Margaret, and so was plunged into the literary set, Tom's genius and interests were focused upon more practical matters than the spinning of words. His inventive brain and master craftsman's hands enabled him to tackle any problem involving design or mechanics and come up with a solution. An outstanding person, in other words, not only to run the manufacturing end of S and S books and to be its art director, but invaluable if your toaster was broken or your tennis racquet needed restringing on a Sunday when the shops weren't open. Since the other three members of our combine were all incapable of driving a nail straight, Tom's gifts won deep appreciation. For example, he and I had children of the same age. When one received a present that had to be assembled, my practice would be to lay everything out, one item well separated from another, and pain-

Tom T. Bevans

fully try to read and follow inadequate instructions written by the Japanese manufacturer. I usually did not score very high on these endeavors and invariably spent hours in the attempts. But Tom would just dump everything out on the floor, look at what the end result was supposed to be, disregard the written matter, and put the whole thing together in a matter of minutes. Positively awesome.

When Walt Kelly's *Pogo* books were sweeping the nation, Tom had the idea of creating a large Pogomobile to hang in a child's bedroom, and he designed a charming one that embodied all the delightful inhabitants of Kelly's Okefenokee Swamp. Tom could assemble it with his eyes shut, but it was very clear that people like me could not. I leaped at the opportunity for once to write a set of instructions that my fellow boobs could follow and, with Tom's patient explanations, did so. I never found out if the product of our collaboration was effective for all-thumbs purchasers, but at least the Pogomobile sold a lot of copies.

Bevans is also credited with a couple of ingenious book-jacket innovations. When the firm published Clifton Fadiman's *Reading I've Liked*, which had a strong but essentially simple jacket containing only lettering, Tom divided the very large first printing into thirds and had jackets run off in three different background colors—green, red, and blue. The result was that the book got triple exposure in store windows and on display shelves, because the sharply contrasting colors produced an eye-stopping effect that the stores were glad to exploit. I cannot produce an affidavit that this was the first time the technique was ever used, but everybody seems to think it was.

Tom used his other apparently original jacket idea to great effect on Jack Goodman's *Fireside Book of Dogs*. He devised a double-size affair which, when folded in half along the horizontal, made a regular-sized, double-thick jacket. A note on the back flap suggested that the reader remove the jacket and open it to full size—something like a twenty-by-twenty-inch square. That would reveal detailed illustrations of the various breeds of dogs, rendered so artistically that a dog lover would probably want to frame and hang it. That turned out to be so effective a sales and promotion idea that Essandess later used it when it seemed appropriate, as for a gourmet cookbook with mouth-watering color illustrations. True, it added a few cents per copy to the production costs, so in the present era of inflation and cost-cutting, it's doubtful if Tom's brainstorm is likely to be repeated soon again.

Bevans never had much to do with the house's editorial decisions, but it should be noted that he was a major factor in S & S's securing a standout title of the period, Wendell Willkie's *One World*. Irita Van Doren, editor of the *Herald Tribune*'s Sunday book section, was Willkie's close friend and speech-writing consultant, and she was Tom's mother-in-law. Publishing often has wheels within wheels.

A final flash of inspiration came to Tom when the firm was planning the first low-priced, full-color list of children's books and was groping about for an attractive name for it. It was Tom who diffidently suggested "Little Golden Books." This may not seem so inspired as to have been worth many millions of sales, but probably neither did "Frigidaire" when someone suggested that.

In the decade or so after World War II, of all the people at Simon and Schuster who had the burden of juggling a number of balls in the air without dropping any, and the drive and personality to do it successfully, none can compare with Albert Leventhal. Of course it's true he was surrounded by people who, in their own provinces, performed stunningly, but if ever a person filled the function of chief operating officer for a bunch of prima donnas, it was Albert. Dick Simon's failing health was reducing his effectiveness. Max Schuster had always essentially been an editor and his involvement in the business didn't extend too far past that role. Leon Shimkin was so completely involved in larger financial visions and Pocket Books that he confined his participation in Essandess trade books largely to help in planning budgets and delighting in, or worrying about, final annual results. That was Emil Staral's essential function too. The other good people around were specialists in their particular individual realms, but generally speaking each shoemaker stuck to his or her last. It was up to Leventhal to see to it that the whole thing stuck together.

Albert was a great sales director, completely worthy of following in the footsteps of Dick Simon. He planned and exploited the spectacular color brochures for specific books and the annual one that brought so much business into the bookstores in the Christmas season. His rapport with booksellers was just as strong as Dick's had been, and he wrote equally inspiring letters to them and made as frequent calls upon them. But at the top of the firm by this time there were myriad misunderstandings and mistrust, personal competition, outright rancor on occasion, so Albert also had the thankless task of becoming the great conciliator. He tried to pour oil on the troubled waters that developed among the three owners. He tried to play fair with Marshall Field, who was receiving virtually no return for the millions of dollars he had invested in the firm. Albert himself had a huge personal stake in the booming children's book division, Sandpiper Press, the editorial end of Golden Books, and this was a complication dealing with the other principals, who had big stakes— Georges Duplaix, the original creator; the Western Printing and Lithographing Company, which produced the books and was equal partner with Essandess; the three S's; and everyone's lawyers. Albert successfully handled these matters separately from his day-to-day performance at running the S and S sales organization, where he was not only its representative in bookstore relationships but often the spokesman for the entire book industry. Few more articulate, agreeable, and convincing speakers ever graced the business stage. He had that unusual combination of being acknowledged and respected as a sometime tough and always realistic performer as well as being beloved, even by his sometime rivals in the trade. He and Jack Goodman were affectionate foils for each other, and it's impossible to say that one or the other was more important to the house.

Jack Goodman was somewhat more casual and flamboyant and, on occasion, would come up with a gag that could boomerang against him. After S and S published Bennett Cerf's first book, *Try and Stop Me*—a huge hit which Cerf's own firm, Random House, didn't publish, because it was having greater difficulties than Essandess under wartime regulations about paper—Cerf had enough unused material to turn out a second book, *Shake Well before Using*. That too was more than reasonably successful. But when he proposed still a third book to Goodman, and discussed what title it should bear, Jack couldn't resist suggesting, "What about *The Bottom of the Barrel*?" Simon and Schuster did not publish that third Cerf book.

Norman Corwin still boasts a deservedly long biography of his writing achievements in *Who's Who in America*, but one does not encounter his name or his works today the way readers and radio listeners did during World War II. At that time he was one of the most inspiring writers and broadcasters in an era when inspiration was a valued commodity. He was a close friend of Goodman's, so Jack was to publish in book form a Celebration Piece that CBS had commissioned Corwin to write and broadcast immediately after the inevitable victory over the Germans.

So on one sunny day in early 1945, Norman was visiting the Goodmans at their home in Rowayton, Connecticut, and announced that he had completed his opus, *On a Note of Triumph*. No one had been privileged to hear a word of it yet, but Jack and my brother Fred, who was also a friend of Corwin's and who lived next door to the Goodmans, were now to be so honored. But Norman needed to deliver the long piece someplace where absolute quiet reigned and there would be no distractions or ringing telephones. An attractive venue was proposed—the middle of Long Island Sound. The Goodmans owned a small sailboat; they could go a few miles from the Connecticut coast, drop anchor, and give Norman's masterpiece the attention it deserved. The party was an exclusive one: Norman, Jack, Fred, and Fred's thirteen-year-old stepson, Mickey, who was brought along because he was the only really reliable sailor among them.

Everything proceeded smoothly. The Great Moment arrived when Norman, in his deep, resonant voice, now muted in keeping with the solemnity of the message, began:

> So they've given up.
> They're finally done in, and the rat is
>     dead in an alley back of the
>     Wilhelmstrasse.
> Take a bow, G.I.,
> Take a bow, little guy. . . .

But before Norman could get on to his next couple of lines, which included

> This is It, kid, this is The Day . . . ,

another voice, even better known than Norman's, was heard coming quietly from the stern of the boat. It was that of the Brooklyn Dodgers' beloved sportscaster Red Barber, and it was saying in equally muted fashion, becoming the seriousness of *that* moment,

So with two out and the count on the batter three-and-two, Pee Wee will be taking off for second on the pitch!

It took the stunned three adults a few seconds to realize how and why this voice had materialized out of the depths of Long Island Sound, but then it was evident. Mickey, a passionate fan of Dem Bums, had brought along a small portable radio so he could listen to something really interesting.

Murder may well have been Norman Corwin's first goal, but laughter from Jack and Fred immediately overrode that reaction and, to do Norman justice, he laughed too. It almost all ended happily, too—*On a Note of Triumph* was a sensational hit, first on radio and then in book form; but it must be reported that the Dodgers lost.

Of the many good things that Jack did for me, the best was to introduce me to his secretary, Antonia Holding, just before I went overseas in World War II. When I returned we got married and have lived happily ever after. Toni quit her job with Jack in late 1944 to go over to the *New Yorker*. But she left behind her "Notes to My Boss's New Secretary," which conveys umplumbed aspects of Goodman's personality. That document, while consistently and charmingly funny, is too long to reproduce here but some excerpts will convey the idea:

"Don't be unduly upset when he calls you in for dictation and then suddenly decides to make many, many telephone calls, sometimes to a character he hasn't even thought of for the last ten years. After all, remember that you're working for a kind of minor genius. And that he is always a good friend to have; although on the other hand he is a totally ineffective and inactive enemy. So don't worry.

"He is an active doodler and it all looks like the kind of things you see under microscopes. Strange, bewhiskered unicellular organisms. Fantastic designs that look like the structure of a maple leaf magnified a hundred times, or the compound eye of a fly magnified two hundred times. There will be a regular parade of them across the letterheads of any correspondence you leave on his desk too long, so be careful about any papers that should be kept nice and clean.

"Don't let him stir his coffee with those scissors he keeps in the desk drawer. He also cleans his nails with them, and it makes the scissors sticky.

"You will have to keep his bank book, which is far from simple. Mr. G. draws checks and then forgets to tell you or, if he does, will gaily say, 'Oh, I did draw a check for $118.26, or maybe it was $126.18. Better make a record of it.' He depends upon your honesty—and accuracy. It's the accuracy that bothers me. There was one time when I told him his balance was $136.03. He raised his eyebrows and said something like "Ah," and looked disappointed in a resigned sort of way. I was pretty embarrassed when I found out that I'd over-looked the existence of a thousand-dollar check not yet deposited, and that his balance really should have been $1,136.03.

"He occasionally writes very funny and—er—very salty letters. Look down noncommittally if he dictates anything low, and put down your pencil and pad if he dictates anything funny. It will be some time before he resumes dictation because he will be consumed with laughter. You must laugh too.

"Rubber bands disappear from his desk, but this is not so myste-rious as it is pitiable. For many months he has been patiently making a rubber ball out of all available rubber bands. He claims that this would be the world's most wonderful golf ball. Of course, I have been defeating this purpose of his, because after he goes home I peel off five or six rubber bands for office use the next day, and there you are. This sets up a nice balance and everybody is happy. True, the ball does bounce around wonderfully well; he brought it out once and was throwing it against the wall and catching it again and I was quite impressed.

"Well, that's all I can think of at the moment. I promise I'll clean out my desk drawers soon, very soon. Meantime, carry on and good luck."

It was typical of Jack that, aside from leaving the notes for his new secretary, he had another copy run off and secretly acted as Toni's agent. As a result, the whole thing appeared in *Vogue* maga-zine, and Toni received a welcome and unexpected check.

When Jack died and a memorial service held for him was a standing-room-only event, the main speaker was his close Hollywood friend, Charles Lederer. Here follows a portion of what Charlie had to say about Goodman:

"What a privilege it was to be loved by Jack! People aren't always proud of what they love, but Jack was. Whether he spoke of his family, or his co-workers at Simon and Schuster, or of his legion of other friends, he spoke with the pride of possession that you might expect from the owner of a thousand da Vincis. Having Jack's affection was like having a whole squad of champions in your corner. And it made you the target for his blessed mania of giving. Making demands on Jack was like giving a girl a rose. 'Makes me feel wanted,' he'd say, grinning, as he wrote the check, or arranged the job, or placed the manuscript, or lent the car, or wrote the check again. Truly, he gave most of himself away. I'm not sure that he didn't give it all away.

"He was always exactly as old as the mood you brought to him. The game was never too juvenile for his elastic, merry spirit, and the conversation might have been adolescent, but Jack never knew how to disdain anything that involved people. His professional achievements were many and remarkable, and more remarkable was how little they meant to him. Whatever the meaning of life may have been for Jack, one fact is certain—it didn't relate to success. The competitive world was another game he could play, and play better than most, but never did he mistake it for more than a game."

Orson Welles wrote an extremely long and moving letter of condolence out of which one short extract struck me as particularly pertinent:

"Nobody was ever better named. Like some character in one of the old comedies, 'Jack Goodman' pegged the man himself. 'John Goodman' would have been too Bunyanesque, too rustically dull. 'Jack' was the saving jigger of lemon juice: it suggests dash and a certain agility. 'Jack' sounds like the hero and sometimes victim of picaresque adventures, and our Jack was surely such a hero and such a victim. 'Goodman' needs no comment. There never was such a good man as Jack. . . . We know that he was almost puritanically godless. Yet if there is no heaven, it will surely be necessary to invent one for Jack."

Jack Goodman and Albert Leventhal both died much too young and something of my own existence, like that of many others, lost luster when they were gone. In my opinion no one ever expressed the emotion a bereaved person feels about such people so movingly as Edna St. Vincent Millay did in her passionate protest, "Dirge Without Music":

I am not resigned to the shutting away of loving hearts in the hard
   ground.
So it is, and so it will be, for so it has been, time out of mind:
Into the darkness they go, the wise and the lovely. Crowned
With lilies and laurels they go; but I am not resigned.

Lovers and thinkers, into the earth with you.
Be one with the dull, the indiscriminate dust.
A fragment of what you felt, of what you knew,
A formula, a phrase remains,—but the best is lost.

The answers quick and keen, the honest look, the laughter, the love—
They are gone. They are gone to feed the roses. Elegant and curled
Is the blossom. Fragrant is the blossom. I know. But I do not approve.
More precious was the light in your eyes than all the roses of the world.

Down, down, down into the darkness of the grave
Gently they go, the beautiful, the tender, the kind;
Quietly they go, the intelligent, the witty, the brave.
I know. But I do not approve. And I am not resigned.

# Across the Far Atlantic

# 12

ONE of the areas that have changed most significantly at Simon & Schuster in recent years is the way foreign rights are viewed and contracted for, and the relative importance given them. This is true in both directions— foreign books republished here, and Essandess books republished abroad—but the latter is a particularly marked change, in fact a complete turnabout.

For the first fifty years of the firm's existence, at least one extensive annual prowl of London and the Continent by one of the editorial bigwigs was a vital part of building each year's list. In the earlier years Max Schuster and Dick Simon took turns at it and unearthed such authors as John Cowper Powys, Bertrand Russell, Isaiah Berlin, Arthur Schnitzler, Franz Werfel, Hans Fallada, Felix Salten, the Aga Kahn, Bernard Berenson, and Nikos Kazantzakis. When Jack Goodman became editor-in-chief, he had no inclination to make such extensive treasure hunts, preferring to concentrate on West Coast authors and Hollywood. Since I had been manager of subsidiary rights, including foreign rights, I knew all the overseas publishers and literary agents well. Being a romantic Anglophile, I took on the yearly three-or-four week expedition and continued to do so for twenty years. Toward the end of my stint Bob Gottlieb did it as well, and following him Michael Korda, but today there is such an abundance of American authors and properties that the emphasis upon acquiring foreign books has lessened. Michael and Alice Mayhew continue to explore overseas territory from time to time, but not as intensively as the Essandess representative once did.

One of the books I found in London which brought me great pleasure—and Simon and Schuster even greater profits—was one I couldn't read at all, because it was in German. Visiting Allen and Unwin one day, I happened upon a volume whose appeal seemed self-evident even if one couldn't read a word of it. On each left-hand page was a clear, detailed, two-color drawing of a commonplace but important object—a refrigerator or a ballpoint pen, for example. On the facing right-hand page was what I presumed was an explanation of how it operated. This, according to Allen and Unwin, was to be entitled *An Illustrated Universal Encyclopedia of Technology*. I bought the American rights and before I ever got back to New York had retitled the book *The Way Things Work*. That book sold almost three-quarters of a million copies in the United States in an expensive trade edition, and that many again through book clubs. This led not only to a second volume that also did very well, but also to several off-shoots about "the way this-or-that works." In England, where my British friends had unearthed the book from Germany, they stuck with the off-putting long title the Germans had used. The British sales were quite good—in the tens of thousands—but that book's publication is not a high-water mark in Allen and Unwin's sales history, while *The Way Things Work* definitely is in Essandess's. Perhaps the reason was that we were able to market our edition more effectively, but I like to think the change of title had a lot to do with it.

There is a reverse story that took place many years before. Ernest Sutherland Bates wrote a book for Simon and Schuster, for which he and Max Schuster agreed upon the title *A Friend of Jesus*. Not bad. But the British publisher who brought out the book the following year thought of a better one, *The Gospel According to Judas*, and his sales were four times better than S and S's. Once again, was it the juicier title that achieved the result? Like so many things in book publishing that can't be proved, I don't know, but I strongly suspect it did.

One of my oldest and best friends in London publishing is Max Reinhardt, owner of the Bodley Head. Max had long been an intimate of Charlie Chaplin and for years had been trying to entice an autobiography out of him. I happened to be on the ground just when Charlie and Oona had finally decided to cooperate; with S and S to escalate Bodley Head's offer, Reinhardt and I jointly secured the book for our respective markets. Chaplin's book, entitled *My Autobiography* (despite semantic protests from us that "My" was redundant when tied to "Autobiography," Charlie insisted upon that title), was a very considerable success and a full selection of the Book-of-the-Month Club. It wasn't as successful as it might have been had the second half of it been as good as the first. The early part was splendid, portraying Chaplin's youth in the East End of London and his first success with much of the feeling and drama of a Charles Dickens novel, but the latter portion, about his major triumphs in Hollywood, was largely name-dropping and was too evasive about his troubles with the United States government over his supposed Communist sympathies. Nevertheless, until Justin Kaplan finishes his current project, the eagerly awaited biography of Chaplin, *My Autobiography* remains the most authoritative record of one of this century's geniuses.

Nubar Gulbenkian, the son and heir of the legendary Mr. Five Percent (because that was his personal share of all Middle East oil production!), was a genial man with a fresh orchid in his buttonhole every day, the sexual mores of a Turkish pasha, the impeccable manners of an Oxford gentleman, and more money than almost anyone else. He wrote an elegantly self-mocking and vastly entertaining autobiography, for which I coined another good title, *Portrait in Oil*, but despite favorable reviews the book made out only moderately well. However, I must recall Gulbenkian for one anecdote. He was asked at the perpetual London residence he maintained at the Ritz Hotel why he had commissioned his special automobile to be constructed with a Rolls Royce engine, but encased in the unbeautiful body of a London taxicab. He replied, "Well, everyone knows that the Rolls Royce is the world's best engine, and I understand that in the narrow London streets the taxicab chassis can turn on a sixpence—whatever a sixpence is!"

I had the piece of luck that every editor is likely to experience if he is around long enough when, in 1972, I was in London just when Bobby Fischer was about to play Boris Spassky for the world's chess championship. An English chess publication had assigned a multilingual Yugoslav grandmaster chess player, Svetozar Gligoric, to cover the event, telephoning in his account every twenty-four hours to be transcribed and set into type immediately. Thus the British publisher would be able to produce a finished book within a couple of days after the final match. To get Simon and Schuster started, I placed an order for a very considerable number of copies to be airfreighted to New York in time to be in American bookstores a week after the end of the match. From then on we could print more books by offsetting the British edition, and in the excitement set off by Fischer's victory, S and S sold over a quarter of a million copies.

The venerable English humor magazine *Punch* had for many years issued an annual cartoon collection. Each book piled up respectable sales in Great Britain, but each time an American publisher had tried to issue an edition the results had been dismal. The cartoons were frequently very funny, often quite up to the standards of the *New Yorker*, but the books didn't work here. The problem seemed to me to be twofold. For one thing there simply were not enough cartoons of top caliber in a single year to justify a book collection; for another, many required amplification to explain them to American readers. Accordingly I persuaded the proprietors of *Punch* to desist from trying to put the annual over in the United States, and instead to allow me to take the accumulation of several years to New York and to turn them over to a pair of imaginative and experienced American humor anthologists, Marvin Rosenberg and William Cole. They were to retain only those cartoons that struck them as gems and also to write short accompanying texts when necessary, to connect British references to the American funnybone. They did a superb job, and in 1952, S and S issued *The Best Cartoons from Punch*. It was a smash hit in the Christmas season—not only in the bookstores but as a Book-of-the-Month Club dividend, as a Reader's Digest Book Club choice, and in syndicated features in magazines and newspapers. The owners of *Punch* were pleased as Punch at this remarkable flow of money after so many years of failure and agreed to continue the arrangement with S and S. Three years later Ron Williams, a Britisher who had lived and worked in the United States as a *Punch* publicity director for many years and knew American taste, assembled a much bigger historic volume, *A Century of Punch Cartoons*. Williams had cleverly divided the jokes into categories (business, husband-and-wife, animals, sports,) which solved the problem a chronological arrangement would have posed. A nineteenth-century cartoon with an involved four-line caption might have seemed riotous to Queen Victoria, but twentieth-century Americans would be likely to quote the queen and say, "We are not amused." So Williams's technique saw to it that really funny modern jokes every few pages leavened the intermittent old ones, which, though interesting and often charming, didn't really set Americans rolling in the aisles. *A Century of Punch Cartoons* became another extremely successful book for Simon and Schuster, and for several book clubs.

This happy relationship with *Punch* might have gone on indefinitely had not my old friend Malcolm Muggeridge become the new editor of *Punch*. Malcolm and I had been close, and I had earlier arranged a contract with him for his own book, so one would have thought that his editing *Punch* would have cemented the magazine's connection to S and S. It didn't turn out that way. Malcolm intended to redesign *Punch* and make it quite a different magazine, and he wanted to display his new direction as quickly and as boldly and as often as possible. And he wanted to do it in the United States, increasing *Punch*'s subscription list here. So he insisted that the annual collection be published here and offered it to me, but I continued to be as adamantly opposed to what I considered a hopeless proposition as I had always been. In the end S and S sadly bowed out. Another American publisher did take on the distribution of the annual and once again struck out; but turning out to be right was small consolation to me when stacked up against the loss of the *Punch* relationship. It also put the first strain on my association with Muggeridge. Things didn't get better when, some years later, he finally delivered his long-overdue manuscript to me. It was supposed to be his full autobiography but it turned out to be merely the first volume of three he intended to write. We were unhappy about the prospect of undertaking so huge and long-drawn-out a project, and Malcolm was unhappy about our reaction, so in the end our ways parted.

Some years later one of the most rewarding author relations Simon and Schuster had ever enjoyed was terminated for almost exactly similar reasons. The firm had been the proud publisher of William L. Shirer's *The Rise and Fall of the Third Reich*, and having Bill Shirer as an author for future books was an exciting prospect. Accordingly a contract was drawn for his autobiography, and nobody was too perturbed when he failed to meet delivery date; there was no time pressure about such a book, and these things happen. We were a little dismayed, though, when he finally did submit a full-length manuscript and it only took him up to the age of twenty-four, long before he became the internationally famous journalist he was to become. However, the book was very good and although S & S was never very keen about two-volume biographies with the second book not in sight, there wasn't much of an option but to go along

William L. Shirer

with the idea. Accordingly, *Twentieth Century Journey*, Volume I, was published in 1976, and it was understood that the second book that would complete Shirer's story would arrive one of these days. Instead he next showed up with a comparatively short manuscript about the year he spent in India with Gandhi. This was to have been a small part of the second volume and it certainly couldn't be termed Volume II in itself. The matter was discussed and it was agreed to publish *Gandhi: A Memoir* as a separate book, and once again to sit back and wait for the completion of *Twentieth Century Journey*. So far, so good. But real trouble arose when Bill eventually delivered his next manuscript. This took his life on another four years, during most of which he was out of work, and it ended not only before World War II but even before the Spanish Civil War! Shirer, it now appeared, had at least a third volume in mind, and possibly a fourth. This was too much for S & S to stomach, and after an unhappy interval of discussion, S & S terminated its contract and was repaid the money it had advanced. Little, Brown has agreed to go ahead with the project; maybe it will be the right firm for Bill. I hope so, for all of us at S & S owe Shirer a debt for having given the firm one of the most distinguished books it ever published.

Possibly the best thing for Simon and Schuster that ever came out of my London trips was the bond I formed in the mid-1960s with a junior editor at Constable, a firm with which we had hardly ever done any business but which I visited every year, just in case. Young James Mitchell and I took to each other on first acquaintance, so when Mitchell had moved to the publishing house of Nelson, he offered me a book that he liked a lot. It was *Wine* by Hugh Johnson, a young but already well-known authority on wine and food. Johnson's book struck me as a highly civilized, unpretentious guide that might do nicely in the United States despite the fact that wine-drinking wasn't all that popular here fifteen years ago. The book was an elegant production job—embodying color photographs, line drawings, and vintage charts—so the safe and economical thing to do was merely to import 10,000 copies of the Nelson edition for our own use and see what happened. Mitchell gladly agreed, but *Wine* turned out to be so successful that almost immediately after those 10,000 copies arrived and went out to the stores, Essandess was flooded with more orders and went on press itself. Bookstore sales have now mounted into six figures, the Literary Guild has enjoyed a very healthy sale of the book to its membership, but all that was merely the curtain-riser for what happened in later years in the relationship between James Mitchell, Hugh Johnson, and Simon and Schuster.

Mitchell, whose talents lay in editing and sales promotion, was a close friend of another young man at Nelson, a genius—and I use that word without reservation—in production, design, and art named John Beazley. Both men were ambitious and chafed under what they considered the rather stuffy, conservative approach that Nelson, largely a publisher of Bibles, brought to book publishing. Accordingly they scraped together enough money to set up shop of their own as the firm of Mitchell-Beazley Ltd., and James Mitchell's prize acquisition, Hugh Johnson, decided to go along with them. The three men embarked upon a fantastically ambitious project, especially for a new firm, a sumptuous oversize atlas with full-color pictures and maps of every great wine area in the world, accompanied by Johnson's penetrating text concerning the features of each vineyard along with reproductions of the vintner's labels. Such a project had no hope of getting off the ground except with a world consortium of publishers willing to commit for their respective shares of the huge first printing of the extensive color pages that would be required to keep costs within practical bounds. Mitchell managed to assemble such a consortium, starting out with Simon and Schuster. It was a huge gamble, but even then it was evident that Mitchell and Beazley were something special in the way of inspired packagers of beautiful and complicated books, and Essandess made its extremely large commitment without undue qualms. *The World Atlas of Wine* became the classic guide and has been termed by most authorities all over the globe as the wine book of the century, a landmark in the literature of wine and spirits, and the standard reference book for both amateurs and connoisseurs. In its original 1971 edition and in later revised and updated ones, the book has sold close to three-quarters of a million copies in nine languages—and at a retail price comparable to a bottle of vintage Château Lafite-Rothschild.

Even this triumph was only the first act of what then developed between Mitchell-Beazley and S and S. In those early years of the fledgling British publisher's existence, we were clearly and justifiably its American favorite and received first consideration on any project planned. Hugh Johnson, a man of many parts, was as passionately interested in, and informed about, matters horticultural as viticultural, and a lovely M-B book came out of that, *The International Book of Trees*, along with some lavish but at the same time instructive books on the art of color photography by John Hedgecoe. The almost exclusive monopoly that S and S enjoyed on American rights for M-B books seemed rather unshakable until two things happened that certainly didn't destroy the bond but did precipitate some loosening of it.

One year James Mitchell tried to persuade Essandess that it would be a good idea if his firm's ten-volume set entitled *The Joy of Knowledge* were abridged, Americanized, and issued in the United States as a mammoth one-volume encyclopedia. It was a staggering proposal involving many hundreds of illustrations and a probable retail price close to $100 per volume, and to get it off the ground would require more money than S & S was then prepared to risk on a single book. So the firm regretfully declined the opportunity. Random House, to whom it was shown next, said a loud "Yes!" The book was duly published some time later as *The Random House Encyclopedia* and it did well, but whether or not it did well enough to return the enormous investment and make a profit is something known only to Random House accountants and their God. In any event that house's enthusiasm and backing of the project naturally impressed Mitchell-Beazley, and S & S had to move over to make room for a competitive M-B favorite. In addition, a third important American publisher, Crown, had come into the picture, both because its list featured gift books and because its chairman, Nat Wartels, was willing to take a chance that his firm wouldn't get into trouble if he published *The Joy of Sex*. That book was a real departure for Mitchell-Beazley and one that had daunted the S & S attorneys when it was initially offered to us. Crown made an immense bestseller of *The Joy of Sex* in hardback. Simon & Schuster made it even greater one later, when it bought trade paperback rights from Crown for many times what it would have paid for all American rights if it had had the nerve originally. But S & S waited until Wartels had tested the waters and proven that a publisher of the book would neither drown in those waters or end up in jail. It turned out that the hefty price Essandess paid for trade paperback rights was academic, because the edition has sold upwards of 8 million copies and was not only the Number One bestseller in the country among trade paperbacks for a very long time, but has set a record of having been in the first ten on that list for just about a full decade. Other collateral joy-of-sex books from Mitchell/Beazley have also fared extremely well on the S & S trade paperback list, but Crown was the publisher that took the original dare and that, as a result, established itself as another prime rival for further Mitchell-Beazley goodies.

Nevertheless, Simon & Schuster retains what it considers among the most desirable of current M-B creations, elegantly produced and handsome pocket guides to a great number of topics, ranging from adaptations of the two old favorites in *Hugh Johnson's Pocket Encyclopedia of Wine* and *John Hedgecoe's Pocket Guide to Practical Photography*, to guides on art museums, calories and nutrition, prescription and over-the-counter drugs, garden plants, antiques, aquarium fish, painting and drawing, gambling, Shakespeare's plays—you name it—and an entire line of travel books, each dealing with a tourist's dream city or region, prepared by American Express. These pocket guides add up to very Big Business and are handled for Essandess today by the house's publisher, Dan Green. The Mitchell-Beazley ramifications have gone a long way past that first meeting of mine in the Constable office with James Mitchell.

In the mid-1970s I stopped making the European trip. To be honest, and speaking specifically of my own emotions, it was a big job each year but it was also fun. Those passages of time, chiefly in London and Paris for me, were no vacation, and I worked much harder and more extensively in Bloomsbury and along the Left Bank than I ever did in New York, visiting publishers and agents and authors and going through piles of manuscripts each evening, but I wouldn't have missed the experience. Some day, if only for the benefit of my family, I may write in greater detail about such joys as soaking in the colossal bathtubs in Browns Hotel, playing tennis on the grass courts of Wimbledon and Queens with Sir William Collins, being a guest at the incredibly star-studded dinners of George Weidenfeld, going to theaters with André Deutsch, playing cricket at Lord's with Ian Harrap, pub-crawling with Ian Parsons and dining more formally with Victor Gollancz, picnicking (after tennis, of course) in Hampstead with Sir Stanley Unwin, and on one memorable occasion, being introduced to the unfamiliar game of snooker at the Savile Club by my friend Max Reinhardt, and holding my own with Alec Waugh and Alec Guinness. All of those except the last two were publishers but they, and their fellow publishers, were instrumental in my picking up something like a dozen British authors each year. From all standpoints—their quality, success, and sheer numbers—the books of British origin on which I secured American rights through the years probably constitute my chief editorial contribution to the company. Among those would be the aforementioned Charlie Chaplin, Ludovic Kennedy, Peter Fleming, Auberon Waugh, Margaret Forster, Adam Hall (Elleston Trevor's pseudonym for his "Quiller Memorandum" books), Christy Brown, Simon Raven, Lynne Reid Banks, Allan Prior, Claire Rayner, Angela Carter, George MacDonald Fraser, Nigel Calder, John Christopher, Anthony Glyn, Malcolm Muggeridge, and Hugh Johnson. London seemed to be fertile ground in those days, and some American publishers actually built the greater part of their lists in such prospecting.

However, as indicated at the outset of this chapter, in today's publishing climate at S & S, less emphasis is placed upon acquiring foreign books. The ones that are picked up in London or at the Frankfurt Book Fair still constitute a reasonable portion of each Simon and Schuster list, but unless they have the potential to be bestsellers, they are likely to be passed by. That is because commercial prospects unhappily but necessarily have become vital in taking on books, and most big commercial books come from authors on this side of the Atlantic. Conversely, that very fact leads into the change in operations these days in the selling of rights to foreign publishers of books of American origin. Once a comparatively minor aspect of the subsidiary rights department, infinitely less important than reprint or book-club rights, the foreign operation was usually delegated to the second or third in command in the department, and he or she used foreign-based agents to shop around and sell what they could. Often really major books commanded no more than an advance of a couple of hundred dollars "against royalties," but those royalities hardly ever seemed to be forthcoming, since a follow-up was not the strong point either of foreign agents or of Simon and Schuster. It all seemed rather piddling stuff, usually not worth the time and effort that would have to be expended upon it to do a better job.

The current, completely different, way of doing things depicts the changing face of publishing as much as any other area of the industry. With American bestselling books in such competitive demand among foreign publishers, that aspect of subsidiary rights has become a major part of original contract negotiations and subsequent efforts.

Historically, almost all big books have been handled for authors by literary agents, and invariably it was their practice to grant the American publisher no more than exclusive book rights in the territory traditionally considered his selling area, the United States, Canada (unless the author was British, in which case dickering might take place), and the Philippines. American book clubs and paperback reprint houses were book rights that would usually be granted, but even rights of sale to American periodicals, or "first serial" rights, were withheld by the agent for the benefit of the author. The idea was that any subsidiary right outside of the book format, or outside the American publisher's staked-out territory, was none of his business, and he wasn't entitled to any share of income that might emerge from a British or foreign-language sale, or a use in a magazine, or an adaptation for a motion picture, television show, or play. Those were the literary agent's business, even if he went at it as half-heartedly as the publisher was likely to do.

The result was that, in negotiating a contract with an American book publisher, the advance was predicated wholly upon what the author's earnings were likely to be be purely out of royalties from U.S. book sales, and it seemed reasonable that a publisher's risk on the advance should be no more than a decent portion of that potential. Therefore, with few exceptions, advances on books were quite modest.

What usually happened? The American publisher did either about what was expected, or better, or worse, paid the author what was coming, and turned his attention to the next book on the list. The traditional old-time agents who had automatically withheld exploitable subsidiary rights were not, by and large, exploiters or hustlers or auctioneers. They were generally pleasant but staid people who spent their working hours having lunch or shuffling papers on their desks.

Although there were some exceptions who did make very good or at least satisfactory deals for their authors in such subsidiary rights as foreign grants, most were likely to "retire" a property after a modest interval of no takers, and forget about it. They may have thought they were practicing their trade conscientiously, and this was true of publishers' subsidiary-rights people too, but not much killer instinct was brought to bear. Like the rest of the business of publishing, the handling of rights was what Fred Warburg had once termed "a gentleman's occupation."

For the past decade or so, the pendulum has swung completely the other way. When a big book comes along, agents demand huge advances for their clients, and get them by submitting manuscripts simultaneously to several publishers and auctioning them to the highest bidder. Publishers pay those sums and more often than not don't live to regret it. Big money is in the air, and the extraordinarily huge advance, which a few years ago would have seemed suicidally perilous, has on the whole turned out to be successful. At least it has at Simon & Schuster, and Richard Snyder must be accorded the credit for sensing early in the game how the world was changing, and taking full advantage of it. He was just about the first to realize that, in an ever-expanding climate of inflation, he could afford to pay what seemed to be extortionate advances if (a) he got *all* the rights, and (b) he had the sort of realistic and tough people to help get back a big part of such an advance by selling rights effectively. But what set up such a situation, and why did powerful agents relinquish their traditional opposition to granting certain subsidiary rights to a publisher?

It seems to me that seeds for it were planted a long time ago by two men, neither of whom was a conventional literary agent but both of whom handled some extremely important authors. The first was the legendary Hollywood movie agent, Irving ("Swifty") Lazar. His real business was the movies and, if he had an author or a book property, he often had no inclination to spend his time or his overhead on what he considered petty details, such as shopping a book's subsidiary rights. So Lazar sometimes played the negotiating game to get the biggest cash advance he could from a book publisher and, if he got it, was glad to give the publisher every right under the sun (except motion-picture rights, of course) and walk away from the operation.

Irving ("Swifty") Lazar

Paul Gitlin

Morton L. Janklow

The second was an excellent New York City lawyer, Paul Gitlin, who attracted more real authors to his firm than Lazar, since Swifty's clients were largely celebrities. Gitlin had the same basic feelings about not becoming involved with book-publishing details after he had consummated a contract for the sort of advance money he was seeking. He too let Simon and Schuster handle rights on books by a number of hugely popular authors—Harold Robbins, Cornelius Ryan, and Irving Wallace, to name just a few. In all these cases the author was credited with the lion's share of income received from the sale of rights, but the credits were applied to the outstanding advance to reduce the publisher's risk. So the precedents for what takes place today on a huge commercial book were established years ago, even though it wasn't then anticipated how far it would later extend. Today many major agents pursue the same trail and many major publishers are eager to pick up the scent. A power in the agency field has been Morton L. Janklow, another attorney who has made the shopping of literary properties a good thing, and a leader among publishers in grasping this sort of big investment opportunity has been S & S's president, Richard Snyder. Janklow is quite content to turn over to Essandess all the things the house is now set up to pursue to the hilt in foreign and other subsidiary rights. Snyder himself, Michael Korda, and Dan Green, top principals in the firm, all keep a keen eye on the selling of rights. The head of the sub-rights department, Susan Kamil, who oversees everything in a charming iron-fist-in-velvet-glove fashion, and the foreign-rights specialist, Marcella Berger, are so expert at the game that Essandess has virtually dispensed with using agents in foreign countries. They do a better job themselves.

Enough cases arose in which this nontraditional way of arranging matters worked out splendidly for all concerned that today, even highly successful and prestigious literary agents are going along. Ones who, in former years, wouldn't have dreamed of granting world rights to an American book publisher now do so if they can get the advance they're seeking and are convinced that the publisher has the push and mechanism to shop rights as well as or better than anyone else. S & S has gained this reputation, so the firm is included in the auctions on virtually every top-dollar-demand book that comes up, and has emerged the winner more frequently than would be likely for any one house. An outstanding example of how it has worked would be the novel *Lace*, a provocative, sexy story by Shirley Conran, who although a published author had never written any fiction before.

Mort Janklow was her agent, and the manuscript had such an atmosphere of sure-fire potential success about it that several publishing houses were violently interested, even though they knew it would cost substantial money. The upshot of intense bidding was that Essandess obtained the book for an advance of $750,000. Three-quarters of a million dollars for a first novel? What word would you use to describe that: absurd? catastrophic? insane? But this is what happened.

Built up effectively by S & S hype among foreign publishers, approximately twenty foreign rights were sold, ranging from a low of a $500 advance to a high of $200,000. The total came to just about $800,000; since most of it was credited to Ms. Conran's account, that meant that the S & S risk of $750,000 was wiped out by British and foreign-language rights alone! Also, before the first copy of *Lace* was ever printed, the *Ladies' Home Journal* purchased magazine rights and

Shirley Conran

the Literary Guild made it a book-club choice. That threw off a $100,000 profit for Essandess in publisher's share of such income. Also remember that in securing all rights, S & S had purchased the mass-market paperback reprint rights for its sister firm, Pocket Books, as well, with no further advance required for that operation! And while S & S had no participation in the two-part television movie released with fanfare by ABC in late February, that certainly was tremendous publicity for the Pocket Books edition of *Lace*, which hit the stands at the same time. This entire story is, as far as I know, just about the most spectacular example of a publisher's being forced to reach for the moon in negotiating for a book, and coming back smelling not of what the moon may be made of, cheese, but of roses.

Even more advance money was agreed to when Dick Snyder, after the great success Random House experienced in publishing Carl Sagan's nonfiction work, *Cosmos*, bought the world rights to Sagan's first (and still unwritten) novel. Scott Meredith, for decades an imaginative, unconventional literary agent, was among the first to appreciate the way the wind was blowing and to take advantage of it. He

got a $2 million advance from S & S for Sagan! Two *million* dollars—
and Sagan was a complete question mark as far as fiction was concerned! But a similar process followed, and even if the $2 million
wasn't completely wiped out, it was reduced to comfortable levels.
Foreign advances brought in over $600,000, and the Book-of-the-
Month Club has made a commitment to take the book, the size of
the advance to depend on how they decide to use it: if it turns out to
be a full selection the club's advance will be $500,000, out of which
the publisher will retain half. So the Carl Sagan risk on the advance
has been very substantially reduced, and even if nothing more is sold
before the book is published, paying $1 million or a bit more for both
hardback rights for S & S and subsequent paperback rights for
Pocket Books looks like a sound investment.

Scott Meredith has always been a maverick sort of literary agent,
never bound by past practices if he sensed something better, so it
might be expected that he'd be among the first to join the merry
gang in this sort of playing for high stakes. Yet more conservative
major agents like Georges Borchardt, a great favorite of the Authors
Guild and Authors League, which indicates whose side he is likely to
be on, have also been pursuing the same tactics when they had the
right sort of juicy package to offer, as Georges did on the Jane Fonda
exercise books. So have established giants such as the William Morris
Agency and International Creative Management (ICM). It's a new
ball game in this respect, and just about the most capable player in the
publishers' line-up is Richard Snyder.

Once, intending nothing more than a compliment, I told him he
was a marvelous gambler. He got quite indignant, maintaining that
he hated gamblers and never gambled, and that any time he authorized a bid that might have seemed excessive, he'd done his home-
work and had made quite sure he was acting professionally. Well, I
must admit that to date results bear him out, and I don't believe he's
ever gone haywire.

# The Phoenixes That Rose

# from the Ashes

# 13

I N the year or two just preceding 1960, Simon and Schuster suffered a series of almost concurrent body blows that might well have laid low a less vibrant firm. Between Dick Simon's illness, Jack Goodman's death, and Albert Leventhal's resignation, morale was low. Even on the purely business side of the company a major figure retired. That was Emil Staral, who for some years had been holding the reins as executive vice-president and treasurer in behalf of Leon Shimkin, because Leon's presence in Essandess affairs had become peripheral due to his primary concern with Pocket Books. Then, a decade later a similar tidal wave swept the quarterdeck of the good ship Essandess, and once again a new crew had to be mustered. Each story follows in turn.

Back in 1959 it was up to me, as the new chief operating officer of the trade-books division, to find replacements for Goodman, as editor-in-chief and advertising director, and for Leventhal, as sales-and-marketing boss. Shimkin had less of a problem in finding a successor for Staral: he had the highly capable and trustworthy Seymour Turk trained and ready to step into that post. I wasn't in that favorable a position, for this was an era when publishing people didn't jump from company to company easily: it was before the current craze for the game of musical chairs had become popular. Today Richard Snyder, faced with the sort of problem I had, would reach out into the field and hire proven top performers from elsewhere, but then S and S didn't have the big money to entice such people—and it had the tradition of promoting from within. That was my attitude too—after all it had happened to me—but whom should I pick?

S and S had several excellent editors on the staff, including the senior editor who, in view of his name, seemed the logical candidate for editor-in-chief—Henry Simon. But sensitive and talented editor that he was, Henry had never seemed to have the sort of fiber that would make him an effective leader. We did have a young man who, with only a few years' experience, was clearly an exceptional editor, Robert Gottlieb. With Max Schuster's approval I named him the new editor-in-chief.

In 1955, only four years earlier, the twenty-four-year-old Gottlieb, fresh from taking his postgraduate degree in England at Cambridge after an undergraduate career at Columbia, had walked into the Simon and Schuster offices looking for a job. He was shuttled routinely to the personnel manager, whose first reaction was wonderment about why this applicant, assuming that he had the money, didn't seem to have the inclination to buy and use a comb. But after a few minutes of interviewing, the personnel manager realized that he was venturing into deeper waters than he cared to enter and, being a perceptive man, did a comparatively rare thing. He phoned the editor-in-chief, Jack Goodman, and diffidently suggested that there was a young man in the reception room who might be worth seeing.

Jack's first session with Bob consisted in the main of a monologue by the latter about himself, and it lasted a lot longer than the few minutes that the personnel manager had asked Jack to give to it. Bob's memory is that it went on through the entire afternoon and ran to four or five hours. At the end of it Jack finally managed to get in a word or two. He said: "Go home and write me a letter telling me why you want to get into book publishing." Bob brooded about this on his way home and exploded in telling his wife about it. "What in heaven's name is Goodman telling me to do? The last time I had an idiot assignment like this was in the sixth grade when the teacher made us write a paper on 'What I did in my summer vacation'!"

However he did sit down at his typewriter, and when he came back to S and S the next day to deliver his letter, this is what Jack read: "Dear Mr. Goodman: The reason I want to get into book publishing is because it never occurred to me that I could work

Robert A. Gottlieb

anywhere else. Sincerely, Robert Gottlieb." He got the job as Good-man's editorial assistant on a six-month trial basis. The same week, a young woman named Phyllis Levy was hired to be Jack's secretary on the same terms. Those two, along with the already established Nina Bourne, Jack's advertising assistant, became "the Jags," a team name inspired by Jack's initials. They formed a trio so talented that it became a major force in an office already well staffed with expertise. On the day exactly six months after they had been hired on the trial basis, Bob and Phyllis walked into Jack's office and announced: "Our six months are up and we've come in to tell you that we've decided to stay."

Phyllis was also an extremely pretty and stylish young woman. I remember when the movie rights to Rona Jaffe's popular success, *The Best of Everything*, were sold to a major film company. Rona's novel was published by S and S and was set in a big publishing office not unlike ours, and the costume designer for the film visited us to see if he could pick up realistic ideas about how the more chic secre-taries dressed at work. The upshot was that in the movie the heroine, played by Hope Lange, wore an exact duplicate of a creation sported by Phyllis.

Phyllis Levy

During his thirteen-year stint at Essandess, Gottlieb revitalized the firm's fiction. He brought in quality authors to an extent that the house could boast a list comparable to that of established prestigious publishers of fiction. Other effective editors like Michael Korda and myself were regularly bringing in and editing good books too, but mainly nonfiction. (In the years since Gottlieb's departure, though, Michael has also turned into very nearly the most successful fiction editor in the profession.) Still, Bob had something special about him—and also, as happens to all of us who are around long enough, he was favored by Lady Luck. Two such cases were unusual enough to deserve recounting.

In the mid-1960s on a trip to London, Gottlieb was staying at the Ritz. As was his custom, he started out on his daily rounds along Piccadilly, and stopped in at Hatchard's book shop a block away to look at recent British publications. Bob has always liked great big blockbuster-length sagas when they are good, and one colossus, almost a thousand pages in length, caught his eye. It was called *A Horseman Riding By*, and was written by somebody named R. F. Delderfield, of whom Gottlieb had never heard, but it was published by the London firm of Hodder and Stoughton, which he was visiting later in the week. By the time he got to their offices, he had managed to read only a hundred pages of the book, but had enjoyed them. He was told that the literary agent David Higham handled the American rights and they were unsold. He immediately got in touch with Higham. David said he was delighted that Gottlieb liked what he had read but that every publisher in New York, including Simon and Schuster, had already turned the book down. It simply was much too long and couldn't be cut without losing much of its flavor. Was there any chance that Gottlieb would take it on, whole, if the conditions were most favorable? Higham said that the size of the advance, for example, could be almost minuscule if S and S would commit to publishing the book. Bob did some computations about what the costs would be to print such a volume and finally said that if Higham would accept a royalty rate that was so low as to make Bob blush at offering it, he'd take a chance. Higham agreed, and an extraordinary publishing phenomenon was launched. Not only did *A Horseman Riding By* become a top bestseller in the United States but, since then, Simon and Schuster has published more than fifteen other big Delderfield novels, most of which have had equal success and have been selections of major book clubs. (Ronnie Delderfield didn't write all those giant novels at the rate of one a year, which is about how quickly they came out here. Many of them had lain dormant on Higham's shelves for years after British publication, but the success of the first one or two in the United States built up a huge Delderfield fan club that took to its bosom every successive title that Simon and Schuster put out.) Gottlieb admits that he never even fantasized that *Horseman*, or any of the other very British Delderfield books, would fare particularly well in the American market—he simply liked what he had read. After Bob left S and S, Michael Korda took over the care and feeding of Ronnie Delderfield and his books and, in the end, he was the editor of many more of them than Bob ever was.

Then there was the time when Gottlieb was visiting his good English publishing friend, Tom Maschler of Jonathan Cape, Ltd., and learned that Cape was publishing a slim volume of almost-poetry by John Lennon, the star of the Beatles, entitled *In His Own Write*. Most people found the text pretty absurd but, of course, the Beatles were by far the hottest thing on the London pop-music scene, and Tom was absolutely certain that the book would be a big success. Well, Gottlieb was knowledgeable about pop music too, and he liked the Beatles, but he had become a little bored with them and he certainly wasn't wild about Lennon's book. He said he'd rather not have S and S take it on, but Tom kept insisting almost to the point of twisting his arm. Bob, just to stall, said he wanted to send the book back and let Max Schuster have a chance to consider it. That was done and, much to Bob's surprise, because Schuster usually was not very involved with projects that fell out of his range of interest, Max reacted—with extremely violent opposition. Bob, who had been quite prepared to go along with a routine negative response, in almost a knee-jerk reaction said all right to Maschler—but only with the small, half-hearted, non-risk-taking acceptance that he felt he could make on his own initiative, despite Max's dislike of the book. He agreed to have S and S import a few thousand copies of the Cape edition at a low price, but that was as far as he would go. Rather surprisingly, considering his own enthusiasm, Maschler went along with the beggarly suggestion, probably because he was bemused by Gottlieb's personality and because he felt the book would have its best chance to go further if published by Simon and Schuster.

And then, right after this quiet scene, Jonathan Cape published the Lennon book in England, and the instant clamor and demand for it was so great that the printing presses couldn't keep up. Any book that was achieving such extraordinary sales in Great Britain could not help but sell more than the meager number of copies that Gottlieb had ordered and were currently being shipped, but one or two copies already were in New York as a result of having been sent earlier for Schuster's consideration. Frantic overseas telephone conversations flooded the wires and it was decided that the production manager, Helen Barrow, should run off a separate first printing in the United States as quickly as possible by offsetting the available copies of the British edition. Helen once again produced a miracle; she whipped the printers so effectively that S and S had 50,000 copies out and in the stores well before the now pathetic few thousand copies from Cape arrived on the ship, and *In His Own Write* went on to sell even better in the United States than in England. Gottlieb, back in New York by publication day, inspired S and S to act the way it invariably did at such opportune times—advertisements, copies to reviewers and booksellers, publicity handouts—but it was clear that neither was anything needed to help sales, nor could anything stop the American public from buying the Lennon book, no matter what S and S did or did not do. After a while Bob said to us all: "This is like standing on a beach and saying to the waves, 'Now come in, now go out.' It's senseless. Let's quit and continue to enjoy it and turn our attention to things upon which we can have an effect." He was right: calling it a day on advertising and promotion had absolutely no effect upon the pyramiding sales, which mounted into the hundreds of thousands of copies before subsiding.

Although Robert Gottlieb is president of Knopf today, and surely bears many of the responsibilities and burdens that title implies, his real passion and sensibilities remain in the editor's chair. He believes strongly that it's the perceptive editor with taste who builds great lists and that, if he does, the commercial good results will follow. Bob feels that it's a mistake when a publisher's decision to take on a book or not is primarily determined by the book's potential in the marketplace. Admittedly that has to be a factor, but it shouldn't be the prime one. Although Gottlieb continues to have nostalgic affection for the old Essandess, and a healthy respect for its present operations, he thinks that too frequently the current firm predicates its choices upon whether a book will work out or not, regardless of its worth. Upon being told this, Richard Snyder made an immediate rebuttal to the effect that it was easy enough, and even laudable, for Gottlieb to hold this view, since he was really in effect Knopf's editor-in-chief, and that the other functions of a publisher or president, such as worrying about cash flow and inventory and warehousing problems, and perhaps dealing with labor unions, were handled for Knopf by Robert Bernstein, president of Random House, of which Knopf is a subsidiary. That is as far as any unscheduled debate has ever gone.

The other person who stepped into the breach at Essandess with triumphant results was Anthony M. Schulte. As far as I know, no one, except possibly his parents, ever called him anything but Tony, for despite his social background and Ivy League schooling, he was always quite definitely one of the boys. He and Bob Gottlieb and Nina Bourne formed the triumvirate that did the most to make Simon and Schuster continue ticking after Dick Simon and Albert

Anthony M. Schulte and sales manager Mac Albert, displaying one of the famous paperweights

Leventhal and Jack Goodman had left the scene. Bob was the consummate editor, Nina had the advertising touch that did something to console one for Jack's not being around any longer to write copy, and Tony stepped right into Albert's shoes and didn't find them too large. In his comparatively quiet and elegant way, Tony became another Albert, respected equally by his peers at S and S and by the book trade. When Bob Bernstein left S and S, first to market "Eloise" products for Kay Thompson and then to join Random House, he became Bennett Cerf's chief adviser about S and S talents that might be weaned away for Random House during this period of crisis for S and S. Bennett knew all about Bob Gottlieb and Nina Bourne, but he was pretty uninformed about Tony Schulte. He did know, though, that the three of them were firm in their determination that they would not move away from S and S except as a package. "Who's Tony Schulte?" Cerf is said to have inquired, and Bernstein's response was, "He's the one you will one day be happiest to have secured." Whether that turned out to be literally true or not, there is no doubt that Tony has been a prodigious figure both at

Michael V. Korda

Knopf and at Random House, executive vice-president of both firms and the best bet to be Bernstein's successor should Bob ever move on to more expansive fields. No one who ever worked with Schulte at S and S could have doubted that if the firm ever lost him, he would be hard to replace. Yet the firm did lose him in 1968, along with Gottlieb and Bourne, in a second cataclysm that rivaled the one a decade before, and new phoenixes had to arise quickly. For Bob not only had departed his critical post himself but had also taken along to Knopf with him an imposing batch of authors who were devoted to him, including Doris Lessing, Jessica Mitford, Charles Portis, Joseph Heller, Robert Crichton, Edna O'Brien, Bruce Jay Friedman, and Chaim Potok. The Simon and Schuster roster of authors who might be counted upon to produce noteworthy books in the future was cut nearly to the bone.

I was Essandess's publisher then, and while replacing Bob Gottlieb might be a monumental task, at least there was one candidate who, for ten years, had been proving himself a terrific editor, Michael Korda. There simply was no one else who could compare with him, so naming him to be the new editor-in-chief was inevitable. Finding a replacement for Tony Schulte was something else again, but there was a tremendously live wire named Richard Snyder who essentially had been working in sales for Pocket Books, but who had moonlighted at Simon and Schuster frequently, working on trade-book operations with Schulte and Gottlieb. I myself really had not seen him in action to any extent, but what Leon Shimkin said about his energy and imagination was extremely impressive, and of course I knew that Tony and Bob rated him highly. So Dick became my associate publisher. Almost instantly I became aware of his hot breath on the back of my neck insofar as my own job was concerned: Dick regularly dropped hints about the opportunities he was being offered to go elsewhere into big positions. Finally we came to an understanding. I told him, "Dick, I am fifty-eight and you're thirty-eight. I've earned the right to continue as publisher until I'm sixty and, overwhelmed as I am by what you've been doing and eager as I am to have Essandess keep you, I want to stay in that spot for the next couple of years. After that you will be only forty, a good age to become top dog. I'll step aside then and invent some prestigious-sounding title for myself that will look impressive, but I'll simply become an editor again and you will be the publisher and my boss. How about it?" We shook hands on it, and that is the way it worked out, to our mutual satisfaction.

Once he was in the driver's seat it was evident that Snyder had his own highly ambitious plans to change the entire face of a publishing company that he felt had been doing little more than coasting along cozily for years, with no driving force to make it expand and grow. He started to sweep the boards almost clear in all departments and install new people, and it was most marked in the editorial department, where lists are built. He had two proven veterans there on whom he relied, the effervescent Michael Korda and myself, but he now set about enticing away from other houses some of the best-known names in editorial ranks, and his batting average was spectacularly high. No matter that something like half of them didn't last too long and either were let go or quit, feeling—as one of the best of them, Henry Robbins, felt—that Snyder set up an adversary situation with both authors and his staff aides. The ones who stuck it out, who realized that having Dick's unusually generous support for those who wanted to be on his team more than counterbalanced a certain aura of frequent put-downs and subsequent concern, were an impressive lot. In a *New York Times* interview with Tony Schwartz, Snyder said: "I demand performance, and I have a low frustration level for people not using all their abilities. My job is to get people to maximize their talents. But I'm a motivator, not a destroyer. In the long run I think people learn more and get more enjoyment from their successes here than they would elsewhere."

The editorial board, a tool that Max Schuster instituted long ago, had been active for decades, but before Snyder it consisted merely of three or four people—the president, the editor-in-chief and another top editor, and an executive with some editorial taste but whose primary role on the board was to give an evaluation of a project's sales and subsidiary-rights potential. These days, depending upon who has recently resigned, been fired, or been hired, the composition of the S & S board is likely to be as many as nine members, but no more, and for good reason. That is about as large a group as can profitably and pleasantly chat about items on the agenda. Then, the board shouldn't be too big, because the distinction of being on it is about the only plum (apart from more money) that can induce an editor-in-chief of another firm to quit his or her established eminence and join S & S without a major title: at least he or she will be recognized as a Chief rather than just an editorial Indian. Finally, and possibly the most practical reason of all, the handsome executive dining room table, at which the Thursday editorial-board meetings are held, can accommodate only nine persons, and even they have to tuck in their elbows while trying to wrestle with their servings of Cornish hen.

In one of his book-publishing articles in the *New York Times* in late 1982, Edwin McDowell wrote about "The Heavy Hitters at Simon & Schuster," likening the editorial-board lineup to the old "Murderers' Row" of the New York Yankees baseball team of the 1920s. That was a term that readers unsophisticated about baseball might have thought opprobrious, but it was, in fact, highly complimentary. The original "Murderers' Row" appelation was bestowed upon the frighteningly powerful Yankee batters who came up to the plate to hit, one after another, and who reached their awesome peak with the 1927 team, generally regarded as the best baseball team of all time. McDowell pointed out that every member of the S & S board had once been or still was the president or publisher or the editor-in-chief either at S & S itself or at another house, with one exception, Alice Mayhew. She had had the title "only" of senior editor at her previous distinguished firm, but had enjoyed a terrific reputation there—one which has been considerably magnified during her tenure at Simon and Schuster.

Why should any editorial board benefit from having so many members? Surely no more than a couple used to be necessary—such as Horace Liveright talking over a potential acquisition with Albert and Charles Boni, or Alfred Knopf doing so with his wife, Blanche, or Dick Simon with Max Schuster. Aren't too many cooks likely to spoil the broth? The answer is that this is an era embracing a wider variety of topics than ever existed before, including fads. Even editors who are the best and most experienced on more or less important world topics are not going to be experts on everything, when viable submissions come along that can range from dog and cat training, through exotic diets and fitness programs, the mystic and occult, to the unproven sexual exploits of rock-music stars; covering the whole universe of possible projects is more than a couple of minds are likely to be able to do with any confidence. That's where such a variety of individual backgrounds and expertise can be invaluable, even if the imposing dominance of the board by Richard Snyder does usually result in Snyder's calling the important shots.

One former S & S editor, before that a power in another publishing house, says he left because he felt as if he were just about the highest-paid first reader of manuscripts ever, and no more than that. He had been enticed away from his previous job by Snyder's tremendously generous salary offer plus the unmatched success that S & S books were enjoying during otherwise troubled times in the business. But he found that whenever he, or some board member, proposed that the firm sign up a book, there really was little discussion. Everybody looked nervously at Dick to sense his reaction, and usually there was little problem in interpreting his concurrence or obvious boredom by any number of small ploys he used to convey how he felt. If he was keen on or even intrigued by a proposal, you could sense it at once. Otherwise he might turn aside and order something from the waiter, or pick up the intercom phone and tell his secretary to remember to do something that afternoon, or perhaps turn a polite but clearly fishy eye at the person making the proposal. No one was inclined to pursue a game which he or she was bound to lose, so, on the whole, the die was cast quickly on most matters. It was as simple as "Dick likes it" or "Dick doesn't like it," and the message came through loud and clear.

Snyder's uncontested sway as the absolute power at S & S extended to all spheres in the office, well beyond the editorial one. Quite early in his tenure, he and the sales director, Al Reuben, arrived at the office at the same time one morning and stepped into the elevator at the ground floor together. They were alone there and Al punched the button for his floor, 10, while Snyder did the same for 14, his floor. The elevator ascended, went blithely by 10 without pausing, and came to rest at 14. Dick stepped out, turned and gave Al a sly smile, and said: "Even the elevator knows!"

Eventually Richard Snyder became so much of a one-man show that he simply had to delegate a considerable area of important responsibility for operations to somebody else, and keep as much out of his hair as his temperament would allow. He was always involved in everything from editorial and contract decisions, through production problems and expenses and jacket-art approval on every book, to office and personnel operations, while constantly having to be on tap for whatever world-shaking demands Gulf & Western might make on him, and a twenty-four-hour day wasn't long enough. So he chose Dan Green, longtime publicity director, to be S & S's new publisher, and Dan, just about the hardest-working executive I've ever seen, has more than shown his ability to cope with the tough challenge of satisfying Snyder.

Dick has claimed that he has achieved what he wanted out of life, but he is so lively and ambitious a man that he will probably never be content to rest upon his considerable laurels. He's a man whose accomplishments have to be respected by everyone familiar with them, but not a man who is adored by everyone. To his credit, he couldn't care less. He has always maintained that being an effective book publisher does not involve one in a popularity contest, and that whatever achieves the most and the best for his company, his employees, and himself is what matters. Snyder does not take too kindly to being crossed by anyone, whether it be in a real or comparatively unimportant difference of opinion. It is lucky for the firm that he is so often right in his viewpoints, because he's in the unique position of being able to get his way uncontested. That never happened before. Simon and Schuster and Shimkin all had to wrestle things to the mat as equal partners when they were all alive, and even when Leon Shimkin acquired sole ownership he relied much more on his top executives and his attorney than Snyder is inclined to do. Michael Korda and Dan Green are the closest to being peers with whom he works in conjunction, but he has no true equals or boss to whom he must answer. Of course Gulf & Western is his boss, but the conglomerate is interested only in results, which happily so far have been splendid, and doesn't interfere with day-to-day publishing. A good example of this took place when S & S published a widely acclaimed and very successful book about international corporations and conglomerates, *Global Reach*, by Richard J. Barnet and Ronald E. Muller. There were sections in that book that were critical of Gulf & Western, but none of the conglomerate's officials ever even thought about discussing the situation, let alone considering pressure from above to influence the authors or the publication. In fact it was months later that Dick, in casual conversation, learned that the G & W people had been unhappy about the book. Another example was when, some time after Seymour Hersh, the Pulitzer Prize journalist, wrote a series of articles in the *New York Times* blasting the actions of certain international corporations, including Gulf & Western, he was signed to a contract to write a book for Summit Books, an S & S subsidiary. No protest was ever aired by the people in the tower on Columbus Circle.

So Dick Snyder gets his way. It is true that he is reasonable and courteous enough to listen attentively to dissents, and I have frequently seen him concede matters when he actually disagrees with a strong opinion voiced by someone he respects, or go along with a majority feeling even if he senses the feeling isn't too sound, but invariably that happens with considerations he actually doesn't feel to be critical.

The person who has the best perspective about Snyder, or at least the most informed one, is editor-in-chief Michael Korda. Although Michael is the same age as Dick and in seniority in the firm tops him by only a couple of years, his background in the trade-books operation at S & S qualifies him as an old-timer as well as a powerful current figure. Michael came aboard twenty-five years ago as Henry

Simon's editorial assistant, and soon afterward became the secretary of the then-small editorial board. That means that he had full perspective about the people who ran the show in following decades: Max Schuster, Leon Shimkin, myself, Bob Gottlieb, Tony Schulte. He was party to the fun-and-games era, whereas Snyder's entry from Pocket Books into trade-book publishing didn't begin until the middle-to-late 1960s, by which time the epoch of wonderful nonsense was fading. Once Snyder really took charge, along about 1970, in Korda's words he took a static company and turned it into an exciting live-wire one. Still quoting Michael, Dick grew immensely and rapidly in an environment somewhat hostile to change and growth and, incidentally, filled with many people hostile to him personally.

It may well be true that back in the earlier days even Michael himself had some qualms about Dick. I don't claim that presumption is true, but it would have been strange if Korda, a man bathed in traditional values in upbringing, education, and years of what seemed to be interesting and viable publishing, hadn't initially reacted negatively to Snyder's revolutionary strong-arm and often abrasive running of the firm. Back then, which is a dozen or fifteen years ago, the general feeling was that while you had to concede that Snyder was an effective and hard-working leader, who certainly produced results, you wouldn't want to be shipwrecked on a desert island with him. Yet even then there was one thing about Dick that has always been true. He had standards and values and integrity about business, and although he pursued his affairs with tough zeal, his word was his bond.

Korda is a man of varied talents and one who could be a success in any number of fields. As an author he has proven what he can do, with two national bestsellers to his credit, *Power* and *Success*, both books taken as literal how-to-succeed guides by ambitious readers who might have been unaware that the calculated advice to the aspiring was written by the sophisticated Korda with his tongue held well back in his cheek. Then he wrote his serious and quite stunning biography of the Korda family, *Charmed Lives*, which was a full Book-of-the-Month Club selection, and an extremely interesting and successful novel on top of that, *Worldly Goods*. Michael is a marvelous mime and extemporaneous speaker who could well have thrived in the theater or in motion pictures had he followed the family tradition. A scholar, with an extensive knowledge of history, multilingual, he even might have been a professor had it suited his temperament, which it didn't. In his chosen career of book publishing he logically could have been content to become a prestigious editor with a focus upon nothing but serious books, but that sort of ivory-tower career didn't appeal either to Michael, who has always had a great affection for working with the good storyteller. So his temperament was perfectly primed and ready to be released to the full when Snyder, a boss whose ideas appealed to Korda, took over. Korda's comfortable fire was kindled into a blaze.

Michael was the first person, I believe, who completely understood what Snyder was trying to do, and appreciated how well he did it. With the passage of years he and Dick have become solidly bonded together, both as publishing associates and as friends. They are of like minds about the book business as a business, and whether a venture turns out to be right or wrong, they invariably act in concert. Yet Snyder, despite equal reciprocal admiration for Korda, plus a solid personal friendship, continued to be realistically tough some time ago when he decided he needed a publisher for the trade division. Since Korda was most valuable as editor-in-chief, Dick named Dan Green the publisher. That caused a lot of speculation about how Michael might react, but the answer was soon apparent. He couldn't have cared less. He might well have been good at the publisher's job, but he found being editor-in-chief a great deal more interesting and rewarding.

Korda is a born pitchman whose presentations at sales conferences have invariably been the highlights. Joni Evans described them this way: "He never prepares anything, but he'll stand up before a hundred or so people, with twenty-five books to present, and summarize the essence of every single one, remembering every last character, dramatizing the whole thing and probably writing half the books himself before they're written while he's talking. He's the only editor who consistently gets enthusiastic applause each time he's done."

Completely true, Joni, and Michael's presentations have unquestionably pyramided advance sales when he had one of his substantial authors to talk about, a Graham Greene or a Joan Didion or a Harold Robbins. He will describe a new Robbins novel so engagingly and so

Mike Korda in action at a sales conference

dramatically that the later actual reading of the book is likely to be an
anticlimax. The small backlash may come when he is equally persuasive about a book that is neither as good nor as potentially commercial and oversells it, but at least he keeps the salesmen awake.

One reason why Michael and Dick Snyder work as a team so well
is that they enjoy a solid friendship quite apart from their office
relationship. Along with their wives they took a three-week safari to
Africa in early 1983 and, I am told, not one single word was ever
spoken among the four of them about Simon & Schuster or the
world of publishing. That seems scarcely credible: it's hard to think it
could have happened with any of their predecessors, who so completely married their working lives with their leisure ones, but perhaps it bespeaks a new kind of professionalism. There is a time and
place for some things and different ones for others, and when the
time is ripe for thinking about publishing, no distraction for fun and
games is in order.

There is one person, however, in the Simon & Schuster framework who occasionally does find time to conceive satirical jests that
are quite in the tradition of the historic Barney Greengrass satire.

That is advertising director Strome Lamon, who claims he does them on the commuting train from Westport because the *Times* crossword puzzle doesn't present enough of a challenge to last the trip to New York. Among other advertising parodies that Strome has turned out in recent years, purely for the amusement of the staff and happily for the targets themselves, were two gems, one lampooning Richard Snyder and the other Michael Korda. (Both men have framed copies of their respective tributes on their office walls.) Each requires a small explanation.

Dick Snyder's was written for his twentieth anniversary with the firm, at a time when Simon & Schuster had just had eight books listed on the *New York Times* bestseller lists at the same time, including one or two at or nearly at the very top. Michael Korda's was written shortly after Michael, an ardent sportsman and a defender of the right to bear arms, had written a real advertisement for the National Rifle Association of America that appeared in a major magazine. On each occasion the irrepressible Lamon sharpened a pencil with his scalpel and went to work, with the results you will see on the following spread pages.

Roger Straus, Jr., hails
the author as

# "A legend in his own mind!"

Not since Xaviera Hollander has there been so
passionate a story of business success. There are
wonderful scenes in this book—and we mean <u>scenes</u>.
We meet some of the great names in publishing history
—briefly—and learn the philosophy that has made Snyder's
name a household word: "You can fool some of the
people some of the time, and that's good enough for me."

"Eight. *Eight?* EIGHT??!!
With a decent sales force,
it could have been nine.
<u>Nine.</u> NINE!!!"

RICHARD E. SNYDER

My Twenty Years
at Simon & Schuster

TOMORROW, THE WORLD

**"This book will be
remembered after
War and Peace is
forgotten. But not
until."** —Bob Gottlieb

**"Yeah, but can he play
first base?"** —Nelson Doubleday

**"It may not be literary,
but then 'literary' is a
dirty word at Simon
and Schuster."**
—Helen Dudar, Dudar, Dudar Day, New York Magazine

**And Gay Talese says:
"Who thought one man
could give sex a bad name?"**

- Soon to be a major motion picture from Paramount,
  starring the late Sal Mineo.
- To be a quality paperback from Touchstone.
- To be a semi-quality paperback from Cornerstone.
- To be published as Silhouette Romance #69.
- Sold to Pocket Books for six figures—$1,248.96.
- A Main Selection of the Science Fiction Book Club.

**Simon and Schuster**

(© 1984 Helen Marcus)

A NATIONAL RIFLE ASSOCIATION OF AMERICA
EDITORIAL BY MICHAEL V. KORDA

# "If God hadn't meant us to have guns, why did he give us plaid caps with ear flaps?

Guns don't kill people. Bullets kill people. It's the bullets you've got to watch out for. As soldiers in both World Wars have testified, nothing stops a bullet like a Bible. All law enforcement officers should be required to wear Bible vests and—yes—Bible belts.

To the charge that guns are not safe: Nonsense! Remember those pre-gun lines:

I shot an arrow into the air,
It fell to earth, I knew not where.

Knew not where? In a crowded playground, perhaps. Or on a hospital. With a gun, you know. Right in some commie, rapist's, flag-burning heart.

And remember, while a ready smile will get you many of the things you want, a ready smile and a .38 will get them faster. With a .38 in your pocket, you are dressed for success.

Guns belong! As Ernest Hemingway said: "When I reach for my gun, I hear the word culture." Guns are part of the good times people have in, say, Beer & Pistol Clubs: 'Drink till two and piss ti'l four.' (A little NRA humor there).

And it is guns that separate us from the animals. By about 200 yards with a decent peep sight. As the Bible says, "I will lift up" —not give up, mind you—"mine arms to the Lord." Think of that, and of the Golden Rule: "Do unto others before they get you," and you can't go far wrong.

## DON'T JUST TALK ABOUT YOUR RIGHT TO BEAR ARMS. PUT YOUR GUN WHERE YOUR MOUTH IS.

# Big Fish That Got Away—

## and Some Faithful

## Galley Slaves

# 14

O
NE of Max Schuster's many aphorisms, when something went wrong, was to issue a plaintive instruction,
"File under 'Grief.' " Over the years plenty of grief occurred, but perhaps the most painful episodes were
when, as happens to fishermen, the Big Authors got away. It's bad
enough to lose a prized employee, but that always did happen to
some extent and these days it happens so regularly that it's hardly
worthy of comment.* However, when a publisher either loses a pet
author, or fails to get one when he or she appears to be hooked, it is
much worse. Let's cast a rueful look backward at some cases.

Maria Leiper, very possibly the best woman editor in book publishing at a time when women editors had rough going trying to
achieve equal recognition with their male counterparts, brought two
brilliant authors to Simon and Schuster in the early 1940s. The first

---

*Hanging on a wall in my apartment is a huge, framed caricature of me, playing tennis,
with the tennis net being composed of a row of the most important books I ever edited for
S & S and, since it was presented to me on my thirty-fifth anniversary with the firm, bearing
the inscription: "35 Years and Still Swinging!" approximately one hundred fifty staff members
signed it. That was in 1980. Now, four years later, I have made a count of how many still are
with the company: thirty-eight. Admittedly the carnage occurred most heavily among people
lower than executive rank, but there were a number of brass hats who have departed too.

Maria Leiper (*right*) and unidentified friend

was Rachel Carson, whose lovely book, *Under the Sea Wind*, came out in 1941. It was successful, but not so outstandingly so that, some months after publication, the unsold copies were disposed of on the remainder market, and neither Miss Carson nor Maria was informed about it. Remaindering books was and is a justifiable and accepted practice, but it's inexcusable not to give an author notice and a chance to buy his or her book at the same low price the remainder house pays. Anyhow, Rachel Carson found it inexcusable and, despite her affection for Maria and splendid working relationship with her, went off in a rage and wrote her wildly successful future books, *The Sea around Us* and *Silent Spring*, for other publishers.

The other outstanding author was Mary McCarthy; *The Company She Keeps*, a collection of her short stories that included "The Man in the Brooks Brothers Shirt," was a smash hit. It was so much so that RKO bought the rights merely so they could use the book's title for a film. As Maria remembers it, S and S, by the terms of a contract not unusual back then, had 25 percent of any movie income, and insisted upon the author's sticking to the agreement and giving the firm its share. Now in today's firm climate of adamant insistence upon legal rights, this may not appear anything other than normal—certainly not villainous—nor was it, really. However, back then, when book publishing was a more friendly sort of thing, a clause in a contract which, with hindsight, seemed possibly unreasonable or unpalatable, was often changed or even waived. Miss McCarthy apparently felt that this was a case where it damned well should have been. It was a title she had coined herself, and the mere title, not the book, was all the movie company wanted. Regardless of the rights or wrongs of the affair, according to Maria Leiper, Mary McCarthy separated from Essandess in high dudgeon, and subsequently went on to write other splendid and profitable fiction for many years.

Mary McCarthy doesn't remember her divorce from S and S that way at all, not even that there was any problem about the sharing of movie money which, in any case, wasn't a tremendously significant sum. Here is how she recalls the event:

"In my memory, the reasons were more emotional than businesslike. Dick Simon, whom I thought was quite a nice man, rather more musical than literary, took my personal situation very much to heart, was greatly worried about my financial future, and frightened by what seemed to him my carefreeness or irresponsibility. I am not sure what the spark was that set all this off, but it may have been a new contract, covering several books, that he wanted me to sign after *The Company She Keeps*, and I suspect I behaved in an airy way, refusing to be pinned down. At that point, in his office or maybe over drinks or coffee in a bar, he shouted something like, 'I can't stand this! Go get yourself an agent!' Calming himself he recommended Bernice Baumgarten of Brandt and Brandt to me. I obeyed, and from then on I was her client. It seems to me that she felt, after hearing the background, that S & S weren't the right publishers for me and after some thought I went to Houghton Mifflin. . . . I do remember Maria Leiper, who was a charming person, good looking and nicely dressed and, unlike most of the others in the firm, truly literary."

In any event, whether Maria's memory or Mary McCarthy's is the more accurate, this gifted author was lost to S and S, but her subsequent relationship with Houghton Mifflin was even briefer, because the editor she knew there, and whose presence had attracted her to that firm, left. The book was shifted to Random House, which he had joined, and was published by that firm, but once again the editor departed to go elsewhere, so in 1949 Ms. McCarthy signed up with Harcourt Brace and has remained there.

The case of Charles Jackson's celebrated novel, *The Lost Weekend*, was a simpler one. The manuscript was submitted on an exclusive basis to Dick Simon by the agent he thought so well of, the same Bernice Baumgarten of Brandt and Brandt, but Dick didn't care for it enough to pass it along to his confrères for other opinions—he simply rejected it. *De gustibus non diputandum est*, and that was surely Dick's privilege, but Bernice didn't forget or forgive, and it was many, many years before another submission to Simon and Schuster came from her.

Another famous modern novel, Walter van Tilburg Clark's *Ox-Bow Incident*, was offered first to S and S by the agent Leland Hayward, but the firm saw more potential in the motion-picture rights than in book sales, and insisted upon some participation if they were to take on the project. Hayward, a major movie agent, absolutely refused to grant any participation at all, withdrew the submission, and next offered the book to Bennett Cerf at Random House. Bennett grabbed it without argument. Score one for Bennett Cerf.

Right after the end of World War II a small agent sent Henry Simon the manuscript of a light novel about advertising that so enchanted Jack Goodman, then the editor-in-chief, that he took it over from Henry, who was by no means as wildly enthusiastic about it as Jack. It was titled *Aurora Dawn* and written by an unknown author named Herman Wouk, and Jack really ran with it, advertising it heavily and promoting it all over town. It became a bestseller and the full selection of the Book-of-the-Month Club and Wouk became, as invariably happened to authors who were favorites of Jack, a man regularly wooed and entertained on weekends by him.

The following year Herman delivered another novel via his new, more major agent, Harold Matson. This was a delightful story rather along the lines of Booth Tarkington's beloved *Penrod* classic, entitled *City Boy*. It received very good reviews, did reasonably well, but wasn't any *Aurora Dawn*, either in Jack's affections or in commercial results. So Jack, beseiged by then with what he thought were bigger fish to fry, turned Herman Wouk over to Henry Simon for further tender, loving care.

Henry and Herman got on well enough, but then two things happened that eventually turned into a tale that Max Schuster would have annotated "File under 'Grief.' " The first was that Herman had

Herman Wouk

written a play, *The Traitor*, which was opening in New York; Henry, although given tickets in the orchestra next to the Wouks for the opening, for some reason didn't attend. That didn't rankle as much as what occurred a little later, when Herman described in great detail to Henry the plot of the new book on which he had embarked—all about a tyrannical naval officer named Queeg on a ship called the *Caine* and the mutiny and trial that ensued. Henry's reaction was as simple as it was infuriating: "It sounds very much like a novel we turned down last week!" Wouk didn't argue but just walked away from the embraces of Essandess and off to Doubleday, and Simon and Schuster never saw a word of the manuscript for *The Caine Mutiny* despite frenzied attempts of Dick Simon and Jack Goodman to repair the damage that Henry's spontaneous but foolish words had wreaked. It was a long time before the possibility of publishing Herman Wouk ever arose again and, when it did, once again it gave rise to unusual undercurrents.

When Harold Matson received the first few hundred pages of a long new Wouk novel called *The Winds of War*, he knew he had something very special to sell. However, Herman was going to take a long time completing the book, and Matson was afraid that the basic idea of weaving a compelling and juicy romantic story into the factual background of World War II was one that might be imitated, possibly quite quickly, by another author for an opportunistic publisher's list. He didn't want the word to get around, so he notified only three major publishers of the existence of the partial manuscript, and insisted upon certain ground rules if they wanted to consider the book. Fearing that with a conventional submission too many eyes would have the opportunity to see the manuscript and an unscrupulous person might have it photocopied to use as a basis for a competitive book, Matson decreed that one person only from each of the three firms, and he or she a principal figure in it, should visit Matson's office separately and read the manuscript there. That way, if any leak occurred, Matson would know pretty well where to look for it. As Essandess's publisher at that time, I elected myself to carry out this enticing chore for the house.

I spent a full day doing this and came back to the office to report to Leon Shimkin, now the sole owner of S and S and more than ever the keeper of the purse strings. Matson had set $1 million as the advance he was seeking, and that was a fantastic sum to pay for book rights in that era. However, I had been extremely impressed by the book and its commercial potential and I told Leon that I thought such a huge risk would indeed justify itself and pay off. I don't know whether Leon disagreed or if he just didn't have a full million dollars tucked away in a sugar bowl in his kitchen at that moment, but he resisted the idea of going that high. Leon was much more involved with the affairs of Pocket Books than he was with hardcover trade books, and in any case he thought that major results would be most likely to accrue from a mass-market Pocket Books paperback edition. So he decided to risk $500,000 on that and let hardcover rights go elsewhere, and he made the offer to Hal Matson, who accepted it. It was most unusual back then for paperback rights to be sold independently before hardcover ones, and for a trade-book publisher to take on a property without having its normal share of paperback income set an uncomfortable precedent, but that is what happened. The two other publishers in the act, Doubleday and Little, Brown, mulled things over and in the end Little, Brown bought the hardcover rights, paying another $500,000, so Matson and Wouk got their $1 million. For a while everybody (except Doubleday) was happy, but only for a while.

For later, when Wouk typed "The End" on the bottom of the final page of his opus, Pearl Harbor was the last historical event of World War II in the book. The entire background story had been about the years before the United States ever entered the war. Matson declared to the very disturbed people at Pocket Books and at Little, Brown that there would be a second volume a few years later that would embrace the rest of the World War II narrative, but that *The Winds of War* stood by itself. This was more unexpected than it was thrilling, and the real question before both houses was, What had they bought for all that money? Leon and I felt solidly that the book as described originally would cover the entire course of the war and certainly would include those years of greatest interest to Americans. The idea that the full story would now come in two volumes, years apart, was a blow, but it was acceptable as long as it was understood that Pocket Books had the rights to the second book as well, and no new contract was necessary. Matson said no—*The Winds of War* was a complete and satisfactory work in itself and the second Volume, *War and Remembrance*, would be another to be renegotiated and sold when the time came. Harold Matson was a fine agent and relations with him had always been very warm, but they suddenly cooled off considerably. The case never reached the stage of going to court, but a bevy of lawyers on both sides spent many hours arguing about it. In the end, because *The Winds of War* turned out to be so huge a success that both Little, Brown and Pocket Books were completely safe and home free on the sums they had paid, the argument became academic and Matson got his way. *War and Remembrance* could hardly help being a comparable success when it was published, so new contracts were drawn for the second book calling for the same sort of advance money, and there have been no regrets. The moral is that even the seemingly most disastrous of experiences can have a happy ending—sometimes.

Another author whose books were published originally by S and S with pleasant but modest success, and who subsequently moved to another house, Harper and Row, and wrote astonishing bestsellers that made Essandess quite rueful, was Shel Silverstein. Somehow, even though they seemed exactly the sort of publications that could benefit from the firm's usual knack of promoting and selling books of humor, his *Uncle Shelby's Zoo—Don't Bump the Glump, Uncle*

*Shelby's ABZ Book*, and *Now Here's My Plan* never made it in really big style. But once at Harper and Row, first with *The Giving Tree* and then with *A Light in the Attic* and *Where the Sidewalk Ends*, Silverstein became a national institution of sorts. *A Light in the Attic* was high on the bestseller list for a full year, dropped off for a while, and then came back to pile up the impressive total of almost seventy weeks on the list.

Then there was Ira Levin, whose stunning suspense novel, *A Kiss before Dying*, was published by S and S in 1953. However, his beloved editor, Lee Wright, switched chairs shortly thereafter and went over to head Random House's mystery line. Ira followed her and was published by Random House thereafter, and while *A Kiss before Dying* was highly admired and quite profitable for Essandess, *Rosemary's Baby* did a lot more for Random House.

Losing an author who then proceeds to write other books for other publishers that puts your performance to shame is embarrassing. But at least one has the consolation that they were different books and might well have been better ones. It is perhaps more distressing to publish a book you esteem, receive lukewarm reviews from the critics, give up and let the book go out of print when modest sales have come to a halt, and then see it reissued a quarter of a century later by another house and hailed as "a modern masterpiece." That happened with Christina Stead's *Man Who Loved Children*, published with little fanfare in 1940 by Simon and Schuster and brought out anew in 1965 by Holt, Reinhart, and Winston. That firm got Randall Jarrell, the late distinguished poet and literary critic, to write a preface in which he proclaimed that the novel was "as plainly good as *War and Peace* and *Crime and Punishment* and *Remembrance of Things Past* are plainly great." With those sorts of associations coming from so eminent a critic as Jarrell, perhaps other reviewers were swept along to join the nationwide acclaim the reissued book received. Regardless of the reasons, *The Man Who Loved Children* will be remembered as a jewel in Holt, Reinhart, and Winston's crown, not in S and S's.

On a less literary level but a more commercial one, Simon and Schuster had the inside track to get Polly Adler's *A House Is Not a Home*, the lively story of her experiences as the madam of her famous brothel. The timing was wrong. In another era Essandess would probably have snapped up that book, but it was submitted to Dick Simon, whose strong puritanical streak made the idea of publishing such a book completely unpalatable.

Finally, let us return again to Maria Leiper, the editor who may have had the hardest luck in losing, or not getting, top-level authors, through no fault of her own. It is said that as many as forty American publishers had the opportunity to sign up *Lolita*, by Vladimir Nabokov, and thought it too racy, before Putnam's finally decided to take a chance on it; Maria was not only among the first to see it but also its most passionate admirer. But arguments, entreaties, tears— nothing could move Max Schuster to authorize offering a contract for what he deemed pornography. Maria very nearly quit over this, and it certainly was a factor in her choosing an early retirement. One can smile wryly when recalling this episode and the mores of the time while looking at modern bestseller lists, including the 8-million-copy sale of S & S's trade paperback edition of *The Joy of Sex*.

The book-publishing business, once hardly more high-pressure than a cottage industry, has recently turned highly competitive and even cutthroat on occasion. Of course money always talked, and valuable authors who liked Essandess and were well liked by the house, such as Irving Wallace and Evan Hunter, were lured away quite a long time ago by offers from other publishers which they could not refuse. Conversely and currently, S & S has done its own spectacular luring, with Dick Snyder making offers that writers like Carl Sagan and Mario Puzo couldn't refuse, to the annoyance of Random House and Putnam's. The quest is for a star who can turn out an instant success with the first book signed up and, in return, a very successful author is quite likely to have his or her next book put on the auction block and sold to a different publisher who bids the most, even though the first publisher has done an exemplary job. It's a two-way street, with the traffic dictated by self-interest; and if that's a fault, which is a debatable topic, the blame can be spread among everyone involved—authors, publishers, and literary agents.

That is not to say that loyalty between author and publisher has vanished. It's simply that there are far fewer cases of a relationship enduring through many years and many books than there used to be, and some publishing houses have a greater gift for tender loving care than others. More often than not it's the relationship of a particular

Graham Greene                    Joan Didion

editor with an author that cements a bond, and while an offer they can't refuse might indeed change matters, I think it would take a lot to induce Graham Greene or Joan Didion or Larry McMurtry or Justin Kaplan to leave Essandess as long as Michael Korda was around, and nothing would have induced Ronnie Delderfield. Bob Woodward and Richard Barnet's warm ties to S & S are Alice Mayhew's doing. Three of my own special treasures, P. G. Wodehouse and Alexander King and Sam Levenson, are dead, alas, but I have had another couple in recent years whose warm relationships with me, ones that now extend to my successors, will continue to bind them to Essandess, or so I dearly hope. One is Robert Creamer, baseball historian supreme, whose *Babe* and *Stengel* are true gems in sports writing. The other is David McCullough, one of the nation's stellar historians, who apart from our personal feelings about each other gives full credit to me on every occasion that offers him the opportunity, for suggesting to him that he write the history of the Panama Canal. That became the book *The Path between the Seas*, and won him virtually every literary and history prize worth mentioning. He has written four smashing books to date for Essandess and is hard at work on a fifth, and may there be no end to them.

Another very special favorite of mine for two decades was Jack Finney. I read his terrific fantasy novel, *The Body Snatchers*, in the early 1950s and, considering it the most enjoyable book of its genre I had ever encountered, kept planting seeds in the mind of his literary agent, Don Congdon, about how much I admired Finney and how welcome he would be at Essandess if he ever came unstuck from his publisher. A few years later the seeds took root and I received the first of the half-dozen Finney books we subsequently published, each one a tremendous pleasure even if not quite the masterpiece in the category that I considered *The Body Snatchers* to have been.*

I didn't truly expect that Jack could ever match or surpass the heights he reached in that book, but I turned out to be wrong. One day a new complete Finney manuscript from Congdon turned up on my desk that literally deserved the usually exaggerated encomium, "I could not put it down." The plot concerned a New York City illustrator who, by means of fantastic methods which Finney managed to make completely believable, stepped out of a twentieth-century apartment building one night right into the winter of 1882, and returned with certain political evidence that the U.S. government was seeking and had devised this way to unearth. The hero drew sketches and took photographs of that world that no longer existed—or did it?

The story itself was a marvelously imaginative, nostalgic, and exciting romance, but the thing that could really make it complete and lift the book into another class of publication than the fantasy category would be if we could include the batch of sketches and photos that Finney had sent along with the manuscript, and publish "An Illustrated Novel." Costs be damned—the project was irresistible. I dreamed up one of my better title suggestions, *Time and Again*, and we were almost off to the races.

Almost. I was enchanted with the sketches and the photographs except for one important thing, which I expressed forcibly to Jack. "What an unattractive woman's photo you've supplied to be the 1882

*For the benefit of my readers who have seen a movie called *Invasion of the Body Snatchers*, two films were made of the Finney novel, each bearing that title. The first, in 1956, was a faithful, extremely well-done picture that is a recognized classic in the field. The second, a 1978 production, struck me as a comparatively arty, pretentious bore, no matter how well it was received by some critics—and particularly by Pauline Kael in a positively ecstatic review in the *New Yorker*.

heroine! Can't you do better than that?" Jack replied that he'd done a lot of research and it was hard. What was regarded as womanly beauty a century ago didn't look so good to us now. Even fabled beauties of the stage wouldn't draw wolf whistles in the latter half of our century. I confidently said that was nonsense and that I'd find a better illustration and Jack shrugged and said it was fine with him if I could.

Do you know what? I couldn't—Finney was absolutely right. Between corseted hourglass figures, bosoms too ample for modern tastes, and unfortunate coiffures, the glamour girls of yesteryear didn't fit the bill. Then I had an inspiration. In the novel the hero, living in an 1882 boarding house where the girl also resides, sees her with her hair uncoiled and hanging down long and loose, and he persuades her to allow him to do a sketch of her. I remembered a photograph I had of a lovely girl who had posed just that way. True, she was a twentieth-century woman and her dress would be wrong, but her face was just right. So why not get an artist to copy the photograph exactly, but change the costume to fit the period? That could then serve as the sketch the hero made in 1882. Finney approved and was delighted with the commercial artist's rendition— and so was I, for the photograph from which the drawing was made was one of my wife, Antonia, at the age of twenty-three, when I first met her!

But did that solve all our problems? No, because when the hero first comes to the boarding house he takes a number of individual pictures of the residents with his box camera, and we had them all to use in the book except for the heroine. Surely he would have snapped her more than any other person. We still needed an attractive photo, and once again I had a lucky jog from my memory. In an old family album I unearthed a woman's photograph I remembered dimly as having been a charming one, taken just before the turn of the century, and indeed she turned out to be attractive by any standards regardless of time. Of course hers was a different face than the one in the drawing, but two factors made that difficulty surmountable. The illustration drawn from Toni's photo was a smiling one, with hair hanging loose. The woman in the formal photograph had a sober expression and her hair was up. And in the book the two illustrations would be sixty pages apart: surely no one would be so eagle-eyed and captious as to point out that these were two different women. (No one ever did.) Perhaps you have guessed that the old family album photo was my mother's portrait. Cleveland Amory devoted one of his "Trade Winds" columns in the old *Saturday Review* to the episode and delivered the punch line. He wrote that it only went to show that Peter wanted a girl just like the girl who married Dear Old Dad.

The publishing history of *Time and Again* has been remarkable and in one respect unique. In its original 1970 hardcover form, it leaped far past what a fantasy "genre" novel could be expected to achieve in sales, and it was chosen as a main selection by two major book clubs. Enthusiastic word-of-mouth recommendations kept the book alive and in print for a number of years, quite unusual for fiction except for books by very important authors. Then, in 1978, S & S put out a quality paperback edition on its Fireside list. It is the only novel that the firm has ever issued in quality paperback. Fiction reprints invariably belong in the province of the mass-market paperback publishers because the higher list price on quality paperbacks is more than the average customer wants to pay for nothing more than an enjoyable reading experience. But this time it worked.

The book had already captured an underground cult, and both the illustrations and the text gave the novel something of the appeal a nonfiction book about old New York would have. The result has been that some 100,000 copies have been sold to date, with backlist sales climbing every year—a remarkable record for this sort of unprecedented book publishing.

So a lot of people not in the Schwed family now possess pictures of my wife and my mother, and if you are not one of them you might as well become one now (see facing page).

The sad fact is that Finney is currently being published elsewhere, but not because of any falling-out in the relationship. I retired from active participation in S & S affairs just about as Jack's next manuscript arrived, and an equally passionate Finney admirer at Doubleday wanted the book more than my successor at S & S did. But from my own standpoint, Jack belongs in the roster of the faithful and I have few more fervent publishing wishes than that he'll pop up one of these days again with another book as outstanding as *Time and Again* and cause S & S sincere regret at having allowed so good an author and friend to depart.

My wife, Antonia    My mother, Bertie

The same close and warm ties that once so often bound authors and publishers existed even more solidly in employer-staff relationships, but that too is very different than it used to be. As has been pointed out, the turnover among staff members is extremely heavy, and S & S is only one example of the general trend in publishing. It's true that a number of highly placed people like Michael Korda, Dan Green, Frank Metz, Sophie Sorkin, and others have unwaveringly held their posts for a couple of decades or more, but the list of the equivalent of one-night stands—talented people who came and went within months—has been long enough to disturb someone who, being intrigued by a bright-appearing new employee one day, inquires about him or her three weeks later, and learns that she or he is no longer on the premises. A secretary who stays with a boss three years is regarded as a veteran old hand—and maybe one without much initiative. Having "get-up and go" is a term that has become more literal than it used to be. When Norman Monath got his first job in the mailroom some forty years ago, business had fallen off and he was about to be let go. Upon being so notified, he stayed throughout the entire sixteen hours between closing time that day and opening the next, took apart every aspect of the slapdash mailroom and reorganized it efficiently, and had it ready for operations as the front doors opened. His boss was greatly impressed, but it was still true that S & S didn't really need a clerk in his subordinate position just then. However he had made himself indispensable—no one, including the mailroom chief, could find anything anymore. So Norman stayed on and did so well that, at the end of his S & S career, he was the president of Cornerstone Library, one of the firm's soundest paperback divisions.

The real Prize for Loyalty and Longevity, however, must go to Sam Meyerson, director of mail-order sales and a vice-president of the trade division. Sam was hired as a stockroom boy in 1924, the year Simon and Schuster was founded, only a few months after the doors were thrown open, and only two weeks after Leon Shimkin was engaged, but Shimkin has been retired for many years, while Meyerson is still actively on the job. Sam was fourteen years old when he came and so good a stockroom boy that he was elevated to bookkeeper soon afterwards while simultaneously attending New York City high-school and college night sessions. By 1937, when Leon Shimkin came up with J. K. Lasser and the first *Your Income Tax* book, Meyerson had become Leon's protégé and he was selected for the massive task of seeing that the torrent of orders, produced from mailings and coupon ads, were filled. He also started to build up lists of buyers of the tax book, and since Lasser's books became annual issues that have dominated the field for half a century and have sold millions of copies, those lists became huge, and very valuable. People who had bought a tax book (and Lasser developed a number of collateral books that extended to tax areas apart from one's personal tax) were prime candidates to buy other quite different books about money, such as investment and business guides and retirement-planning books. The lists not only were used by Simon and Schuster but, as is the practice in mail-order operations, were rented to other companies at so-much-per-thousand names and addresses, and that became a profitable source of income. Sam Meyerson ran it from the very beginning and still does, along with all the other phases of mail-order advertising and selling. He is not only a consultant on any financial and investment book that is submitted to the house but acquires many himself and acts as editor or co-editor. Among such

Sam Meyerson

for which he receives credit are immensely successful books like William Nickerson's, Al Lowry's, and Robert Allen's real-estate books, every one of which has topped half a million copies in sales. He also edited Gerald Loeb's classic in the field, *Battle for Investment Survival*, and is regarded as an authority in the promotion and selling of books by mail order by the American Association of Book Publishers, frequently being asked to deliver a speech or run a seminar.

Admirable as all these details are, the real point is that Meyerson has been at it, unflaggingly and with enthusiasm, for sixty years! I propose he be proclaimed Dean of the Faithful Galley Slaves,★ and a toast be drunk to him, not in champagne but in water from Old Man River!

---

★If any readers think of "galley slave" as an opprobrious term, it would be because they are unaware of a collateral definition of the word "galley." A galley is the tray for holding composed type from which printer's proofs are run off, so a galley slave in this context is a publisher's devoted employee.

# Render unto Caesar the Things

# That Are Caesar's

15

IF Richard Snyder had not been around to take over in 1975, Gulf & Western would have had to invent him. Stupendous, successful growth has been the hallmark of the decade in which he's been in charge at Simon & Schuster, and one need only toss out a few figures to show why the conglomerate must be extremely happy today that Snyder was chosen as the new head of the book publishing company it acquired that year.

At that time the firm's sales volume was in the neighborhood of $44 million; in 1983 it was roughly $210 million. In 1975 about 800 people were employed by the various divisions of S & S, but today there are over 1,100 people on the regular payroll. Apart from the two major bulwarks of the company, the Simon and Schuster trade books division and Pocket Books, for years there had been several subsidiary imprints such as Cornerstone Library, Julian Messner, Monarch Press, and Washington Square Press, and they have continued to exist, but they have been supplemented by something like a dozen new imprints that have thrived so vigorously that they now constitute an impressive segment of the whole. To single out the most spectacular financial child that Richard Snyder has sired, Silhouette Books, its 1983 net sales came to approximately $53 million. Silhouette, which produces paperback romance novels for mass-market outlets, was created to replace the loss of the United States distributorship of Harlequin Books, which Leon Shimkin had negotiated a dozen years before and which S & S had built up from a $1 million business to a $60 million one, along with forming the nucleus for a successful book club. But after those dozen years Harlequin, a Canadian firm, decided to pursue the United States market itself—a grievous loss for S & S. Deciding to compete head-to-head with Harlequin, Snyder founded Silhouette, which flourished, but in June 1984, during a weakened market, it was unexpectedly announced that S & S was selling Silhouette to the very corporation that owns Harlequin! It is not yet clear as we go to press if this is a triumph or a disaster or a little of both, but what is clear is that it's tough for a book to keep up with Snyder's moves.

In more traditional and prestigious book publishing, the American distributorship of the Webster's New World Dictionaries in all languages, published by the noted British house of Collins, was acquired by Snyder when the U.S. operations of Collins were on the edge of bankruptcy. Snyder poured money into marketing research and found out that advertising dictionaries was wasted expenditure; featuring the name "Webster" in point-of-sales displays was all that mattered. Using this technique the dictionaries were so much more successful than they had been that S & S recovered its purchase price to Collins, and started tossing off healthy profits, in less than two years. Since "Webster" is a name that isn't exclusively the New World's, and is used by several competitive lines, one might wonder why the apparently simple idea of blazoning the magic name all over the place didn't occur before.

A firm believer in building a big publishing company on a horizontal basis rather than building it up vertically, Snyder has inaugurated new publishing imprints which are quite independent of the mother firm in how they choose books and operate. They are subsidiaries and have the benefits of using service arms such as accounting and warehousing and clerical and computer functions, but each maintains its own publishing integrity, and can even be competitive with each other and with S & S in possibly going after the same book. Two of these new houses had short lives, for different reasons. Larry Freundlich's Wyndham Books was terminated because it simply didn't work out as successfully as hoped. Kenan Press, to be headed up by Dan Green, never got around to publishing a book, because before its first title could be issued, Dan was appointed publisher of Simon & Schuster and the books he had signed up were transferred to its list. However, Summit Books, run by James Silberman, the much admired former editor-in-chief of Random House, is a prestigious and successful new face on the trade-book publishing scene, and the same is true of Linden Press, which Joni Evans manages. Jim and Joni are so good at their respective jobs that one can appreciate Snyder's decision to cut them loose to run their own shows, since by this tactic he has eliminated any possibility of rivalry or friction between them and S & S's own editor-in-chief, Michael Korda.

No one could be more supportive of this than Michael, and certainly not out of shying away from rivalry. He is the first to recognize that the company as a whole has to be supplied with good books all the time and with hugely successful ones frequently, and that it's dangerous to have one strong editor's taste dominate the selection of manuscripts, particularly in the area of fiction. Any one person is certain to be fallible, and having Silberman and Evans on the team, but acting apart from the S & S editorial board, solves the problem constructively. Of course, the board also boasts other excellent judges of fiction, but in his position as editor-in-chief, an acknowledged fiction expert, and an editor relied upon so solidly by Snyder, Michael's judgment is likely to carry the most weight.

In other spheres, Snyder strongly supported the expansion of the two quality-paperback lines, Touchstone and Fireside, both of which have become infinitely greater contributors to the common weal. And he had S & S plunge back into the arena of children's books. A contractual restraint had been imposed upon Essandess back in 1958 as a part of the transfer of Golden Books to Western Printing, so for some years the firm was out of the business of publishing children's books. When S & S was able to begin edging back with conventional titles, it no more than dabbled at it, but now Snyder went at it full tilt. Once again, using the horizontal tactic, he set up three separate imprints for juveniles: Little Simon (picture books for the very youngest, many only a few pages long, constructed of some impervious material that's immune to bathtub water and very possibly also to high explosives); Wanderer (real books for children from 8 to 12 to read, and for which Dick was able to wrest away from Grosset and Dunlap the ever-popular, classic Tom Swift and Nancy Drew series after a bitter publishers' imbroglio); and a third line, Windmill (imaginative, colorful playbook packages, such as pop-ups). Robert Kraus, the founder of Windmill and its most prolific author, has since left S & S, so those books have gradually been merged into the Little Simon list, but in any event Simon & Schuster is once again solidly back in certain areas of children's books.

Nor is Dick Snyder ever likely to be content to leave well enough alone and coast upon hard-earned laurels. The new project that is getting off the ground currently is the one headed up by Frank Schwartz along with Alvin Reuben, previously sales director, to produce software for the computer market—books on floppy disks and other paraphernalia that tie in to everything from office and home computers to arcade games: it is felt that these can be sold successfully in bookstores. They take a number of forms, so many that the last thirty pages of the S & S Spring/Summer 1984 catalogue are devoted to nothing else. There are "Computer Books," which are exactly what the term implies—books about computers. There are "Microsoft Books," put out by the major software developer in the country, which has now entered the book field as well, and these will be distributed by S & S. Finally, there is "Computer Software," which is Simon & Schuster's first thrust into producing and publishing software itself, and this also encompasses the distributorship of "The Learning Company," educational software for young children.

Essandess is by no means alone in embarking in a big way into this unproven field, but Snyder has always been conscious that in a technological era the publishing industry has been amazingly slow to take advantage of technology, and the mere publishing of books in an old-fashioned way will not suffice in the future. Even now an astonishing statistic is available: 20 percent of all books sold are books about computers! It's obviously a fertile field for textbook publishers but S & S, even before securing a real textbook division, did have some special factors going for it. It has established entree in both mass-market and traditional bookstores that is stronger than most publishers'. It has a flock of "brand names" books that lend themselves to this new use, such as the Lovejoy Scholastic Aptitude Text (SAT) books, the J. K. Lasser income-tax books, the Webster's New World Dictionaries, and many standard reference books such as medical guides, over-the-counter-drug information books, almanacs and statistical-record books, volumes of familiar quotations, and quite likely one of my own pets, *The Timetables of History.*

Getting into the field of computer software undoubtedly acted as an impetus for Dick Snyder to pursue an action that had long been considered desirable, though too expensive. That was to acquire a textbook house, the one very significant branch of book publishing which Essandess didn't have, since it is an operation which an existing trade-book publisher's staff is not equipped to undertake. The only practical way to add a textbook line is to go out and buy an existing one, but that requires the sort of money that's out of reach for a firm that generates its own capital, which continues to be true of S & S despite the Gulf & Western conglomerate ownership. G & W money is not sought or required for the Simon & Schuster publishing operations. However it is there if and when an opportunity arises that requires such tremendous financial backing as buying a large textbook house. So Gulf & Western, impressed by Snyder's vision of bigger worlds that could be built, late in 1983 bought Esquire, Inc., a group of educational publishers whose flagship is the venerable and prestigious Allyn & Bacon, for $200 million. Their sales volume that year was about $120 million, which means that, assuming both it and the Simon & Schuster performance were to continue at the same level, a new year would see S & S becoming a $350 million company! Perhaps even more significant for the firm's future is the fact that S & S is unique in now being able to publish books in every area of importance: trade books, mass-market paperbacks, quality paperbacks, romance paperbacks, children's books, dictionaries, and now technical books and textbooks. With such diversification, any disappointing year suffered by one division is likely to be counterbalanced by good performances in others. Snyder's S & S has come a long way from the almost cottage industry of the early years.

After reading the account of Dick Snyder's achievements in the initial proposal I drew up for this book, one reader commented that I was positively hagiographic in my attitude about him. After checking my dictionary to make sure the word meant what I thought it did—that I wrote about him as if he were a saint—I took stock of how I felt. The word seems unduly strong, but it's true that as far as performance goes, I have unbounded admiration for Dick. He is an incredibly hard worker and insists upon others measuring up to his standards using methods that some find distressingly domineering, but he has integrity, taste, and judgment. Certainly he is the most effective boss that S & S has ever had, and the record proves it.

The image that Dick projects as a person probably traces from his boyhood background and subsequent struggle to the top. The son of a middle-class coat manufacturer, he tended to rebel when his parents felt he was going on the wrong track. In his *Times* interview with Tony Schwartz he said: "They were very permissive, and I guess I kept wishing they had exercised more authority. I can remember going to *Annie Hall* with Joni when it opened. There was that great line when Woody Allen gets a ticket from a cop, rips it up, and says, 'It's not your fault, I just can't deal with authority.' I poked Joni and said, 'That was me.'"

After an undistinguished college career at Tufts University and brief service in the army, he got a job in the marketing department at Doubleday, but less than two years later he was fired. "I've never really understood why," he said. "I guess I was brash and stepped on a lot of toes by telling them how wrong they were doing everything. They didn't care to hear that, of course, and told me to look for another job."

That was in 1961 and Dick found a new job—third assistant to the sales manager at Golden Press, the children's-book division of Essandess. He moved up fast; after a series of promotions he became publisher and executive vice-president of the firm as the 1970s began. When Charles Bluhdorn, the chairman of Gulf & Western, purchased S & S in 1975, a critical aspect of his negotiations with Leon Shimkin was insistence that Richard Snyder would be president.

Since then Dick has established himself and the company he has rebuilt so solidly that he no longer needs to make an extravagant public-relations gesture to show the flag, but at the outset he made one that produced book-page headlines for a day but not much else. That was the hiring of Eugene McCarthy, the defeated but wildly popular and esteemed presidential candidate, as an editor. Gene, a delightful, civilized man, was just as well liked and admired as an individual in the S & S office as he had been nationwide among intellectuals during the campaign, but although he effected some high-level political introductions, that was about as far as his tangible editorial contributions went. He was a knowledgeable and passionate devotee of poetry, but that wasn't quite what S & S had hoped to gain from his services and, after a fairly short hitch in an editor's chair, Gene and S & S parted company on mutually regretful terms. Yet the hiring of McCarthy was the first indication of Snyder's own particular passion in publishing, the political book. For decades this had been the almost exclusive purview of Doubleday, and while firms like Harper and Row and W. W. Norton and even to a lesser extent S & S had an occasional plum of a political book, whenever a truly major property was in the offing, Doubleday was the best bet among book publishers to secure it. It was Snyder's first and prime editorial directive to change this and to make S & S the company that people in Washington, and their literary agents, would think of first. The story of how he did it follows shortly hereafter.★

Michael Korda has said that S & S is in the business of buying stars as authors of the company's big books, and Snyder and Korda's

---

★Just about as this book was going to press, a political book inspired by the joint efforts of Snyder and Korda created a sensation throughout New York City more than two months before it was scheduled to be published. That was *Mayor* by Ed Koch, which originally must have been thought of as a book that might be quite fascinating to readers bemused by urban government but which, like the book former Mayor John Lindsay wrote some years ago for W. W. Norton, would be so insular as to have little appeal past the New York market. In preliminary planning a substantial but by no means extravagant print order was proposed with publication slated for late March 1984.

No one had dreamed that Mayor Koch would write the uninhibited, wild-swinging, and vicious book that he did, which lashed out with specific charges against a number of the biggest political figures in the state and city administrations. Nor had it been anticipated that, when galleys were sent out in mid-January to reviewers, every newspaper would leap upon them as the juiciest sort of scandalous news and run front-page stories about the contents of the book with utter disregard of the scheduled release date. That is what happened and the *New York Times*, which had purchased first periodical rights to print excerpts from the book at publication time, thought seriously about breaking the contract in view of the news stories that obviously took much of the wind out of their sails. There had been a recent precedent for such an action: when Harper and Row was about to publish former President Gerald Ford's memoirs, and had sold periodical rights to *Time* and to *Reader's Digest*, the *Nation* magazine scooped them by printing material lifted from galleys sent to the reviewer, and the sales of periodical rights were aborted. However, in the case of *Mayor*, the *New York Times* ran its own major news story so as not to be left out in the cold with the competition, and after reflection decided to go ahead with the fuller use of the book as planned.

Dates, however, were changed with rapid-fire decisions and work. Essandess's production department accomplished a miracle and got books in two weeks, in time for early February publication, and the *Times* rescheduled its use. Simon and Schuster increased its first printing very substantially, but not nearly enough, for the book became a sensational success requiring five printings in its first month on sale, when about 100,000 copies were sold in New York alone. The demand in that city was understandable, but more remarkable has been the nationwide interest that has made *Mayor* a top bestseller everywhere.

life-styles furnish the backdrop that expresses book publishing as show business. Many envy it and some deplore it, but it's hard not to admire what they achieve regardless of the razzle-dazzle that accompanies it. They know their job, and the flashy stuff like huge advances and hard-sell promotion is invariably supported by almost obsessive attention to details that matter and make for better publishing, such as meticulous copy-editing, layout, and design, and individual review of every jacket sketch and proof, the last frequently calling for the scrapping of what the very talented but often harassed art director, Frank Metz, has presented, and an order to go back to the drawing board.

Despite grudging respect for Snyder's extraordinary publishing success with S & S, many people hold him in little affection. Most of these are outsiders who once worked at S & S, or people who have encountered him only peripherally but who are aware of the reputation he built as a tyrannical and abrasive boss. My own feeling is that a decade ago, while he was cutting the wide swath that would lead him to his present pinnacle, the reaction of some who suffered his displeasure and subsequent put-downs, or firings, was understandable. It hardly mattered whether Dick was right or wrong in a disagreement, because his method was not to placate or even debate; he seemed invariably to override imperiously. That acknowledgedly superb editor, Henry Robbins, who in a brief time had brought the house the most prestigious authors since Bob Gottlieb's day, stalked out of an editorial board meeting in a fury one day as the result of his feeling of humiliation, and Snyder has been pictured as the villain of the piece. The fact is, however, that regardless of his unquestionable editorial talents, Henry could be a pretty intolerant and irascible man himself, often not endearing himself to coworkers like Frank Metz or the subsidiary-rights people when he saw things differently than they did. On this occasion Robert Evans, then the head of Paramount Pictures, with whom it was planned S & S would be working closely, asked to attend an editorial board meeting. It was a request that could hardly be denied, so Evans came and sat through most of the meeting quietly, but near its end he asked to say a few words. The words turned out to be that Paramount had had such a smash hit in *Love Story* that its primary goal was to find another such property as soon as possible, so if any Simon & Schuster editors happened upon that sort of manuscript, he or she was to drop everything and call him collect on the telephone immediately. Henry Robbins threw down his napkin, smacked his plate, launched into a tirade about the sort of insidious, disgusting, nonliterary, and vilely commercial influence that was being allowed to hold forth in board meetings, and departed in high dudgeon. Evans salvaged the embarrassment that shrouded the table by grinning and saying, "Happens every day in Hollywood!" That particular spectacular separation of an editor from S & S can hardly be blamed on Snyder, but there have been other cases which might have.

Still, it is hard to argue with success, and it's quite possible that harsh methods were required to resurrect a firm that was more or less treading water when Dick took over. Once he had built the team he wanted and saw the company zooming in growth and prosperity, this leopard had both the ability and sagacity to change his spots. Dick hasn't mellowed—he dislikes the word, thinking that it implies complacency—but he surely has matured. Memories are long and first impressions hard to change, though, so there inevitably will be some who continue to think less than the world of Snyder, but the majority of them will not be those who have observed him and worked with him in more recent years. Yet one man who has, who was once his best friend, is no longer on speaking terms with him. His name is David Obst.

Obst and Snyder met in 1971 and instantly hit it off together, each seeing the other as a window through which to view a bordering generation. David soon came to think of Dick as an older brother and mentor: Dick found David a fascinating introduction to a younger group familiar with the scene that intrigued his exploratory interests. Over the ensuing years they became the closest of friends, often vacationing together with their families at Fire Island and at Gulf & Western's luxury resort in the Dominican Republic. Their relationship was somewhat unusual for Snyder, for he is more apt to be surrounded by colleagues and business associates than warm personal pals, but David was an outstanding exception, and each man had reason to feel gratitude to the other as well as deep affection.

At the time of their meeting, Obst was a young radical newspaperman who acted as agent for a number of *Washington Post* reporters. One of them was Daniel Ellsberg, whose *Papers on the War* had

David Obst

been sold to Dell, but trouble arose about it and the contract was canceled. Obst then brought the project to his new friend, Snyder, who saw this as a first step to securing political books. S & S took it on, and not long afterward Snyder and Obst started to wonder if there might be a book that could emerge from all this vague Watergate stuff that was going the rounds. That eventuated in Obst's submitting a queer, hazy proposal to S & S in October 1972, one which gave no hint of what was going to transpire. After all, only one month later Nixon was going to be reelected president by the most overwhelming majority in American political history. Four other publishers were approached by Obst about the book but he didn't get any action, and Snyder became his last hope, so David orchestrated a meeting for Dick to meet the *Post* reporters on the story, Carl Bernstein and Bob Woodward, at the Hay Adams Hotel in Washington.

It was a disaster. Snyder had been out late, hadn't slept, and was in a foul mood. Bernstein and Woodward had broken a story in the paper that was inaccurate, the *Post* was in trouble, and their jobs were on the line. They were on tenterhooks and Snyder was extremely insecure about going along with their ideas, but Obst implied more

Carl Bernstein and Bob Woodward

or less that if Snyder didn't buy this book from him, they'd never do business together. Dick inquired, "Do you really feel that strongly?" Upon being assured that David did, he said "Okay."

An apparently disproportionately large advance of $55,000 was agreed upon with some reluctance, but Snyder understood that the writers required time off from their jobs and considerable money for research. Apart from that there were other worries: it didn't seem such a very big story at all to begin with, there was no peg on how it should be written, and February 1973 came and went with not a single word being put down on paper. Snyder kept asking where the book was.

Then, in March, the principals in the Watergate scandal cracked and talked, and the entire affair came unglued. Suddenly Bernstein and Woodward were the heroic fair-haired boys and Snyder was quick to visualize the potential for S & S. After telling Obst, "This is it! We're going all the way with it!" he assigned the editorial role to Alice Mayhew and cut her loose to work night and day with Woodward and Bernstein. Alice was the one who told the authors that the peg was to build up the Deep Throat character and make him interesting, and she knocked herself out working with them. Her efforts, backed by Snyder's putting his money where his mouth was, sparked the crash publishing program that launched *All the President's Men.* The very large first printing of 75,000 copies ran out of stock immediately, and an immense second printing of 150,000 copies was hustled through the presses. Snyder rolled up his sleeves and made the book work in every direction. The bookstore sales shot the title right up to the Number One position and kept it there a long time, and every conceivable subsidiary right was exploited to the hilt under Snyder's constant spurring. Big contracts were negotiated with book clubs, newspaper and magazine syndicates, and some twenty foreign publishers, and Milly Marmur ran a masterful auction for paperback reprint-rights while Dick breathed over her shoulder, finally selling the rights to Warner for a $1 million advance, the first seven-figure sum ever achieved by a nonfiction book.

Richard E. Snyder and Alice Mayhew (© *1984 Helen Marcus*)

John Dean

*All the President's Men* was the real turning point for Simon &
Schuster on its subsequent climb to new heights, and it made
Richard Snyder the force and power he has became and remained.
The book is as much a benchmark of his administration as the first
crossword puzzle book was for the founders of the firm.

Just about the time the book was being issued, John Dean, who
was on the eve of going to prison, contacted David Obst about
writing his book, and David alerted Dick Snyder, who flew out to
California to listen to Dean outline his ideas. After hearing him out
Dick said, "Forget it—do it *this* way and call it *Blind Ambition*," and
made a contract with Obst calling for a $300,000 advance. When the
first four or five chapters were received it was clear that Dean had
embarked upon a catastrophe and Snyder wanted his money back.
Obst prevailed in arguing that the book could be salvaged and would
be worth it, but Snyder was adamant and insisted not only that
Taylor Branch be called in to doctor the writing but also that the
advance be cut in half. In the end the size of the advance made
no difference, because *Blind Ambition* became another phenomenal
success.

Snyder's trip to the West Coast to get the John Dean book happened to be concurrent with the assignment given to him to be Leon Shimkin's emissary in an effort to sell S & S to the Music Corporation of America (MCA), which owned Universal Pictures. The first item on his agenda, however, was John Dean, so he and Dean and Obst met for dinner in the fashionable Polo Lounge, where they drew an uncomfortable avalanche of attention from reporters and gossip columnists. Dick and David decided to duck so much unwanted publicity and took off in a car to Palm Springs for a breathing spell, arriving there at four in the morning. At five the telephone rang: it was Shimkin calling from New York at eight o'clock his time. Leon reported that he had enjoyed a good session with Charles Bluhdorn of Gulf & Western and that everything was set for the firm to be sold to G & W *if* Snyder were to meet with Bob Evans, the head of another G & W subsidiary, Paramount Pictures, and they got along well together. Accordingly Shimkin had arranged a breakfast meeting for the two of them at eight o'clock Los Angeles time at the Polo Lounge!

Charles Bluhdorn

Snyder, with one hour's sleep, hopped back into the car and drove back at breakneck speed, and over coffee a few hours later he and Evans agreed that they could love each other and the path was cleared for the takeover by Gulf & Western. Obviously the MCA exploration died aborning, and with G & W becoming the owner, Richard Snyder took control of S & S as president, and Leon Shimkin retired into a nonfunctioning honorary title of chairman with a bundle of money to console him.

Both men were more than ready for a change after their scratchy relationship for a number of years. An amusing example of the friction took place after the paperback reprint rights to *All the President's Men* were sold to Warner Books for a record $1 million. Leon, in reporting to the board of directors, played down the importance of the sale. No doubt he was trying to keep a lid on the upstart prickly nettle Snyder had become. He spoke of the fact that the authors got half the money to begin with, and that after overhead and other expenses were taken into account, the net profit to S & S wasn't so very spectacular. Probably not much more than a quarter of a million dollars. Dick, who had been sitting as solemn as an owl while this oration was going on, spoke up. "Mr. Shimkin—I promise that I'll never do it again!"

Even the John Dean book was not the closing chapter of the Watergate–S & S saga. Woodward and Bernstein had another project in the works, *The Final Days*, but contract terms were hard to work out because they felt by now that Obst was in Snyder's pocket and wasn't doing his best for his authors. In the end once again, the size of the deal turned out to be academic, because the reading public couldn't get enough juicy information about Watergate, and *The Final Days* had a first printing of 200,000 and in its turn became a top bestseller. On that book Scott Armstrong had been the chief researcher for Bob Woodward, and a couple of years later the two of them collaborated to write still another smash hit about the Washington scene, this time about the Burger Supreme Court, *The Brethren*.

With such a record of fantastic mutual benefits, it's easy to see why Dick and David would have grown close even if they hadn't liked each other personally as much as they did. So a peculiar situation was set up when Random House, persistent wooers of Obst, hoping he would steer some properties their way, answered "We will" when David half-facetiously suggested that he might shift his allegiance if given his own publishing imprint. When Obst reported the offer to Snyder, Dick agreed that he should accept—it was too good an opportunity to turn down—but a little later thought better of it and told David to refuse because S & S was prepared to do the same thing. Torn by indecision about which way to turn, Obst accepted the Random House proposal because, as he now is frank to admit, he didn't want to spend a lifetime in Snyder's shadow and he felt he had to grow as his own man.

Dick, his fury over what he considered flagrant betrayal being compounded by concern over an eye operation he was about to undergo, ruled Obst out of his life on the spot. Obst was very fond of Snyder's entire family and saw them all the time, but Dick decreed that he was never going to talk to David again and was forbidding his children ever to do so too. However, in fact it turned out that it didn't take Obst very long to realize that he had made a bad mistake. He didn't do nearly as well with Random House as he had with S & S and he was contrite and wanted to return. He needed what Snyder had given him—a long leash held in a tight grip, and he didn't get that at Random House. By this time Dick's anger had reached the cooling point and he agreed to welcome home his prodigal son. He said to David: "You were very good in Washington. Why don't you go out to California and be equally good there?" He set Obst up in his own house, and the relationship flourished again as strongly as before between Obst and the Snyder family, even though there was now a new Mrs. Snyder, Joni Evans.

The Snyder-Obst entente came to a second end in the late spring of 1982, after a joint enterprise to produce films named S & S Productions didn't get off the ground and sputtered to a halt. Things were not good in films just then, and it's difficult to pinpoint the reason. In any case, Simon & Schuster not only had co-financed Obst's house on the West Coast but had advanced him money on which to operate. Snyder wanted David to get out of it all, sell the house, and return the money, but there were no buyers for the house. The longer the situation went on, the angrier Dick got, despite David's pleading, "Let's stay friends—it's only a house." But at the same time, despite having landed a new job at CBS, he wasn't repaying his note either, even on the long-term installment basis to which

Dick Snyder in contemplative mood

Snyder had agreed. One day Obst telephoned and received a message from Dick's secretary: "Mr. Snyder wishes you neither good nor ill but do not call again."

Despite this unhappy conclusion, Obst continues today to esteem Snyder highly and retains affection for him. He feels Dick has such an unusually strong sense of right and wrong, and proper and improper conduct, that he simply won't put up with anything or anybody who doesn't meet his exacting standards. He is an extremely hard-nosed man, David says, and if you say something to him you had better live up to it, which makes him rough on employees who are encountering him on a day-to-day basis.

Still, the lot of employees who can survive and thrive under Snyder's sort of autocratic administration is infinitely better in material ways than any Essandess employees have ever known in previous managements. Starting salaries, regular reviews for raises, office conditions, perquisites, retirement planning, and solicitude for employees in trouble, all are immeasurable improvements over the sometimes paternalistic, but generally slipshod, methods exercised by Snyder's predecessors. One disgruntled long-time associate of Leon Shimkin's said of him, "He was like the butcher who keeps all the best cuts of steak for himself." Leon indeed had his own individual generosities, such as buying Noel Lynch, longtime supervisor of the mailroom, a house and a business in the West Indies upon his retirement, but he had nothing like Snyder's appreciation of how the entire crew aboard Essandess should be treated. In an unsolicited testimonial in my possession, a veteran salesman, Jack Lovell, writes: "Dick Snyder is the best thing that ever happened for salesmen. Dick got us profit-sharing, health benefits, expense accounts, the use of a car supplied by the company, and I could go on and on." Those plaudits have been echoed by other old-timers among the sales representatives, such as Saul Gilman, who has seen publisher/presidents come and go.

On two occasions, there have been attempts to unionize Simon & Schuster. The first occurred just before World War II when the Book and Magazine Guild approached Dick Simon and Leon Shimkin with a proposed contract. Leon said, "What's the bottom line to us?" and hearing that it entailed nothing more than a $2-a-week raise to one person in the mailroom, said "Okay." But then, when the staff was shown the contract for a vote, it was the mailroom personnel who screamed a strong protest. "What's this about regular hours and being committed to report on time? We come in pretty well as we please, and as long as we do our work, which usually involves staying late, no one has ever kicked. We don't want this contract!" Result—the contract was repudiated, the underpaid mailroom employee got his $2 raise anyhow, and Essandess's *laissez-faire* handling of its staff continued on its merry way.

The second attempt to unionize S & S came almost immediately after Snyder's taking charge, and Dick is frank to admit that the contention that the company's wage scale was low in the industry was justified. It was his job to fight inroads by a union so he did so successfully, but the moment the matter was settled he instituted an entirely new and generous program on salaries. If you work for

Essandess these days your remuneration is above the going rate paid by other book publishers, and that may be something of an understatement.

In their penetrating book, *Life and Death on the Corporate Battlefield: How Companies Win, Lose, Survive,* authors Paul Solman and Thomas Friedman point out that the key to survival is the ability to adapt to a highly complex, unpredictable, and constantly changing environment—a Darwinian imperative rules in business as it does in nature. Dick Snyder is one book publisher who understands this and is not content to stand pat with a comfortable environment—he acts. If a staff member doesn't like it, or Snyder doesn't like the staff member's performance, he or she goes. But in one respect nothing has changed over sixty years, whether Dick Simon or Max Schuster or Leon Shimkin or Dick Snyder was running the show. Essandess alumni and alumnae thrive once they leave and go elsewhere: the firm has always appeared to be the best training ground in book publishing. Apart from those who have escalated their earnings handsomely, approximately a dozen former S & S people head up other firms today. And as far as current conditions back at home base are concerned, you may not be able to live with the experience—but if you can, you couldn't buy the experience anywhere else.

# l'Envoi

These days, in a publishing climate that has changed so substantially from that experienced by people through the earlier years at Simon and Schuster, the main aspect to be noted immediately is the difference. Those who feel sentimental about the older regimes might claim that the atmosphere today is considerably clammier and less enjoyable, and I, a sentimentalist, would agree. Realists, conscious of the excitement and benefits of the current administration, would claim that everybody concerned, from management through staff to authors, is much more solidly secure and better off—and I, a realist, would agree. Other times, other customs.

One thing is apparent, however, about the present-day hardworking body that has made Simon & Schuster the power in book publishing that it has become. That is its sole dedication toward doing the best and most effective job possible today, and doing better tomorrow. But there is so little knowledge of or interest in past history that most of what has been recorded in this book will be unfamiliar and startling news, even to people who have been working at S & S for some years. The firm not only doesn't possess a library worthy of the name but, since 1980, hasn't even had a complete catalogue of what the house has published in the past. It isn't felt to be (to use an obnoxious but valid word under the circumstances) relevant. Nor is the matter of how long-lived S & S publications may be in the future of much interest, past what the next couple of balance sheets may show. We live for today.

So in coming to the end of this story of Essandess's sixty years up to now, simply as a matter of contrast and with no intention of drawing any moral from it, I would like to recount a perhaps insane but charming action of one of the firm's founders about half a century ago.

On Saturday, May 23, 1936, a new wing of Max Schuster's beautiful country house, Green Laurels, in Sea Cliff, Long Island, was completed and a small ceremony arranged for the laying of its cornerstone. This wing was to house Max's impressive library, which, apart from thousands of other books he revered, would contain every S and S book published up to that time, not only in its original format but also with a leatherbound copy of each one. Max's irrepressibly grandiose mind had conceived an idea in connection with this great event, and with Max to think was to act.

For some months he had been approaching distinguished people associated with Simon and Schuster to write him letters that would fit into his concept, which was to inter memorabilia about S and S so securely in the cornerstone that there would be a reasonable chance that it all might be unearthed and read by scholars a thousand years from then. A sophisticated cynic might wonder what reaction a man like Albert Einstein must have had when approached with such a request, but the fact of the matter is that not only did Einstein pen such a letter (in German and accompanied by a translation), but it was a delightful letter. And others came from an impressive roster of literary figures including (in alphabetical order) Harry Elmer Barnes, Charles A. Beard, Thomas Craven, Abbé Ernest Dimnet, Theodore Dreiser, Will Durant, Walter Duranty, Clifton Fadiman, H. L. Mencken, Christopher Morley, Lewis Mumford, Donald Culross Peattie, Walter Pitkin, and Hendrik Willem Van Loon. There were others too, including Dick Simon and a couple of other top Essandess editorial figures. No one seems to have turned down Max's request despite its dreamlike quality.

Schuster took these letters and, along with other items such as the *New York Times* of that date, press clippings and photographs relating to S and S, the 1936 catalogue, clippings about other publishers' books he admired, a sample of every United States coin minted, and God knows what else, had them all hermetically sealed in a copper box which was then encysted in the concrete block which formed the cornerstone of his new library. The covering letter was some dozen pages long, written carefully in Max's clear hand, and began as follows:

"*To an Unknown Mortal of 2936 A.D.* (Notes to Be Left in a Cornerstone):

"This letter is an impertinence, a defiance, an arrogance flung in the face of time. Perhaps it will never see the light of day. Perhaps it will never be examined by human eyes. But there is always the possibility, the remote chance, that our hopes will not betray us, and that these words will be deciphered by some surprised and bewildered excavator or research worker one thousand years from now. This is the life expectancy which the chemists, in this year of grace, grant to the paper on which these lines are written, and to the waterproof India ink with which they are set down."

(Max supplied Einstein and all the other letter writers with those same materials, and had other items laminated as thoroughly as possible.) His letter then went on to describe things and events, particularly publishing matters in 1936, and to pose queries about how comparable things might be in 2936, even though it seemed unlikely he could ever learn the answers. The letter concludes with the statement: "This is an idle and sentimental gesture, but an honest instinct impels me to try it."

A copy of the first *Crossword Puzzle Book* would surely have been in that box, and I hope it will entertain that Unknown Mortal of 2936 to try to wrestle out some of the answers to definitions such as "Spanish water wheel" in five letters. Let us wish that there will be someplace for fun and games in the first half of the thirtieth century as there once was in the comparable part of the twentieth, even though the odds today don't seem to make it a particularly attractive bet.

# Photograph Acknowledgments

A majority of the photographs in this book were supplied by the individuals themselves, taken from family albums and the like, and the author is profoundly grateful. Some, particularly a few unearthed in the files of Butler Library at Columbia University, bore no credits and were impossible to trace to a source. These were of quite ancient vintage and the likelihood is that they, too, came from private files or are in the public domain. If any photographer has been overlooked the correction will be made in any future printings.

In a few cases, certain photographers stipulated that their credits plus copyright notice be printed adjacent to the photographs in the body of the text; this has been done.

Appreciation is herewith extended to the other following photographers for permission to use their work:

*Peter Simon* for the photographs on pages 43, 91, and 140
*Victor H. Schneider* for the photograph on page 82
*Rob Levine* for the top photograph on page 83
*Hans Namuth* for the photograph on page 102
*Chris Little* for the photograph on page 112
*Maria Martel* for the left photograph on page 118
*Ed Wakely* for the photograph on page 131
*Thomas R. Koeniges* and *Newsday* for the photograph on page 155
*Alan Porter* for the photograph on page 180
*Clemens Kalisher* for the photograph on page 221

*Karsh, Ottawa* and *Woodfin Camp & Associates* for the left photograph on page 263

*Quintana Roo Dunne* for the right photograph on page 263

*Ron Batzdorf* for the photograph on page 279

*Joan Bingham* for the photograph on page 280

*George Chinsee, M Magazine,* for the photograph on page 286

*Douglas Kirkland-Sygma* for the top photograph on page 229

*Dirck Van Sickle* for the bottom photograph on page 229

*Henry Grossman* for the photograph on page 232

*David Kennerly* for the photograph on page 258

# Index

Addams, Charles, 44, 118, 177
Adler, Polly, 261–62
Aga Khan, The, 185, 216
Alexander, Herbert, 82, 179
Allen, George, 30
Allen, Woody, 275
Allen and Unwin, 217
Allyn & Bacon, 274
Amory, Cleveland, 266
Armour, Tommy, 30, 59$n$, 177
Armstrong, Scott, 16, 284
Arno, Peter, 44, 118
Atheneum, 80
Atwood, Margaret, 15

Baker, George, 118
Baker, Russell, 117
Banks, Lynne Reid, 226
Bannister, Constance, 197
Bantam Books, 165
Barnes, Harry Elmer, 290
Barnes, Joseph, 55, 154–55, 175–76, 181, 183
Barnet, Richard J., 247, 263
Barrow, Helen, 55, 121, 151, 152, 154, 155, 156–160, 187, 239
Barrow, Roz, 151
Bassett, Jack, 39–41
Bates, Ernest Sutherland, 53, 217
Baumgarten, Bernice, 256, 257
Beard, Charles A., 290
Beazley, John, 223–25
Bellamann, Henry, 103
Belloc, Hilaire, 15
Berenson, Bernard, xviii, 185, 216
Berger, Marcella, 231
Berlin, Irving, 21
Berlin, Isaiah, 216

Bernstein, Carl, 16, 279–81, 284
Bernstein, Robert, 170–71, 240, 241, 242
Bespaloff, Alexis, 183
Bevans, Tom Torre, xviii, 55, 123, 150–51, 155, 167, 206–09
Bischof, Werner, 193
Bleeker, Sonia, 183
Bluhdorn, Charles, 86, 275, 283
Bodley Head, The, 217–18
Bolger, Ray, 198
Bombeck, Erma, 117
Boni, Albert, 245
Boni, Charles, 245
Boni and Liveright, 66, 73
Book-of-the-Month Club, xix, 35, 39, 53, 57, 80, 137, 153, 218, 219, 233, 248
Borchardt, Georges, 107, 108, 233
Boston Women's Health Book Collective, 16
Bourne, Nina, xviii, 44, 55, 58, 88, 91, 97, 99, 121, 187–88, 240–41, 242
Branch, Taylor, 282
Brand, Millen, 11
Brandt & Brandt, 256, 257
Brendler, Ralph, 81
Brockway, Wallace, 64, 181, 182–83, 193
Broun, Heywood, 88
Brown, Christy, 226
Buchwald, Art, 117
Buranelli, Prosper, 2
Burgess, Anthony, 15
Busch, Ronald, 165
Bush, Vannevar, 177
Butler, George, 33
Butterfield, Roger, 97, 177

Calder, Nigel, 226
Cambridge University, 235

Cantor, Eddie, 58, 118
Capp, Al, 97, 118, 177
Carnegie, Dale, 75–76
Carroll, Lewis, 149
Carson, Johnny, 101, 105
Carson, Rachel, 11, 255
Carter, Angela, 226
Cartier-Bresson, Henri, 193
Castañeda, Carlos, 138
Cerf, Bennett, 73, 80, 118, 171, 190–91, 210, 241, 257
Cerf, Christopher, 80
Chambers, Whittaker, 42
Chaplin, Charlie, 217–18, 226
Christopher, John, 226
Clark, Walter van Tilburg, 257
Cole, William, 183, 219
Colmore, Julia, 183
Collins, Alan, 123
Collins, William, 225, 271
Columbia University, xvii, 7, 19, 20, 45, 48, 235
Computer books and software, 273–74
Congdon, Don, 183
Conran, Shirley, 231–32
Consolidated Book Company, 80
Constable Ltd., 222
Cornerstone Library, 268, 270
Corwin, Norman, 211–12
Craven, Thomas, 44, 51–52, 96, 290
Creamer, Robert, 263
Crichton, Robert, 242
Crosby, Bing, 170
Crossword Puzzle Books, 1–7
Crown Publishers, Inc., 224–25
Culbertson, Ely, 22, 24–25
Curtis Brown Ltd., 123

Dalton, B., 100
Darrow, Whitney, Jr., 44
Davies, Joseph E., 177
Dean, John, 282–84
de Graff, Robert Fair, 162–65, 174, 178
Delderfield, R. F., 237–38, 263
Dell Publishers, 279
Delmar, Vina, 60
de Seversky, Alexander, 177
Deutsch, André, 225
Didion, Joan, 15, 249, 263
Dimnet, Abbé Ernest, 11, 290
Disney, Walt, 42
Dolger, Jonathan, 183
Donahue, Phil, 110
Doubleday & Co., 80, 123, 138, 258, 259, 266, 275, 276
Duplaix, Georges, 166–69, 210
Dreiser, Theodore, 139, 290
Dreyfus, Jack, 110–14
Dunn, Alan, 44
Dunne, John Gregory, 15

Durant, Ariel, 15
Durant, Will, 7–8, 11, 15, 48, 64–65, 96, 290
Duranty, Walter, 96, 290
Durocher, Leo, 30

Eastman, Max, 46–47, 118
Ehrlich, Leonard, 11
Einstein, Albert, 11, 96, 142, 290, 291
Eisenhower, Dwight D., 176
Ellsberg, Daniel, 278–79
Erskine, Rosalind, 139–42
Esquire, Inc., 274
Evans, Charles, 30–33
Evans, Joni, 107–08, 185–86, 249, 272, 275, 285
Evans, Robert, 277–78, 283
Eveland, Wilbur Crane, 129

Fadiman, Clifton, xviii, 10, 48–51, 55–62, 64, 123, 134, 148, 181, 183, 208, 290
Fallada, Hans, 11, 216
Farrar, Straus & Giroux, 11, 80
Faulk, John Henry, 16
Feirstein, Bruce, 119
Felipe, 71
Fernandel, 196–97
Field, Marshall, 67, 79, 80, 173–78, 190
Finney, Jack, 264–66
Fireside Books, 35, 272
Fischer, Bobby, 218–19
Fisher, Dorothy Canfield, 39
Flint, Jeremy, 26
Fonda, Henry, 109
Fonda, Jane, 35, 106–09, 233
Ford, Gerald, 276n
Forster, Margaret, 226
Fortune, 10, 17
FPA (Franklin P. Adams), 88
Fraser, George MacDonald, 226
Freundlich, Larry, 271
Frey, Richard, 25
Friedman, Bruce Jay, 242
Friedman, Thomas, 288

Gaines, Charles, 33
Gandhi, Mahatma, 222
Gann, Ernest K., 177
Geis, Bernard, 103
Gendel, Evelyn, 183
Gershwin, George, 19–20
Gilman, Saul, 287
Gitlin, Paul, 82, 84, 230
Gligoric, Svetozar, 218–19
Glyn, Anthony, 226
Goldberg, Vicki, 183
Golden Books, 79, 92n, 166–72, 205, 210, 272, 275
Golden Records, 170–71
Gollancz, Victor, 114–16, 225

Goodman, Jack, xviii, 22, 25, 35, 44, 55, 58, 88, 90, 91, 97, 122, 125, 148, 179, 183, 201–06, 208, 210–15, 216, 234, 235–36, 241, 257, 258
Goren, Charles, 25–26, 177
Gottlieb, Robert, 44, 53, 55, 103, 179, 216, 235–243, 248, 277
Grann, Phyllis, 184, 185, 187
Gray, Francine du Plessix, 15
Green, Dan, 55, 101, 107–09, 225, 231, 246, 247, 249, 267, 271
Green, Elinor, 187
Greene, Graham, 15, 110, 249, 263
Greengrass, Barney, 46, 121–24, 142, 250
Grew, Joseph C., 177
Gross, Leonard, 33, 99
Gross, Ronald, 183
Grosset & Dunlap, 272
Grossman, Richard, 143–46, 183, 191–95
Guinness, Alec, 226
Guinzberg, Harold, 73, 80
Guinzberg, Tom, 80
Gulbenkian, Nubar, 218
Gulf & Western, xix, 68, 69, 72, 85, 86, 180, 246, 247, 270, 274, 275, 283–84

Haldane, J.B.S., 149
Haldeman-Julius, E., 7–8
Halsey, Margaret, 36–39, 183
Halsman, Philippe, 195–98
Halsman, Yvonne, 198
Hamilton, Hamish, 124
Harcourt, Alfred, 10–11, 15, 16
Harcourt Brace Jovanovich, 60, 85, 256
Harlequin Books, 270–71
Harper & Row, 151, 260, 276, 276n
Harrap, Ian, 225
Harris, Diane, 183
Harry N. Abrams, Inc., xix, 89
Hart, Lorenz, 20
Hartswick, F. Gregory, 2
Hayward, Leland, 257
Healy, Raymond J., 183
Hedgecoe, John, 224
Heller, Joseph, 15, 155–56, 242
Hellman, Geoffrey T., xix, 60, 190
Hepburn, Katharine, 109
Herblock, 177
Hersh, Seymour M., 16, 247
Higham, David, 238
Hill, Morton A., 141–42
Hirschfeld, Al, 97
Hobson, Laura Z., 97, 103, 177
Hodder and Stoughton, 237
Hodgins, Eric, 103, 118, 152–53
Holding, Antonia, 212–13, 265–66
Holt, Reinhart & Winston, 261
Hope, Bob, 118, 177
Horn, Alfred Aloysius (Trader Horn), 134–36

Houghton Mifflin, 108, 185, 256
Howe, Quincy, 64, 122, 181–82, 183
Howe, Wallis E. (Pete), 163–65
Huebsch, Ben, 10
Hunter, Evan, 177, 262

Ickes, Harold L., 154–55
Infeld, Leopold, 11
Information Please, 57
Inner Sanctum, 58–59, 61, 87–95, 98
International Creative Management (ICM), 233
Irwin, Edman, 7
Iseman, Joseph, 160–61

Jackson, Charles, 257
Jacobson, James M., 69, 178
Janklow, Morton, L., 230–31
Jarrell, Randall, 261
Jeans, Sir James, 148
Jensen, Paul, 183
Jersey City Printing Company, 151–52
Johnson, Hugh, 222–24, 226
Johnson, Josephine, 11
Johnson, Lyndon Baines, 147
Johnson & Johnson, 172
Jolliffe, Norman, 143
Jonathan Cape Ltd., 238–39
Jovanovich, William, 85
Judelson, David, 86

Kael, Pauline, 264n
Kamil, Susan, 231
Kaplan, Justin, 12, 62, 64, 74, 183, 218
Kasner, Edward, 148
Kazantzakis, Nikos, 15, 216
Kelly, Walt, 44, 97, 124–29, 177, 208
Kenan Press, 107, 271
Kennedy, Ludovic, 226
Keynes, John Maynard, 149
King, Alexander, 101–03, 132–33, 153, 263
King, Margie, 101
Kinney System, Inc., 85
Klopfer, Donald, 73
Kluger, Richard, 55, 183
Knickerbocker, Julia, 101
Knight, Hilary, 97, 124, 130, 130n
Knopf, Alfred A., 11, 80, 97, 99, 103, 240, 242, 245
Knopf, Alfred, Jr., (Pat), 80
Knopf, Blanche, 184, 245
Koch, Mayor Ed, 276n
Koehler, O., 149
Korda, Michael V., xix, 72, 101, 103, 104, 105, 138, 183, 216, 231, 237, 238, 242, 243, 247–51, 263, 267, 272, 276, 276n, 277
Kraus, Robert, 183
Kroch, Carl A., 18
Kunhardt, Dorothy, 158

Laing, Arthur Everard, 92
Lamon, Strome, 55, 97–99, 251
Lange, Hope, 236
Larrick, George, 144–45
Lasser, J.K., 77–78
Laver, Rod, 30
Lazar, Irving, 228–29
Leacock, Stephen, 149
Lederer, Charles, 214
Leiper, Maria, 48, 64, 120, 121, 122, 183, 185, 254–56, 262
Lennon, John, 238–240
Lenz, Sidney S., 22
Lerner, Max, 177
Lessing, Doris, 242
Levenson, Sam, 119, 263
Leventhal, Albert Rice, xviii, 22, 24, 25, 36, 39, 44, 52, 55, 122, 123–24, 166–69, 170–71, 179, 183, 201–06, 209–10, 215, 234, 240–41
Levin, Ira, 261
Levin, Meyer, 177
Levitan, Selig, 84
Levy, Phyllis, 236
Lewis, Ethelreda, 134
Liebling, A. J., 177
Liebman, Joshua Loth, 79
Linden Books, 107, 186, 272
Lindsay, John V., 276n
Literary Guild, 80, 123, 223, 232
Little, Brown, 259, 260
Little Simon Books, 272, 273
Liveright, Horace, 245
Lohf, Kenneth, xvii–xviii
Lovell, Jack, 287
Lowell, Joan, 136–37
Luce, Henry, 54
Lynch, Noel, 287

Maloney, Russell, 149
Mansfield, Irving, 105–06
Marmur, Mildred, 55, 186, 188–89, 281
Marshall, General George C., 151–52, 177
Maschler, Tom, 238–39
Mason, Jerry, 193
Matson, Harold, 257–60
Maude, Louise and Aylmer, 60
Mayhew, Alice, 187, 216, 245, 263, 280–81
McCarthy, Eugene, 275–76
McCarthy, Joseph, 125, 176
McCarthy, Mary, 255, 256
McCullough, David, 12, 263
McDowell, Edwin, 244
McGovern, Artie, 35
McMurtry, Larry, 15, 263
Mead, Shepherd, 118
Mencken, H. L., 290
Meredith, Scott, 232–33
Messner, Julian (Publisher), 270

Metz, Frank, 105, 267, 277
Meyerson, Sam, xvii, 121, 122, 124, 268–69
Millay, Edna St. Vincent, 215
Mitchell, James, 222–25
Mitchell-Beazley Ltd., 223–25
Mitford, Jessica, 141, 242
Moberg, Vilhelm, 15
Monarch Press, 270
Monath, Norman, 20–21, 40–41, 59n, 267–68
Morehead, Albert, 25
Morehouse, Laurence E., 33, 99
Morley, Christopher, 290
Morrison, Alex J., 29–33
Morrow, William (Publisher), 21, 185
Morton, Joe, 164–65
Muggeridge, Malcolm, 220, 226
Muller, Ronald E., 247
Mumford, Lewis, 290
Murrow, Edward R., 177
Music Corporation of America (MCA), 283, 284

Nabokov, Vladimir, 192–93, 262
Nancy Drew series, 272
Nelson Publishers, Ltd., 222
Newman, James R., 15, 148–50
New Ventures, 193–200
*New Yorker, The,* 10, 44, 57, 60, 149, 190
New York University, 73, 78
Nicklaus, Jack, 30, 177
Nixon, Richard M., 125, 279
Norton, W.W. (Publisher), 276, 276n

O'Brien, Edna, 242
Obst, David, 278–86
Oppenheimer, George, 73
Oppenheimer, Robert, 177
Oxford University Press, 61, 114

Paar, Jack, 101, 132–33
Paramount Pictures, 86, 277, 283
parsons, Ian, 225
Paul, Weiss, Wharton, Rifkin & Garrison, 160
Pearlroth, Norman, 51
Peattie, Donald Culross, 96, 290
Peck, Gregory, 194–95
Pell, Arthur, 66
People's Book Club, 80
Perelman, S. J., 15, 72, 97, 119, 132, 177
Perkins, Maxwell, 176
Petherbridge, Margaret (Farrar), 2, 5–6, 183
Pitkin, Walter, 290
Plaza Publishing Company, 2
Pocket Books, 50, 74, 79, 82, 85, 86, 113, 162–66, 173, 175, 177, 178, 180, 204, 209, 232, 233, 234, 243, 248, 259, 260
Polshek, James Stewart, 70
Popular Library, 85

Portis, Charles, 242
Potok, Chaim, 242
Powys, John Cowper, 11, 15, 55, 148, 216
Price, George, 44
Prior, Allan, 226
*Punch*, 44, 219–20
Putnam's G. P., 184, 185, 262
Puzo, Mario, 262

Ramon, Simon, 226
Rampa, T. Lobsang, 137–38
Random House, 73, 80, 107, 171, 186, 210,
   224, 232, 240, 241, 242, 256, 257, 261,
   262, 284–85
Rayner, Claire, 226
Reader's Digest, 219
Reagan, Ronald, 112
Reese, Terence, 26
Reinhardt, Max, 217–18, 226
Rembar, Charles, 139n
Reuben, Alvin, 246, 273
Rickey, Branch, 30
Riggs, Bobby, 30
Ridge Press, 193
Ripley, Robert L., 51, 99
Robins, Harold, 82, 99, 110, 230, 249
Robbins, Henry, 243, 277–78
Robinson, Henry Morton, 103, 153–54, 177
Rodgers, Richard, 20
Rose, Carl, 44
Rosenau, Mickey, 211–12
Rosenberg, Marvin, 219
Rovere, Ernest, 26
Rukeyser, Merryle Stanley, 7
Russell, Bertrand, xviii, 15, 92, 148, 177, 216
Russell, Lillian, 200
Ryan, Cornelius, 82–84, 177, 230

Sagan, Carl, 232–33, 262
Salten, Felix, 11, 42, 216
Sandpiper Press, 210
Scarne, John, 177
Schenken, Howard, 26
Scherman, Harry, 39
Schnabel, Artur, 11, 20
Schnitzler, Arthur, 11, 138–39, 216
Schonberg, Harold, 15
Schulte, Anthony M., 55, 179, 240–42, 243
Schuster, M. Lincoln, xv, xvii–xix, 1–3,
   7–8, 10–11, 17, 42, 45–65, 66, 67, 68, 73,
   74, 77, 80, 81, 88, 91, 94, 96, 105, 117–18,
   120, 122, 123, 124, 134, 138, 141–42, 146,
   147–48, 162, 174, 178, 179, 180, 183,
   184–85, 190, 198, 201, 203, 209, 216, 235,
   239, 244, 245, 248, 254, 257, 262, 288,
   290–91
Schuster, Ray, 64–65, 81, 184–85
Schwartz, Frank, 273
Schwartz, Tony, xix, 275
Schwarzenegger, Arnold, 33, 107

Schwed, Fred, Jr., 205, 211–12
Schwed, Peter, xvii–xix, 55, 146, 179, 183,
   188, 206, 216–26, 234–35, 242–43, 248,
   263–66
*Scientific American*, 15
Scully, Frank, 118
Sears Roebuck Company, 80
Seitlin, Charlotte, 185
Seligman, Elizabeth (Simon), 36, 156n, 191
Seligman, Mary, 156n
Sheehan, George, 33
Sheinwold, Alfred, 26
Shepherd, Jack, 146–47
Shimkin, Arthur, 170
Shimkin, Leon, xvii, xix, 3, 6, 10, 25, 35,
   41, 54, 57, 60, 66–86, 88, 122–23, 162–66,
   166–67, 169, 170–71, 174, 175, 177–79,
   180, 190, 203–04, 209, 234, 243, 248, 259,
   260, 275, 283, 284, 287, 288
Shimkin, Michael, 80–84
Shirer, William L., 14, 176, 220–22
Silberman, James H., 186–87, 271–72
Silhouette Books, 270–71
Silverstein, Shel, 260–61
Simon, Alfred, 36
Simon, Andrea, xviii, 41–42, 81, 139, 143,
   174
Simon, Carly, 41
Simon, George, 36
Simon, Henry, 36, 41, 48, 64, 183, 235,
   247–48, 257–58
Simon, Joanna, 41, 156n, 174
Simon, Leo, 198–200
Simon, Lucy, 41
Simon, Norton, Inc., 84–85
Simon, Peter, xviii, 41, 81
Simon, Richard L., xv, xvii–xix, 1–3, 6–7,
   10–11, 17–44, 54–55, 58, 59, 59n, 66, 67,
   68, 73, 80, 81, 88, 91, 94, 96, 115–16, 122,
   124, 134, 138–39, 142–43, 152, 161, 162,
   173–74, 176, 178, 183, 190–200, 201–03,
   209, 216, 234, 240, 245, 256, 257, 258,
   262, 287, 288, 290
Sims, P. Hal, 22–25
Sloane, William J., 21
Snyder, Richard E., xix, 11, 69, 70–72, 86,
   94, 103, 107, 120, 165, 180, 185, 186, 228,
   230–31, 232–33, 234, 240, 243–51, 262,
   270–88
Soglow, Otto, 44
Soliman, Patricia, 187
Solman, Paul, 288
Sorkin, Sophie, 153, 183, 267
Spassky, Boris, 218–19
Spengler, Oswald, 148
Staral, Emil, 180, 209, 234
Stead, Christina, 261
Steichen, Edward, 193
Steig, William, 44
Steinkraus, William, 183

Stern, Philip Van Doren, 150, 183
Straus, Roger, 80
Straus, Roger, III, 80
Streeter, Edward, 177
Sullivan, Scott, 183
Summit Books, 16, 187, 247, 271
Susann, Jackqueline, 103–06

Talese, Nan, 108, 185
Tallchief, Maria, 198
Taller, Herman, 143–46
Tarkington, Booth, 257
Thompson, Kay, 97, 124, 130, 171, 177, 241
Thurber, James, 177
Tilden, Bill, 7, 29, 30
Tolstoy, Leo, 60–61
Tom Swift series, 272
Touchstone Books, 35, 272
Trevor, Elleston (Adam Hall), 226
Trotsky, Leon, 11
Tufts University, 275
Turk, Seymour, xix, 179–80, 234

Unitas, Johnny, 30
Universal Pictures, 283
Unknown Mortal of 2936, 291
Untermeyer, Louis, 96
Unwin, Sir Stanley, 226

Van Doren, Irita, 209
Van Doren, Margaret (Bevans), 206
Van Loon, Hendrik Willem, 41–42, 55–56, 96, 290
Vaughan, Bill, 129
Viking Press, xix, 73, 80

Wallace, Irivng, 82, 84, 103, 177, 230, 262
Walsh, John E., 183

Wanderer Books, 272
Warburg, Frederic, 137–38, 228
Warner Communications, Inc., 85, 281, 284
Wartels, Nat, 224–25
Washington Square Press, 270
Waugh, Alec, 226
Waugh, Auberon, 226
Webster, H. T., 44
Webster Dictonaries, 271
Weidenfeld, George, 225
Weidman, Jerome, xviii, 62–65, 121, 123, 183, 200
Weinstock, Herbert, 182–83
Welles, Orson, 214
Werfel, Franz, 216
Western Printing & Lithographing Co., 166–68, 169, 172n, 210, 272
White, Patricia, 183
Whitehead, Alfred North, 148
Whyte, William Holly, 156, 177, 194
William Morris Agency, 233
Williams, Ron, 219–20
Willkie, Wendell L., 11, 16, 176, 177, 209
Wills, Ridley, 7
Wilson, Sloan, 177, 194
Wind, Herbert Warren, 30
Windmill Books, 272–73
Wodehouse, P. G., 15, 95, 98, 119, 156, 177, 263
Wolfe, Thomas, 176
Wolff, H., Co., 159–60
Wolff, Helen, 183
Woodward, Bob, 16, 263, 279–81, 284
Woollcott, Alexander, 88
Wouk, Herman, 97, 257–60
Wren, Christopher S., 146–47
Wright, Lee, 22, 24–25, 38–41, 55, 123, 185, 190, 261
Wyndham Books, 271